JUDGMENT CALLS

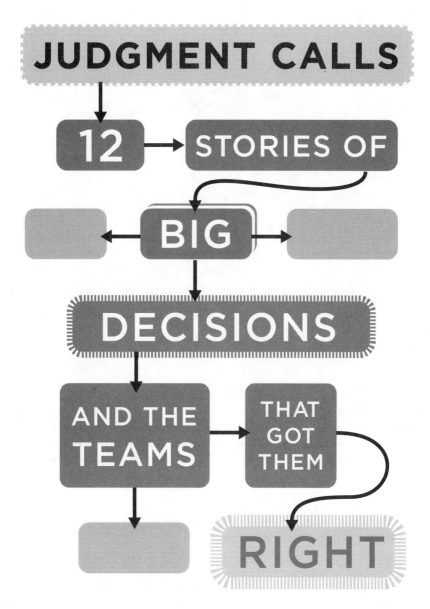

JUDGMENT CALLS

12 → **STORIES OF**

BIG

DECISIONS

AND THE TEAMS → **THAT GOT THEM**

RIGHT

THOMAS H. DAVENPORT & BROOK MANVILLE

Harvard Business Review Press • Boston, Massachusetts

Printed in the United States of America

10 9 8 7 6 5 4 3 2 1

No part of this publication may be reproduced, stored in or introduced into a retrieval system, or transmitted, in any form, or by any means (electronic, mechanical, photocopying, recording, or otherwise), without the prior permission of the publisher. Requests for permission should be directed to permissions@hbsp.harvard.edu, or mailed to Permissions, Harvard Business School Publishing, 60 Harvard Way, Boston, Massachusetts 02163.

Library of Congress Cataloging-in-Publication Data

Davenport, Thomas H., 1954-
 Judgment calls : twelve stories of big decisions and the teams that
got them / Thomas H. Davenport, Brook Manville.
     p. cm.
 ISBN 978-1-4221-5811-1 (alk. paper)
 1. Decision making. 2. Problem solving. I. Manville, Brook, 1950- II. Title.
 HD30.23.D3718 2012
 658.4'03—dc23

                                                                   2011040344

The paper used in this publication meets the requirements of the American National Standard for Permanence of Paper for Publications and Documents in Libraries and Archives Z39.48-1992.

Contents

Foreword

At the outset of a book of stories about judgment, perhaps the way to begin is by telling the story behind the book itself. In the spring of 2010, Tom Davenport and I met for lunch, not with any thought of embarking on a new project but only to catch up. But with two disasters much in the news at the time—the continuing fallout from the global economic meltdown and the explosion of BP's Deepwater Horizon oil platform in the Gulf of Mexico—our conversation kept returning to the question of why it is so hard for organizations to do the right thing.

Our prior research together, spanning two decades, was a source of pride for us. We had focused on knowledge in organizations rather than the more prevalent subjects of information technology and data management and felt we had made a serious difference in at least some management thinking, conversation, and actions. Knowledge, we had argued, was the most valuable asset in modern organizations, and their success depended on their attention to cultivating it, sharing it, and using it.

Now, however, we had to admit that the catastrophes being visited on the world weren't owing to failures of knowledge. Not at all. Who knew more about finance than the employees of the firms that precipitated the financial crisis? Their halls were full of Ivy League graduates rubbing shoulders with the world's leading economists and finance professionals. How could anyone say there wasn't sufficient know-how? And who knew more about how to rein in the risks of their operations than the regulators? Often hired directly from the very entities they were to regulate, they had not only the requisite intellectual tools to understand complex financial structures but intimate familiarity with how they were being applied. Yet all this knowledge, the product of the very strong investments in human capital these organizations made, had brought us to our collective economic knees. So what was missing if it wasn't information or even knowledge? Try judgment.

As that conversation led to others, it wasn't long before Tom and I asked Brook Manville to join the discussion. Not surprisingly, given how long we have been friends and colleagues, he had also been thinking along the same lines. All of us knew something of the existing literature on judgment, which is not unsubstantial. We wondered whether its lessons had simply gone unheeded, or whether it fell short in some way of offering the right lessons for today's organizations.

What we discovered, first, was that the wealth of material already published on judgment treated it as only an individual capacity and exercise. Whether the source is an ancient one, like Aristotle's inquiries into "practical wisdom," or a thoroughly modern one, like Dan Ariely's fascinating behavioral economics studies, the focus is on the sole actor and his or her ability to choose a wise course of action. At the same time, most writing on judgment conflates judgment and decision making, to the former's disadvantage. People chipping away at the subject tend to opt for one of two modes, approaching it either as an application of mathematics (following the hugely influential Howard Raiffa) or as a branch of individual psychology (building on Herbert Simon's cognitive science).

We discovered, in other words, that no one was looking into the workings of what we term *organizational judgment*—the collective capacity to make good calls and wise moves when the need for them exceeds the scope of any single leader's direct control. We wanted to know why some organizations manage to display good judgment while others seem to lack it. If a group's judgment is something other than the sum total of the practical wisdom of individuals in the group, then we wanted to know what it is, how it is called upon in moments of need, and how to get more of it.

Very briefly, organizational judgment is to group decisions what individual judgment is to individual decisions. It is what guides organizations when information alone cannot. It is the context in which group decisions are made—the atmosphere of collective experience, bias, and belief that sets the boundaries, the limits, the methods of analysis, the very conversations and vocabularies and stories that are the heart and soul of so many decisions.

Think of a recent decision you were party to. Whether it related only to your own life or to the direction of a group, it was not made in a vacuum. I am willing to bet you did not approach it with Cartesian purity, plotting coordinates and noncontextually weighing factors as if you were considering some crystalline structure. No, you made that decision in a social setting. It is that setting which differs from organization to organization, and which is the focus of this book. All the experiences and emotions and histories and individual stories add up to a "climate of opinion" in any organization that is the soil from which decisions emerge.

All this, Brook, Tom, and I agreed, was uncharted territory and important to explore. We agreed that the way to begin was by going out and talking to real people about the judgment calls their organizations had made. And as we began those visits, we realized that the best way in which we could share what we were learning with others would be to tell those organizations' stories in all their richness.

In terms of my personal involvement, this was a point where the story of the book took a turn. Soon after we began this fieldwork, I became ill for a time and decided I could not responsibly commit to a full share of the research and writing. It was a tough admission, but in the end, the right call. I instead offer this Foreword in gratitude—both for Tom and Brook's understanding and support, and for the discoveries that populate the pages that follow.

The important news that they bring back from their investigations is that the background and context we call organizational judgment can not only be discerned, it can be *managed*. Maybe not as much as some might like, but in meaningful ways. Things can be done to ensure that the courses of action taken by organizations are more grounded in reality and a shared sense of what is right. In particular, Tom and Brook found the evidence of what we had suspected: that honing organizational judgment means creating processes and mechanisms that allow discussion and debate and conversation to work its own collective chemistry.

I'm proud to say, then, that I was present at the beginning of something big. Across the history of theorizing about how decisions are best made, we have already seen three eras. First, there was the "great man" school of thought (a folly that Tom nicely summarizes in chapter 1.) According to its teachings, judgment was surely accorded central importance, but the judgment was assumed to be an individual characteristic—indeed, one of the distinguishing characteristics that separated truly great men (yes, alas, always thought to be men) from the rest of mankind.

The corrective to that way of thinking came later, marking a second era. The key to good decision making was understood to be more abundant information relevant to the decision, and much later, to be the ever-snazzier technology that could make it possible to process immense amounts of potentially relevant data. Even as investments in analytics yielded many triumphs, however, they also revealed that not every nuance of a decision could be nailed by numbers.

It's a lesson we were reminded of anew when the 2009 death of Robert McNamara, architect of the Vietnam War, spurred so many reflections on his singular career. In many ways he was emblematic of a type of executive all too common in the post–World War II world: very smart and achievement-driven, but overly convinced that problems of any kind would yield to rational analysis. The group of men that formed around him were labeled the "whiz kids" for their acumen in using operational analysis to solve logistical problems during the Vietnam War. On top of McNamara's predisposition to disregard the role of judgment, he worked in environments—first Ford Motor Company, then the U.S. Department of Defense, then the World Bank—where there was no real sense that judgment was a capacity worthy of development and conscious exercise. Thus, sadly, there were virtually no mechanisms or processes in these environments that could systematically challenge decisions that were, in fact, judgment calls—and bad ones. Famously, McNamara came to understand this late in his life, as he struggled to comprehend how moves he supported intellectually had produced so much damage and tragedy.

McNamara's high-profile mistakes were hardly the death knell of a data- and IT-smitten era. And indeed the advances in these fields should continue, because decision making always benefits from better information. At the same time, the awareness grew that not every important input to human decision making and action had been or could be practically expressed as data. Knowledge, largely tacit, always dynamic, went beyond the concrete capture of databases. The realization that this did not mean it was *unmanageable* ushered in a third era.

And now, we see the dawn of a fourth era of thinking about organizational decision making, in which the importance of judgment is acknowledged. As with knowledge, and before it, information, the new thought is not that judgment matters. It always did. The breakthrough is that judgment has become tractable enough to analysis, even at the organizational level, to be worth discussing.

It's easy to see why, historically, judgment hasn't been talked about much in the academy or in firms. For one thing, it's hard to settle on the right "unit of analysis" as a basis for work on the subject. The question of where judgment resides is elusive and resistant to the type of analysis academics need to produce for their professional advancement. And so there has been much more focus on individual decision making: it is just easier to deal with.

Another hurdle in studying organizational judgment is that it's hard to find the evidence to distinguish good practice from bad. Failure is an orphan, says the proverb, while success has many parents. When one wants to investigate bad judgment, in a systematic rather than individualistic way, one has to search pretty hard to find a live example. It is much easier to say, "Well, the former CEO was a fool" than "We really need to look at how our own judgment capabilities failed us."

And certainly, given the lack of widespread vocabulary and frameworks about the subject, it is hard to find organizations who can talk about their judgment capabilities and how they are developed. Enterprises and teams that exercise good judgment usually "just do it"—either by unconsciously following a tradition, or by taking conscious actions but not using the language of judgment in their deliberations.

Our hope is that this book will begin to lower these hurdles. It will not be the last word on organizational judgment, we hope. (In fact, it cannot even claim to be the first. For those who know James March's work, it is not surprising that he has already ventured into this territory. The models of organizational decision making he has developed are true syntheses of decision modeling and humanistic common sense.) Rather, in telling the stories of judgment calls that worked out, and the capabilities that made them routine rather than extraordinary events, we hope to introduce many others to a new field for study, full of concepts and practices that are not taught today, but are powerfully needed.

Introduction

Great Men, Not So Great Decisions

MORE OFTEN than any of us might care to admit, the course of human affairs relies on great judgment. Even in this age of abundant data and rocket-science analytics, many, many decisions force people to draw on their accumulated wisdom to make the right call. Sometimes that's because the absolute right answer can't be known; the question at hand relates to a future too full of uncertainty. Other times, the optimal solution could be determined based on accessible information, but the urgency of the situation means it can't be assembled in time. In still other cases, conflicting values come into play and the trade-offs defy easy quantification.

As societies and their organizations experience ever-accelerating rates of change, we suspect all these conditions will apply more often, and more decisions than ever will come down to judgment calls.

The question is, how can we make sure those calls are made well? Is it enough to choose smart leaders who seem to have their people's interests at heart, and trust their wisdom?

A look at one particularly pure example of that approach, firms' pursuits of mergers and acquisitions (M&A), suggests the answer is no. This is a realm where we see top leaders of enterprises making the highest-stake decisions with the least input from others, and the results hardly vindicate the process. Estimates based on reliable studies indicate that between 50 and 70 percent of M&A deals fail to realize their goals, and many destroy value outright. As we embark on a book about how good judgment happens in some situations, it might be useful to reflect on why, in M&A decision making, it so reliably doesn't.

Take, for example, the 2000 decision by Time Warner CEO Jerry Levin to merge his company with America Online (technically a purchase of Time Warner with inflated AOL stock). While AOL had been a high-flying Internet access company in the 1990s, by 2000 it was already beginning to look stale. But Time Warner was a media conglomerate without a lot of online assets, and the prevailing notion was that it had to have Internet-related businesses to compete.

When Levin began to explore options with AOL's founder and chief executive, Steve Case, however, he'd had little discussion with the rest of his management team. By reputation, Levin was something of a loner to begin with. He was also wary about heavy involvement of his board in the decision, in part because of tensions with board member Ted Turner, whose company Time Warner had acquired in 1996. Levin and Case eventually concocted a $164 billion deal, the largest in history at the time. Having arrived at terms satisfactory to himself, Levin prevailed upon his board, persuading even Turner, to support the acquisition.

Normally, in volatile markets like those during the dot-com boom, deal makers would put a "collar" on the deal so that one party could back out if the other's stock declined too much. And AOL's stock was tanking on almost a daily basis before the deal closed. But Levin neither sought nor obtained a collar.

Indeed, even as the shares of the combined company began to decline in value almost immediately after the deal, Levin wore his missing collar as a badge of honor and commitment. In an interview ten months down the road—by which time AOL's stock had already declined 38 percent—Levin was asked about the matter and gave this explanation:

> With a collar, the implication is that you are really not sure—your commitment to the valuations is somewhat insecure, and you need this kind of protection. I wanted to make a statement that I believe in it. It . . . means a total commitment to the deal come hell or high water.[1]

No doubt Time Warner shareholders were greatly comforted by the leader's unwavering faith. But by 2002, the combined company declared a $99 billion loss from a write-down of its goodwill value—at that point the largest corporate loss in history. Levin was forced to resign in 2002, with Ted Turner's calls for his head ringing loudest. AOL Time Warner never thrived with the decline in AOL's fortunes, and the company's stock value decreased from $226 billion to as low as $20 billion. Eventually AOL was spun off as a separate company in 2009.

Once that happened, even Levin got the picture that he had used poor judgment. By 2010, on the decade anniversary of the deal, he admitted it:

> "I presided over the worst deal of the century, apparently, and I guess it's time for those who are involved in companies to stand up and say: you know what, I'm solely responsible for it," said Mr. Levin. "I was in charge. I'm really very sorry about the pain and the suffering and loss that was caused. I take responsibility."[2]

Better late than never, we suppose.

Bad choices about acquisitions and what to pay for them get egged along by ego, pressures to grow, and the well-known phenomenon of "deal fever."

But it's interesting to note that decisions made in isolation *not* to deal can be just as poorly judged. Consider the acquisition of Yahoo! by Microsoft that never happened.[3]

By 2008 Microsoft had been circling Yahoo! for several years for the same reason Jerry Levin had wanted AOL: to add some Internet assets. Also like AOL, Yahoo! wasn't quite the catch it would have been earlier; the exclamation point in its name seemed sadly inappropriate. By the time of the Microsoft offer, the company's stock was trading at 44 percent below its fifty-two-week high, and Yahoo! had recently shed 10 percent of its staff.

By all accounts (except apparently one), the Microsoft offer was a heck of a deal for Yahoo!. On February 1, 2008, Microsoft proposed a friendly takeover of Yahoo! Inc. for $31 per common share—a $44.6 billion offer. The proposed price was 62 percent above the previous closing price for Yahoo!.

In this story, the Jerry Levin role was played by Jerry Yang, a cofounder of Yahoo! who had taken over as CEO a few years earlier. Yang, who was obviously enamored of the company he led, turned down the $31 offer in discussions with Steve Ballmer, Microsoft's CEO. Microsoft upped the offer to $33 a share—a 70 percent increase above the closing price preannouncement.

Yang, however, felt that the right price for the deal was at least $4 per share higher. He was so confident in the price he was holding out for that he didn't put either the $31 or the $33 offer to a proxy vote. Why ask the owners of the company what their investment was worth?

On May 3, 2008, Ballmer pulled the offer, which was probably his smartest move. Yahoo! stock slid, and has never found its way back out of its trough. The only event that lifted it significantly after the Microsoft offer was the announcement that Jerry Yang was being replaced as CEO by Carol Bartz (who was herself fired in 2011). Just after assuming the job, Bartz was asked in a CNBC interview whether she would have taken the Microsoft offer. "Sure," was her reply, "you think I am stupid?"[4]

Beyond M&A

We could go on and on about poor M&A decisions, and probably many of our readers could, too. The stories become infamous precisely because they are the kinds of "big swings" that make or break reputations, and often bring out the worst in managerial decision making. The merger machinations have to be kept at least somewhat close to the vest, and the rationale for the deal is all rooted in future potential, not past experience (or data based upon it). Therefore such decisions are routinely entrusted to solitary leaders at the top—and they are thus the greatest case against the ability of those solitary leaders to exercise great judgment at the scale of the organization.

But M&A decisions are hardly the only kinds of moves that single-minded enterprises make badly. Missteps occur in every sphere of business and organization—in matters of strategy, innovation, operations, and people—most of which are minor, and some of which have huge consequences.

Strategy making is probably most rife with poor judgment, though the flawed deliberations behind most dumb decisions never come to light. Sins of omission—roads foolishly not taken—surely outnumber sins of commission. When these do become known, they become sources of acute embarrassment, even to leaders long acknowledged to be great, as Ken Olsen, the cofounder and longtime CEO of Digital Equipment Corporation, found out.

Olsen guided the company to dominance of the minicomputer category over its first thirty years.[5] As a testament to his vision, Digital became the second-largest computer company in the world after IBM. But by the mid-1980s, it became obvious to most observers that the world was moving on to personal computers.

Not to Olsen, however. He doggedly maintained that the mini remained the next big thing. His words are amusing at this point: "Customers don't want a computer that sits on a desk. Customers want computers that sit on the floor."[6] Even if they did want computing on their desktops, Olsen argued that "most people in an organization want terminals."[7] Olsen also stuck by Digital's proprietary VMS operating system while the rest of the world shifted to Unix and Windows.

With a leader with his head in the sand, Digital couldn't stay in business for long. By 1998 the company was sold to Compaq for $9.6 billion, well below its peak annual revenues of $14 billion.

Olsen was surely not the first great industrialist who erred by believing his gut was unimpeachable and his vision reliable. Henry Ford, who built one of the world's largest and most successful car companies, committed his share of bad judgment, though he obviously also made numerous good decisions. He perfected the assembly line, virtually defined vertical integration, and doubled the wages of his workforce to $5 a day, thus making them much more loyal as employees and consumers of his cars. But Ford also made some truly awful decisions. He stopped improving the Model T, declaring it "already correct" and the only car anyone could ever need—and it rapidly lost market share in the 1920s. He decided to build a prefabricated industrial city in the rain forest of Brazil that he called Fordlandia, intending it to be a cheap source of cultivated rubber for tires. But according to historian Greg Grandin, Ford was too distrustful of experts to consult even one on the subject of rubber trees.[8] It was an agricultural and social disaster, was sold at a $20 million loss, and rotted in the jungle. Worst of all, he allowed his name to be used for anti-Semitic causes and arguments, and met with associates of Hitler from Germany.

Even the late Steve Jobs of Apple, the contemporary decision maker most acclaimed for his golden touch over the last decade or so, had moments when his judgment failed him. In the 1980s, he hired John Sculley to succeed him as CEO of Apple, and Sculley presided over a period of slow growth and product missteps in the ensuing years. Jobs later commented, "What can I say? I hired the wrong guy. He destroyed everything I spent 10 years working for, starting with me."[9] Jobs sold all of his Apple stock when Sculley pushed him out, which cost him billions. Few would call Next Computer, the start-up he founded during his hiatus from Apple, a success. And when he came back as CEO, he allowed the backdating of stock options. Jobs certainly redeemed himself with a string of fantastically successful products from Apple—and as one of the company's founders, he got a bit of slack for a bad call now and then—but he was hardly immune to faulty judgment. One factor that Jobs attributes his good decisions to was greater reliance upon others. In a summary of a 1997 interview, a *New York Times* article published after he resigned for health reasons in 2011 noted:

> In his early years at Apple, before he was forced out in 1985,
> Mr. Jobs was notoriously hands-on, meddling with details and
> berating colleagues. But later, first at Pixar, the computer-
> animation studio he co-founded, and in his second stint at Apple,
> he relied more on others, listening more and trusting members
> of his design and business teams.[10]

Why the Fixation on Great Men?

Human judgment, it appears, is frail and fettered no matter which humans the judgment comes from. Even the greatest of leaders can't get out of the way of their own egos. Neuroscience and behavioral economics now tell us that all humans fall into a common set of decision traps or cognitive biases—from, for example, *anchoring* (overreliance on familiar but irrelevant information for a decision) to the *zero-risk bias* (a penchant to reduce a minor risk to nothing, but missing the opportunity to reduce proportionately instead a much bigger risk).[11] A recent article suggests that while leaders may be able to identify the cognitive biases in others' decisions and recommendations, they have virtually no chance of seeing their own.[12]

Yet no matter how many mistakes are made by individuals, the single leader and decision maker prevails as a paradigm. History still puts the Great Man (or, less common, the Great Woman) on a prominent pedestal. Management theorists still praise the solitary, heroic leader. Indeed, there's a long philosophical tradition behind the Great Man theory.

Thomas Carlyle, the nineteenth-century Scottish philosopher, began his 1840 book, *On Heroes, Hero-Worship, and the Heroic in History*, with these words:

> We have undertaken to discourse here for a little on Great Men,
> their manner of appearance in our world's business, how they have
> shaped themselves in the world's history, what ideas men formed
> of them, what work they did.

Carlyle, who was known earlier in his career as a curmudgeonly and satirical writer, abandoned all pretense of satire when writing about Great Men (we'll continue to capitalize the term in a somewhat satirical fashion). Later in the introduction to the book, he writes worshipfully:

> One comfort is, that Great Men, taken up in any way, are
> profitable company. We cannot look, however imperfectly, upon
> a great man, without gaining something by him. He is the living
> light-fountain, which it is good and pleasant to be near. The light
> which enlightens, which has enlightened the darkness of the world;
> and this not as a kindled lamp only, but rather as a natural luminary
> shining by the gift of Heaven; a flowing light-fountain, as I say, of
> native original insight, of manhood and heroic nobleness;—in whose
> radiance all souls feel that it is well with them.[13]

Carlyle already sounds a bit nutty in his enthusiasm for Great Men, and this is only page 1 of his book. Indeed, Carlyle's views increasingly diverged from those of polite society as he aged. He maintained that democracy was an impossible form of government, and that slavery should never have been abolished. Adolf Hitler found Carlyle's biography of Frederick the Great (a generous gift from Joseph Goebbels) inspiring and comforting in his last days in the Berlin bunker.

Fortunately, most of Carlyle's ideas have been left behind, but not the Great Man notion. It lives on in both theory and practice.

That is, of course, because it is such a convenient fiction in some ways. In a society that depends on its members' taking initiative and suffers when they indulge in free riding, it helps to hold up role models and dangle the incentive of fame and fortune for individual achievement. As David Ogilvy was fond of saying, "Search your parks in all your cities/You'll find no statues of committees." There is no denying, too, that most would rather listen to a good yarn about a maverick taking on the world and beating the odds. As much as we might revere a studiously deliberative body—like the Supreme Court—there tends to be little romance in its triumphs.

Thus we see publishers shelling out huge advances to leaders willing to tell their tales—as GE's former CEO Jack Welch did in *Jack: Straight from the Gut* and, more recently, George W. Bush did in *Decision Points*. But it isn't only the public at large that hangs on such words; many a leadership scholar has written almost as worshipfully as Carlyle about the charismatic power and decision-making genius of great corporate and governmental leaders. One of the more tempered appreciations of leadership decision making is Noel Tichy and Warren Bennis's *Judgment: How Winning Leaders Make Great Calls*, but still the focus is on famous CEOs and the approaches they personally embrace.

The leadership literature's Great Man obsession might be harmless enough—the management equivalent of romance novels—if it were not for the fact that it fuels real disparities and painful disappointments in society. In the corporate realm, boards of directors, desperate to boost bottom lines, seize upon those few candidates whose track records suggest they are in possession of some fairy dust to sprinkle, and the ensuing bidding war pushes chief executives' salaries sky-high. In 2010, the average CEO in the S&P 500 made $11.4 million in total compensation—343 times the median income for workers in all occupations.[14] Modern-day CEO perks often exceed Frederick the Great's—they have airplanes, limousines, security forces, massive expense accounts, and large retinues at their disposal. This despite the fact that, in many cases, the fairy dust never materializes.

And in government, while we don't pay our Great Men so much, we continue to believe—despite much evidence to the contrary—that they are the solution to all the world's (or at least the country's) problems. We devote an increasing amount of attention to them in presidential campaigns. We ascribe (at least if they represent our party and political beliefs) heroic traits to them. We hold them accountable for realizing all our dreams and aspirations, for finding us jobs and making our house prices increase. Like the image dreamed by Nebuchadnezzar, King of Babylon, the reality on the ground is not as impressive:

> *Thou, O king, sawest, and behold a great image. This great image, whose brightness was excellent, stood before thee; and the form thereof was terrible.*
> *This image's head was of fine gold, his breast and his arms of silver, his belly and his thighs of brass,*
> *His legs of iron, his feet part of iron and part of clay.* (Daniel 2:31–33)

The Antidote to the Great Man Theory

We offer this book as an antidote for, and even the counter to, the Great Man theory of decision making and organizational performance. We view no individual man or woman as uniquely and solely responsible for wonderful outcomes; CEOs, political leaders, visionary thinkers, like all of us too, are living examples of at least occasional human frailty in thought and deed. Even the best leaders sometimes make bad decisions; the worst make them frequently, and perhaps one or more can bring down massive and hugely successful organizations.

Instead of Great Men, we'll preach the virtues of Great Organizations— organizations that build the ongoing capability to make great decisions again and again, reflecting the judgment to more consistently than not make "great calls" in difficult situations. Great Organizations expand the number of people involved in important decisions, because they know that while individual humans are fallible, in the aggregate they are usually more effective. They tap into their employees' (and customers' and partners') broad range of expertise, and they ask for their opinions; they deliberate and problem-solve toward a better answer, instead of "going with the gut." They also employ data and analysis to make decisions, because they know that on the whole, the scientific method is the single best guide to decisions and actions the world has ever known. They employ sound decision-making processes, including investigating multiple alternatives, seeking out dissent, and fostering a decision culture of inquiry rather than advocacy. In short, they become effective decision machines in which Great Men aren't necessary or desired, at least in the sense of dictating an answer "just because s/he's the boss."

When such organizations employ these approaches on an ongoing basis, we call it good organizational judgment.

Of course, leaders are still important (though perhaps not 343 times more important as the average worker, as today's salary scales imply). Good leaders create the agenda of decisions to be made. They set the tone for culture and decision processes. They encourage the diverse members of their organizations to step up and participate in deliberations and decisions. We are not dismissive of leadership and leaders in this book at all, but we think they have a new set of roles to play. The Great Man (or Woman) of the future knows the role of the great leader is not to decide important questions alone—but rather to ensure that all the right things happen across their organizations so that the best thinking and the best problem solving results in a better answer.

Patterns of Change in Today's Organizations

A sea change is under way in many organizations today, as we observe where and from whom judgment is valued, and how it gets exercised in contemporary decision making. The changes—decision making more among frontline workers, more distributed, more team based, and so forth—are consistent with the decline of the Great Man and the rise of the Great Organization and good organizational judgment. At least four major trends are beginning to shape a new pattern that we think will define good decision making in the future:

- The recognition that "none of us is as smart as all of us." Social media, prediction markets, involving customers in product development—all of these are evidence that leading organizations want to tap the wisdom of the crowd, as Jim Surowiecki put it in his seminal book.[15] While involving multiple people in decisions can be unwieldy and doesn't always yield a better outcome, it is often both possible and likely to yield a better result.

- The second trend is tapping not just the wisdom of the crowd, but the leadership of the crowd. While hierarchy and leadership from CEOs and presidents are not going away, there are increasing settings in which "collective leadership" is being employed. Of course, we are all familiar with the "open innovation" technologies of Linux and Firefox, but that is only one model. As Mehrdad Baghai and Jim Quigley, the former CEO of Deloitte, have noted in a recent book, there are a variety of collective leadership "archetypes" based on whether the work structure is emergent (as in, for example, community organizing with volunteers) or directive (as in the relationship between a general and soldiers), and whether the work itself is scripted (as in an orchestra) or creative (as in an improv play).[16] These dimensions open up multiple ways for many to work as one, and for organizations to benefit from leadership and decision making by multiple contributors. This means, of course, that the organization would also benefit from efforts to improve the decision-making capabilities of its collective leaders.

- The use of data and analytics to support—and sometimes actually make—decisions. Intuition will never vanish—nor should it—but there is plenty of evidence that when data or scientific evidence is available, they lead to better decisions than intuition alone. Some organizations are "competing on analytics," while others are simply using them as an occasional aid to better decisions.[17] It may be romantic to believe that we can "thin-slice" our way to better decisions, as Malcolm Gladwell argues in *Blink*, but the fact is that good decisions typically require systematic analysis. Even some of Gladwell's examples of supposed thin-slicing actually used detailed analysis—such as the marriage scientist John Gottman.[18] He can tell you in a few minutes of observation whether you are likely to stay married to your spouse, but he can only do so after decades of behavior and speech coding, and deep statistical analysis of it.

- The fourth relatively new factor is one that has continued to alter so many aspects of business and life more generally: information technology. It doesn't create better organizational judgment directly, but it's definitely an enabler of the other changes we have mentioned. While early applications of IT have primarily been about better transactions, over the last decade or so they have firmly entered the realms of knowledge, insight, and judgment. Technology makes possible the changes above of increased participation and analytical decision support. It also allows for the capture and distribution of many forms of explicit and even implicit knowledge. While judgment has historically been a subject that addressed human rather than technological capabilities, no current account of the nature of judgment would be complete without significant mention of the latter's role.

All of these changes come at a time when external conditions in the world have made getting decisions right more important than ever. Businesses face ever-higher levels of competition, and in a climate of increasing economic uncertainty and volatility, markets and customers move faster than ever before. Further, the same technologies that make it easier to tap collective wisdom within organizations also create more transparency into them; the punishment for getting big decisions wrong is swift and stern.

Of course, many things haven't changed in the world of organizational judgment. As we hope our stories will demonstrate, good judgment and consistently good decision making require such eternal verities as good leadership, strong culture and values, accountability, and good decision processes. These are widely emphasized in the decision-making literature, but rarely in combination with the four new factors that have transformed the judgment environment.

How Organizations Are Responding

In response to these changes, some organizations are taking the usual "head in the sand" approach. On the issue of more participation, insecure senior executives are simply reminding themselves that they are the boss, and insisting that only their judgment and decisions count. On social technologies, instead of figuring out how they can facilitate collaboration and group judgment, many firms still ban their use altogether. One survey of chief information officers found that 54 percent ban all social media use at work (though it's likely that many of their employees find a way to access Facebook anyway).[19] With data and analytics, many senior executives continue to trust their gut; another survey suggested that 40 percent of decisions are still based on it—and we think that's probably lower than the true number.[20]

But many executives have looked around, have seen that the world is changing, and are moving with, or even ahead of, the patterns of change. The organizations we describe in this book have embraced new approaches to judgment building and have already applied it to important decisions. They're consulting more people and drawing from their expertise, adopting some form of collective leadership, applying data and analysis to decisions, and supporting it all with new technology. They are focusing on either big, strategic decisions or the daily tactical decisions that

are critical to successful execution of strategy. Leaders are still exercising their responsibilities, but they are doing so in more participative and
humble ways. There is no gimmickry here—the organizations we describe
are all simply doing their homework in various ways, and they are getting
better decision results.

Why Look at Good Decisions?

This book has twelve stories of how particular decisions were made and
improved through activities designed to build organizational judgment.
Decisions are an important lens for these judgment-building activities
because they are the objective of them. If you think about it, a vast amount
of organizational activity these days is ultimately intended to improve
decision making. Many IT projects, for example, have this as at least an
implicit goal. If you're putting in an expensive new enterprise system,
building a data warehouse, constructing a knowledge management system, or installing business intelligence software, your ultimate purpose
is to support better decisions within your organization. Outside of the
realm of IT, perhaps your organization is trying to improve decisions via
decision role clarification, reengineering a decision-oriented business
process, or addressing a particular decision, such as those in a business
strategy. If you have undertaken such activities and those better decisions are not actually happening, something is wrong. Perhaps you need
to establish a closer connection between those activities and the actual
decisions that need to be improved.

But despite occasional problems, decisions can be improved and made
well with good organizational judgment. We chose to tell stories of good
decisions because we think the world needs some good examples to emu-
late. It's all too easy to focus on bad decisions (as we have done at the
beginning of this chapter), and there is certainly no shortage of them. But
we thought that readers might be tired of reading (and hearing and watch-
ing) about the bad decisions made by banks in the financial crisis, the poor

judgments made by BP and its business partners that led to the oil spill in the Gulf, or the bad calls at NASA that led to the *Challenger* and *Columbia* shuttle disasters. Yes, bad decisions happen, and sometimes they can be very instructive. And we all like to read about human frailty and the troubles that ensue from it. But the world doesn't seem to be getting better at decisions, even after these poor examples have been studied in great depth. So we decided to "accentuate the positive." The organizations we describe in this book are surely not perfect, but they seem to be making headway in the journey to better decisions.

Instead of providing you with a checklist, we are recounting stories— perhaps not the most rigorous form of evidence, but often the most memorable type. We subscribe to the power of narrative for learning and modeling. We also believe that stories incorporate necessary context and human fabric. And does the world really need another management framework?

That said, there is an implicit framework that emerges from these stories, or at least some common themes that we think define the new paradigm for organizational judgment. They are:

- *Decision making as a participative problem-solving process.* Organizational judgment at its core depends on a disciplined (if not always highly structured) process. In its various steps, the process will include, at the outset, framing the problem to be solved; pursuing the problem through iterative steps that progressively refine the questions that must be answered; engaging diversity of opinion; using fact-based analysis to weigh benefits and risks, and generate and test hypotheses; and pursuing all appropriate options based on continuous deliberation and learning until the best answer emerges. Equally important as the process per se is the need for it to be (albeit in varying degrees in different situations) participative. When organizations with good judgment make important decisions, they routinely engage a broader group than just a few top executives, if not "the crowd"; they seek multiple points of view, including contrarian ones; they work especially to include people with the best knowledge and experience, regardless of status or hierarchy; they embrace the perspective of the "front line" or key stakeholders (including partners, suppliers, and customers) who must implement and live with the decisions made.

- *The opportunities of new technology and analytics.* As more companies recognize the power and value of technology-enabled analysis and analytics for defining their strategy, marketing, or making other key decisions, a new standard is emerging about the integration of data analysis into the "front office" of every business. No longer the rarified provenance of "the geeks downstairs," technology is becoming integral to decision making, and the overall judgment exercised by the organization, whatever the industry or sector.

- *The power of culture.* Organizations that practice great judgment inevitably have many of the key attributes and values mentioned embedded in their operating culture (respect for the problem-solving process; inclusiveness; leaders as facilitators of decisions, not "monarchs," etc.). Some organizations come by the new kind of values and behaviors more naturally than others; in some cases, as the need for better decision making and new patterns begins to emerge, cultural change evolves hand in hand with more "democratic" and analytical approaches.

- *Leaders doing the right thing and establishing the right context.* The role of the leader in creating organizational judgment is often first about reframing decisions as indeed not their own exclusively. But great leaders also work to ensure that the processes and mind-sets of more distributed, problem-solving approaches key to judgment are in place and part of the norms of doing business in their enterprise. In many cases they can be seen instituting cultural change to migrate their organizations toward overall better judgment.

We see these themes at work in different ways in different dimensions in the stories we have collected, and each chapter will exhibit some of the variations in them. Of course, as an evolving paradigm, organizational judgment can be found in various, often incomplete forms; it would be foolish to expect any single organization to have all of these ideas complete, perfect, and implemented at a 100-percent level. Our stories show the outlines that are emerging—and you and your own organization can fill in the details as you consider how decision making in your own work might benefit from the ideas of this new approach.

Why You Should Read This Book

If you think that you have a "golden gut," that you always make excellent decisions on your own, that you are the only person whose opinions matter within your organization, and that social technologies are purely a waste of time, you probably won't be comfortable with this book—and you should drop it immediately. If you have only read this far, we are confident you can get your money back.

But if you're still reading, that means you believe in the possibility that other people in your organization just might have expertise or opinions that could help in your decisions, and that evidence and data analysis might be helpful in decisions too. Maybe you'd simply like to get a better understanding of the iterative and deliberative decision processes that successful organizations employ. If you are a senior manager within your organization, with responsibility for making the organization better, you have really come to the right place. You naturally would like to help your firm or agency or school make better decisions over time. We hope to convince you that undertaking activities to improve your organization's overall and collective judgment is the best way to bring that about.

If you are an individual contributor or educator or consultant, of course you make decisions too—and you can probably benefit from hearing about better ways to make them. You may not have a large organization that you are trying to get into shape, but everybody is a member of a social network (not Facebook, but the social relationships themselves) from whose wisdom you can benefit, and in the age of the Internet, anybody can gather and analyze some data to help with a difficult problem. We believe that knowing about the organizational context of judgment will help more junior or even free-floating individuals improve their ability to make decisions.

No matter what your employment situation, we think you'll enjoy reading these stories about how organizations are making increasingly good decisions with the new and old tools at their disposal. So we invite you to read through our stories and see where this new world is headed.

Part One

Stories About the Participative Problem-Solving Process

THE FIRST PART OF THE BOOK begins with a few stories of organizations that showcase the first two themes of the new pattern discussed in the introduction: framing decisions as an iterative problem-solving process, and engaging in a more self-consciously participative approach to getting to a good answer. The segment begins with the tale of NASA, and a difficult launch decision its personnel had to make one time about the (recently retired) space shuttle. We'll see how NASA—an organization known for some bad decisions with tragic consequences in the past—learned from its mistakes and embraced a better approach to organizational judgment. After that we'll focus on an interesting and innovative small business whose leader turned a home-building business challenge into a value-added problem-solving process. And we'll conclude the segment with a case study of the global consulting firm McKinsey & Company—and a major decision its partners made about acquiring and developing their most precious of assets: their people.

1

NASA STS-119

Should We Launch?

I N FEBRUARY 2009, the engineers and scientists of NASA were wrestling with a grave, potentially life-or-death decision: whether to green-light the launch of mission STS-119, the next flight of the space shuttle *Discovery*. Every launch of a NASA manned spacecraft puts astronaut lives and millions of dollars of equipment on the line; reputation, political capital, and scientific standing also ride on a successful launch, but catastrophe can undo them all. For every mission, NASA would like the maximum possible certainty, but there are project pressures against endless debate and analysis to unravel every possible concern. Operational schedules are tightly wound and project milestones are critical. The issue here was whether STS-119 might have a faulty valve in the systems supplying fuel to the engines, integral to maintaining pressure in the all-important hydrogen tank. The previous mission (STS-126) had experienced such a problem, which had happily not affected the success of that flight. But NASA engineers do not bet on good luck—and the risk of possible disaster with this next mission was very real. The piece of equipment in question, no longer manufactured, could not be easily replaced—but it was buttressed by some system redundancy with other valves. Should STS-119 be launched? Could the flight readiness review team get to the right "go or no-go decision" with the appropriate level of confidence?[1]

Looming over these critical questions was the history of NASA itself, some fifty years of pioneering scientific triumphs punctuated by a few, but heartbreaking, accidents—where an occasional bad decision led to historic tragedy. How to be sure that this decision didn't become another tragedy? The real story of the launch of STS-119 is not about what finally happened, but about the power of how NASA personnel finally decided what to do—a process of disciplined and iterative decision making, buttressed by a strong but pragmatic culture of inquiry, things NASA developed in the morning-after clarity and learning following some historic and very public errors in judgment.

Learning from History

As the whole world knows, the first of those errors in judgment resulted in the fireball in the sky on January 28, 1986, when the space shuttle *Challenger* exploded in its second minute of flight, killing its entire crew. Despite concerns that cold weather could reduce the effectiveness of the O-ring pressure seals at the joints of the space shuttle's solid rocket motors, NASA managers had approved the launch of *Challenger* on that day, when the temperature at the Kennedy Space Center was barely above freezing. The spacecraft was destroyed as the failure of an O-ring to seal its joint allowed a jet of hot flame to escape and breach the shuttle's external fuel tank, causing a fatal ignition of the liquid hydrogen and liquid oxygen it contained.

Like every shuttle launch, the January 1986 mission was preceded by a flight readiness review (an FRR, in NASA acronymspeak), whose purpose was to evaluate issues that might threaten mission success and to withhold launch permission until those issues are resolved. Two weeks earlier, an FRR had certified *Challenger* ready for flight. Of course, participants in that meeting could not foresee how cold it would be two weeks hence. The day before the launch, NASA personnel became concerned about the weather; the solid rocket motor manager at Marshall Space Flight Center asked Morton Thiokol, the manufacturer of those motors, to review their safety in cold weather. In a series of teleconferences that evening, Thiokol engineers initially recommended against a low-temperature launch. But after their view was challenged by NASA shuttle managers, an offline "caucus" among engineers and managers at Thiokol reversed that recommendation. *Challenger* lifted off the next morning and was destroyed seventy-three seconds later.

The presidential commission set up to examine the *Challenger* disaster found that pressure to maintain the shuttle program's launch schedule led managers to minimize the seriousness of engineers' concerns about the O-rings.[2] The perceived need for shuttle "productivity" certainly contributed to the error in judgment. Sociologist Diane Vaughn's detailed study of the launch-approval process in *The Challenger Launch Decision* offers a fuller and more nuanced explanation. Vaughn points to what she calls "the normalization of deviance" as a key factor. Because earlier cold or cool weather flights that suffered O-ring problems did not result in disaster, that initially unexpected damage was gradually accepted as normal. FRR participants had come to view it as an acceptable risk. In other words, the success of nearly two dozen previous missions led to complacency that failed to take the danger seriously enough. The result, says Vaughn, was "an incremental descent into poor judgment."[3]

She also points to problems in the deliberative process during the January 27 teleconferences. NASA managers at Kennedy and Marshall Space Flight Center could not see the engineers at Morton Thiokol who had concerns about the O-rings. They missed the "body language" that could have helped expressed the engineers' unease; they were unaware of the local conversations between calls that might have given them a better grasp of the technical issue. As a result, the level of the engineers' concern was not clearly communicated. In addition, NASA's technical culture tended to discount the engineers' partly intuitive argument about the dangers.

So the multiple causes of bad judgment in this disastrous case include reluctance to credit "bad news" that would thwart schedule and productivity goals, complacency resulting from a history of success, and ineffective communication.

Seventeen years later, the only other fatal shuttle accident—the *Columbia*—occurred. It is unclear whether the crew could have been saved if NASA had understood the damage to *Columbia* while it was in orbit, but the board that investigated the disaster attributed the agency's failure to try to assess possible damage to many of the same factors behind the *Challenger* decision, especially the complacency born of many successes and communication failures.

This second accident and the criticisms in the Columbia Accident Investigation Board report strengthened NASA's resolve to address the cultural as well as the procedural flaws responsible for those fatal errors, and multiple changes to both process and culture were instituted over time.[4] Looking now at the flight readiness review—for STS-119, the *Discovery* mission originally scheduled for launch on February 19, 2009, and finally launched nearly a month later, on March 15—will illustrate what the space agency has done to ensure the soundness of its judgments about flight viability and safety.

The Flight Readiness Review

Today, the flight readiness reviews held at Kennedy Space Center before a scheduled launch date bring technical teams and managers together in one room, including representatives from three domains: program, engineering, and safety—about 150 people in the case of the STS-119 review. The importance of gathering them in one place, face-to-face, is clear when you contrast such a meeting with the *Challenger* teleconference, or any teleconference for that matter, where inattention, misunderstanding, and incomplete communication are common.

The FRR is preceded by a series of smaller team meetings and technical reviews to discuss and analyze issues that will come up in the formal FRR. There are likely to be fifty teams working on specific technologies, projects, and subsystems. These meetings are part of an ecology of decision-making redundancies, integrated tightly into an overall and well-orchestrated process of problem solving. Overlapping authorities and tasks increase the odds of exposing potential issues and uncertainties—they can't fall through the cracks if there are no cracks. This way of working, and the culture by which the entire process is facilitated, also gives early and ample opportunity for people to speak out when they see a problem. Mike Ryschkewitsch, NASA's chief engineer, says, "You know one of the things that NASA strongly emphasizes now is that any individual who works here, if they see something that doesn't look right, they have a responsibility to raise it, and they can raise it . . . for example, you have whole communities of experts throughout NASA whose whole life is about maximizing safety to the crew."

In large part thanks to all that preliminary work, many FRRs are fairly routine. Problems have been identified, analyzed, and solved beforehand. Representatives of the teams that carried out that technical work present their results to the group as a whole and have the knowledge they need to answer the questions their colleagues may raise. The STS-119 review— which actually became a series of reviews—was unusual. The technical problem about the engine valve first noted was barely understood at the time of the first FRR and not resolved to the satisfaction of many partici- pants at a second, marathon session. It took three meetings to arrive at "go" for launch. That "decision about the decision making" showed that the FRR is not a rubber stamp on a foregone conclusion; it demonstrated Ryschke- witsch's claim that people at NASA felt free to delay flights over technical concerns, putting flight safety ahead of schedule and productivity. Though the process of problem solving and decision making is well structured, the culture of dissent and open exchange balances and gives critical flexibility to what might otherwise be a dangerously rote activity.

The Problem of the Faulty Valve

The problem that faced the engineers and scientists who took part in the FRR for STS-119 came to light during the previous shuttle mission, STS-126. Shortly after that spacecraft, *Endeavor*, lifted off from Kennedy Space Center on November 14, 2008, flight controllers noticed an unexpected hydrogen flow increase related to one of the shuttle's three main engines. Because three control valves work together to maintain proper pressure in the hydrogen tank, the other valves compensated for the malfunction and the flight proceeded safely. But before another mission could fly, the shuttle team would need to understand why and how the problem occurred, whether it was likely to happen again, and just how dangerous a recurrence might be.

Bad weather in Florida forced *Endeavor* to land in California on November 30 and the shuttle was not returned to Kennedy until December 12, delaying examination of the faulty valve by almost two weeks. X-rays showed that a fragment of the valve's poppet (a tapered plug that moves up and down to regulate flow) had broken off. So the risks engineers had to consider included not only the kind of hydrogen flow anomaly they had seen on STS-126, but the possibility that a poppet fragment racing through propellant lines might rupture one of them. The level of risk depends on two factors: the likelihood of a problem happening and the seriousness of the consequences if it does. The consequences of a ruptured line would be disastrous, so the likelihood had to be extremely low to make the risk acceptable. The necessary technical analysis would have to have two major components: studying the valve to determine why the poppet broke, as a way of understanding the probability of a similar failure; and figuring out whether a poppet fragment was at all likely to breach the propellant system.

Because the valve is part of a system that included the shuttle, the main engines, and the external fuel tank, responsibility for understanding its failure lay with teams at the Johnson Space Center in Houston, the

Marshall Space Flight Center in Huntsville, Alabama, and several NASA contractors, including a division of Boeing. They began work on these issues. The process proved challenging.

The first flight readiness review for STS-119 took place on February 3. It quickly became apparent that the technical teams did not yet understand the problems well enough to certify that the next shuttle spacecraft for this mission, *Discovery*, was ready to fly. Steve Altemus, director of engineering at Johnson Space Center, said, "We showed up at the first FRR and we're saying, 'We don't have a clear understanding of the flow environment, so therefore we can't tell you what the likelihood of having this poppet piece come off will be. We have to get a better handle on the consequences of a particle release.'" The launch was rescheduled for February 22—overoptimistically, as it turned out—and the technical teams kept working.

They faced tricky problems. X-ray analysis had determined that the poppet failed because of high-cycle fatigue—that is, damage caused by repeated use. Unfortunately, these components were no longer manufactured and were in short supply, so the option of acquiring new, unstressed poppets did not exist. Given that fact, a reasonable approach could be to examine poppets for cracks that might indicate potential weakness; a poppet with no cracks seemed extremely unlikely to fail. But even electron microscopes could not reliably locate tiny cracks unless the poppets were polished first, and polishing subtly changed the hardware, invalidating its flight certification.

Trying to determine whether a poppet fragment might puncture a fuel line was made even more difficult because of the complexity of the fluid dynamics analysis necessary to determine the velocity, spin, and probable path of fragments of different sizes. The behavior of rapidly moving fluid is notoriously hard to predict. NASA's Glenn Research Center, Stennis Space Center, and the White Sands Test Facility began impact testing to simulate and try to understand the problem.

A second FRR was scheduled for February 20. Scott Johnson, chief safety officer for the shuttle, noted that "the majority of the safety community was concerned about the amount of open work in front of us. As a result, I recommended that we delay the FRR. We still had a lot of analysis work going on. We weren't really that close to being able to quantify the risks."

The Marathon Flight Readiness Review

The review proceeded as scheduled, however. More than 150 people gathered in the cavernous Operations Support Building 2 at Kennedy Space Center: engineers and managers from NASA centers, international partners, contractors, consultants, and former employees—"graybeards," in NASA parlance—whose practical wisdom was valued by the generations that followed them. The astronauts who were to fly on STS-119 were there as well. Bill Gerstenmaier, head of space operations, who facilitated the meeting, wrote afterward, "I worked with all the astronauts very closely . . . their kids went to school with my kids, and here they are in the very room where we are discussing their safety." Mike Ryschkewitsch remembers, "The kind of pressure we were under says if we make a bad mistake, people die . . . These are our friends and acquaintances and we are saying to them, 'This is good enough for you to fly.'"

Ed Hoffman, director of NASA's Academy of Program/Project and Engineering Leadership, which is responsible for the knowledge sharing and project management development throughout the agency, observed that the immensity of the building, the sense of purpose, and the muted but palpable anxiety present that day reminded him of a service in a cathedral.

The meeting lasted nearly fourteen hours, far longer than any earlier FRR. It was an indication of both continuing uncertainty about technical issues and the openness of management to full and free discussion.

Despite the tremendous amount of analysis and testing that had been done, technical presentations on the causes of the broken valve on STS-126 and the likelihood of recurrence were incomplete and inconclusive. Unlike at most FRRs, new data streamed in during the review and informed the conversation. A chart reporting margins of safety included TBD (to be determined) notations.

Doubts about some test data arose when Gene Grush, lead of the Johnson Space Center's Concept Analysis Team, received a phone call from NASA's Stennis Space Center informing him that the program to evaluate the danger of material broken off a poppet breaching a fuel line had used the wrong material. "I had to stand up in front of that huge room and say, 'Well there's a little problem with our testing. Yes, we did very well, but the hardness of the particle wasn't as hard as it should have been.' That was very critical because that means that your test is no longer conservative. You've got good results, but you didn't test with the right particle," he said.

While presentations and discussion continued in the Operations Support Building, Mike Ryschkewitsch brought more than one hundred other engineers into the conversation by way of an e-mail thread. He recalls, "People thought I was doing my own e-mail, but of course I wasn't. I'm sending messages out to all of these guys, with things like 'I just heard this; do you all agree?' . . . I sent maybe two to three hundred messages in all. It allowed me to have my own equivalent of a back room caucus . . . We are in the kitchen talking and having little arguments back and forth. Right at the very end of the very long day I put a poll out to everyone and said 'Are we ready to go or not?' "

Commenting on the length and openness of the session, NASA chief safety and mission assurance officer Bryan O'Connor remarked, "Gerst [FRR chairman Bill Gerstenmaier] was absolutely open. He never tried to shut them down. Even though he could probably tell this is going to take a long time, he never let the clock . . . appear to be something that he was worried about."

That is not to say that Gerstenmaier was indifferent to the launch schedule. *Discovery* was scheduled to deliver the final set of solar arrays needed to complete the International Space Station's electricity-generating solar panels, enabling the station to support an expanded crew of six. If STS-119 launched later than March 15, it would interfere with the March 26 mission of the Russian Soyuz vehicle to transport the Expedition 19 crew to the station, and would push back future U.S. launches. Late in the day, Gerstenmaier reminded the group of these risks to the Space Station program and the shuttle schedule. A few participants perceived his comments as pressure to approve the flight. Others saw it as appropriate context setting, making clear the broader issues that were part of their collective judgment. After he spoke, he gave the groups forty minutes to "caucus," to discuss what they had heard during the day and decide on their recommendations. When they came back, he polled the groups. The engineering and safety organizations and some center directors in attendance made it clear that they did not find adequate rationale to fly STS-119.

NASA manager Steve Altemus summed up the decision: "as a community we never really got our arms around the true risks." Bill McArthur, safety and mission assurance manager for the space shuttle at the time, said, "The fact that people were willing to stand up and say 'We just aren't ready yet' is a real testament to fact that our culture has evolved so that we weren't overwhelmed with launch fever." That syndrome in the past had led dissenting voices to be discouraged and, even worse, treated with disdain. As the participants filed out of the meeting, Joyce Seriale-Grush said to Mike Ryschkewitsch, "This was really hard and I'm disappointed that we didn't have the data today, but it feels so much better than it used to feel, because we had to say that we weren't ready and people listened to us. It didn't always used to be that way."

Clearly, the culture and norms around open discussions and speaking truth to power had changed considerably from the days of *Challenger*.

Discovery Mission Success

After the FRR, Gerstenmaier had doubts about making a March 15 launch date, but he decided to "kick it back to the team, give them the action, see what they can go do and see how it comes out." Approximately one thousand people worked intensely on the problem.

A breakthrough came when an eddy current system, typically used to test the integrity of bolts, was successfully adapted to check for cracks in valve poppets without affecting that hardware. Results of those tests gave engineers and managers confidence that the risks of another valve malfunction were acceptably small.

The third FRR, on March 6, led to a "go" decision. "By the time we eventually all got together on the last FRR the comfort level was very high," said O'Connor. "For one thing, everybody understood this topic so well. You couldn't say, 'I'm uncomfortable because I don't understand.' We had a great deal of understanding of not only what we knew about, but what we didn't know about. We had a good understanding of the limits of our knowledge as much as possible, whereas before we didn't know what those were."

In the final decision-making session, the astronauts slated to take the controls of *Discovery* were also in the room. Sitting before the scientists, engineers, and managers, they were a powerful and visible reminder of the stakes of the decision. They too had a vote for readiness. If ever there were an example of a decision-making process engaging—critically—the people who had to live with the judgment made, this would be it.

STS-119 was approved for launch on March 11. After delays due to a leak in a liquid hydrogen vent line (unrelated to the valve problem), *Discovery* lifted off on March 15, 2009, and safely and successfully completed its mission.

The Persistence of Good Judgment

Several elements of the process used to analyze, delay, and eventually approve the launch contributed to NASA's good judgment. Overriding all was the design of an FRR problem-solving process, which brought together so many and varied experts and interested parties in one room and also through a series of well-orchestrated offline working sessions. Discussions were artfully facilitated so stakeholders could listen to one another and discuss their findings and opinions in a "truth first, hierarchy later" kind of way. Widespread, "democratic" polling (rather than, say, providing information to a few senior managers who would make the decision themselves) was another hallmark of the process. The FRR designed into the process the presence and influence of multiple viewpoints and sets of expertise—an important component of judgment, and one that study after study has shown to be critical to successful decision making.[5]

The extent and quality of testing and research, including having separate groups take different approaches to the same problem, were also important. The scientific culture of NASA, and its commitment to having the best possible factual information, was another critical aspect.

Understanding the importance and potential consequences of a decision—in this case, seeing the astronauts whose lives depend on the shuttle technology and, at the same time, understanding the legitimate need to fly as soon as it is possible to do so safely—was a living example of another invaluable dimension of building judgment into this process: tightly linking the stakes of the decision to the accountability for what would be decided.

The leader's approach and style in managing this entire process was also fundamental.[6] Decision-making processes are often subverted by a leader who pays lip service to consultation, going through the motions of openness while pushing the group toward the choice he's already made. Similarly, some attempts to create a decision-making process fail because they go to the opposite extreme—encouraging endless discussion and lowest-common-denominator consensus building.

NASA colleagues praised Gerstenmaier's openness to discussion and debate while still keeping his eye on the need to find the best possible answer in the context of project constraints. Several of the participants in the FRRs commented generally on how NASA's culture has been changed, learning from the tragedies that came before—away from "launch fever" and much more balanced toward safety; away from discouraging or disregarding dissent from engineers and others, but rather embracing scientific inquiry as a critical partner in final decision making.

The earlier, fatal errors in the shuttle program happened in part because of the agency's tendency to think of space flight as routine—operational rather than experimental—when it in fact remains a risky endeavor that tests the limits of complex technology designed to control immense forces. Gerstenmaier notes that the probability of failure of a shuttle mission with no obvious technical problems is about 1 in 77—not odds that any of us would accept in commercial aviation. In "Some Safety Lessons Learned," Bryan O'Conner writes about the importance and difficulty of fighting complacency:

> Countering complacency is arguably harder than recovering
> from a mishap. We have to find creative ways to counteract the
> common psychological tendency to assume that a string of
> successes means that we have somehow reached a state of
> engineering and operational perfection—and, therefore, immunity
> from failure.[7]

Sustaining a commitment to safety—and to good judgment—requires constant, vigilant attention to both processes and culture. It also requires what writer Edmund Gosse long ago described as "higher modesty"—the recognition that, no matter how smart and knowledgeable you are, you can still be thoroughly wrong about important issues.[8]

Reflections on Organizational Judgment in NASA STS-119

In a recent study, Karl Weick and Kathleen Sutcliffe analyzed what they called "high-reliability organizations"—and what they do to perform consistently at a high level of quality control.[9] The mind-set and processes of organizations like hostage negotiation teams, emergency medical teams, nuclear power facilities, and firefighters are integrated and designed to perform better than many organizations; they have to be, because their price for failure is high. A major barrier they constantly fight to overcome is complacency and arrogance. Weick and Sutcliffe note five attributes of these organizations, all of which we can identify in this NASA case: commitment to tracking small failures, the ability to recognize and understand complex issues, real attention to frontline (operational) workers, the ability to learn from and rebound from errors, and the ability to improvise effective response to crisis.

A major part of NASA's ability to do all those things was its problem-solving process, as seen in this case. It both followed a clear and logical analytical approach, in appropriate sequence, and also counterbalanced the sequence by flexibility for change as needed. The overarching culture was one of open exchange, honoring of diverse opinions, and the embrace of the right to dissent. Today we admire NASA not just for its successes but for its ability to rebound from the horrible tragedies of *Challenger* and *Columbia*. If ever there has been a resilient and high-reliability organization, it is the National Aeronautics and Space Administration—and the judgment it has built is clearly a very important part of what it is.

2

WGB Homes

How Can We Sell This House?

GREG BURRILL IS the owner and founder of WGB Homes. WGB has built over 1,800 homes in the western and southern suburbs of Boston. Boston is known for its "Route 128" technology corridor, but in fact most of the technology activity in recent years has taken place near Interstate 495, the "outer loop" that when originally built, ran through farms, fields, and small towns. Now it's the home of EMC, Hewlett-Packard, Staples, and other large employers, and Greg Burrill has built a lot of homes for their executives and employees. The area—alternatively known as MetroWest or the Blackstone Valley—also has good access to downtown Boston via the Massachusetts Turnpike and commuter rail service. It's been the primary growth area for residential real estate in Boston over the last twenty or thirty years, since there was plenty of both open space and jobs in the area.[1]

Burrill's been in business for thirty-nine years—through good times and bad for home builders—so he must be doing something right.

He's conservative in his approach to his business, never going into deep debt like many home builders. "You have to have low loan-to-value ratios, and you have to have cash," he notes. He also simply slows the pace of development and construction down when times are tough. They've certainly been tough over the last several years; Burrill doesn't remember a period of decline in residential real estate that lasted this long.

WGB Homes is primarily a family business. Greg Burrill's brother Steve is its vice president. His two daughters, Erica and Vanessa, both work for the company, as does one son-in-law. In a newspaper article about the company, a buyer of one of their homes described them as "nice, honest, fair people."[2] The company's pattern is to build one development project at a time—enough to keep all members of the family and company busy, but not anything that will bankrupt the company in a residential construction turndown. They do it all—buy the raw land, develop the land, build houses, and market them. They will occasionally even resell a house in one of their neighborhoods if approached by the owner.

WGB's current development project is called Brookmeadow Village. It's in the semirural town of South Grafton. Grafton was one of the Massachusetts towns known for "praying Indians"; the Pilgrim missionary John Eliot established a church and school for the Nipmuck tribe there in 1671. It was later known briefly for woolen manufacturing. Today it's mostly an exurb for young families who can't afford the high housing prices nearer Boston. It's still not cheap, however; new houses in Brookmeadow Village average just over half a million dollars.

Brookmeadow Village is a ninety-one-lot neighborhood. Burrill prides himself on building neighborhoods, not subdivisions, and the company sponsors parties and picnics throughout the year for the neighborhoods it has built. Brookmeadow Village is located on one hundred thirty acres and includes a small retail complex, seventy-five acres of open space, and over two miles of walking trails leading down to baseball and soccer fields. All houses are Energy Star certified—Burrill's first development with that qualification. Overall, the selling of the project has gone well given the difficult economy; over twenty homes have been built and sold—including one to Erica Burrill and her husband.

The House That Wouldn't Sell

Despite the success of the project overall, one of WGB's spec houses in Brookmeadow Village sat unsold for much longer than the usual period. Priced at about $550,000, it was a substantial investment to carry for a family firm. WGB had tried something new with this particular home, but given what Burrill knew of changing demographics and customer preferences, it seemed like a safe bet. But if so, why wasn't it selling?

A nonselling house is an occasional but important problem for a small business like WGB. The way the company tackled the challenge reflects perhaps the most core element of great organizational judgment—pursuing a decision through an iterative process of problem solving. But the way it did that also reflects the special culture and leadership style of founder Greg Burrill.

Burrill's sales staff heard regularly from empty nesters and couples with older children that they enjoyed the community feel of a suburban neighborhood, but had different needs than young families. The wish for a master bedroom on the first floor came up repeatedly. Besides anticipating the day when they would not want to climb stairs so frequently, many customers thought the aging of the baby boom generation would give such houses high resale value. So WGB designed this house—called the Oxford—with a first floor master suite. It also had three other bedrooms upstairs, and a relatively small backyard—again, for baby boomers who don't want to spend all their time cutting grass—that looked out over forested land.

And indeed, interest in the house was high. But despite a significant amount of traffic through it, after six months it hadn't sold. At that point, Burrill worked with his sales office to figure out alternative ways to market the house, and also reduced the price a bit. That brought even more traffic—but months later, still no sale. Clearly the location was not the issue, but was it the lot size, or the price, or something about the design?

Burrill thought systematically about what he could change in the house. The lot size was fixed. He'd already lowered the price a bit, and lowering it further might reduce perceived values of all the other houses and lots in Brookmeadow Village. He leaned toward the design as the problem. Two other houses in the Grafton area with similar designs, built by other local builders, weren't selling either. Yet changing the design would be difficult, so he needed more information.

Sourcing the Wisdom of the (In) Crowd

Burrill had faced similar situations before during difficult housing markets, so he knew what to do. Whenever a house doesn't sell, he calls on the wisdom of the crowd. The crowd, in this case, is anyone who might have an informed opinion on the issue, including:

- His wife and the family members who work for the company, including his brother, his two daughters, and his son-in-law

- The other twelve or so employees of WGB Homes

- Subcontractors who have worked on the house and on others in the development

- Customers who purchased other houses in the neighborhood

Burrill asks everyone who's seen the house to furnish opinions about how to improve it. "Everyone is a designer or an architect at heart," he says, "so why not learn from them?" Most are happy to volunteer a perspective. At times Burrill has even undertaken larger-scale surveys of customers; his firm recently surveyed about four hundred customers, for example, about issues around the sales process and their perceptions about WGB's model homes.

Burrill had always been interested in other people's ideas about his houses, but as his business has grown, and as his own family members have become more involved in it, he has realized that the insights and opinions of everyone involved in building and selling the houses are extremely valuable. "I try to surround myself with people who are smarter than I am," he notes modestly, "and I get as many opinions as I can. But then I have to make the decision."

The Group Discussion

After the solicitation of multiple opinions, Burrill assembled a meeting of WGB family members, aiming for some collective decision making. Everything people had heard or thought was put on the table. Some of the informal advisers who had toured the house thought there just weren't as many boomer buyers as Burrill had counted on. Comments by younger families who'd been turned off by the first floor master were recalled.

Burrill's daughters, Erica and Vanessa, who handle sales and marketing for him, had also picked up signals from older couples. It seemed that while those target buyers might imagine they wanted a first floor master, when it came down to buying, they ended up purchasing what they were used to—especially when the trade-off sank in, that they would lose space on the first floor to entertain. "Half my first floor would be the master bedroom," one buyer commented. Erica and Vanessa recalled several instances where they would have people who were very interested in the Oxford model and then decided to buy a second floor master from them—or worse, a second floor master from another builder. It led Burrill and his family to believe that as much as a first floor master is what buyers said they wanted, their buying habits reflected otherwise.

By the end of the meeting, the team had concluded that the floor plan was the problem, and had come up with ways to improve it. The specific changes to the house involved adding a bathroom to the second floor and expanding an area over the garage to accommodate it. That made it possible for parents with small children to have their bedroom on the second floor and then move downstairs at whatever point they chose. At any stage, the second "in-law" suite could be put to good use. Burrill also improved the view from the back of the house by changing some windows, and expanded the entertaining space by opening up the kitchen to the family room. The downside of making multiple changes at once is that you never know exactly what leads to a successful outcome. But Burrill had no time for academic experiments involving only one change.

The implementation of the agreed-upon changes by Burrill and WGB was also a lesson in organizational judgment. The prospect of reversing a decision that wasn't working out wasn't as painful as it would have been for many companies. This is because WGB practices what is called, in other industries, *late configuration.* Just as Benetton once used white yarn to produce sweaters, and only dyed them after retailers placed orders for specific colors, Burrill completes only the outsides of houses on landscaped lots for the spec houses he builds. This allows the buyer to specify interior details to their tastes, and WGB can complete the home after it's bought in as little as thirty-two days. The fact that the houses aren't fully completed also makes it feasible to alter the unfinished frame more substantially—as WGB needed to in the case of the house that wouldn't sell.

The Outcome and the Embedded Learning

The changes seem to have worked. A baby boom couple bought the house a few months after the redesign—even in a difficult housing market. The couple responded well to the design and expanded the house even more by having WGB finish off their basement. Some of the features that they liked most about the house were ideas that had been generated and implemented through the participative decision-making process.

The two other houses in the area with first floor master bedrooms that were being sold by other builders did not use participative decision making to make adjustments and customize the plans. At the time we write, one is still on the market and the other recently sold for substantially less money than the asking price and surrounding houses.

Greg Burrill thinks they might have hit on a winner with the revised version of the house, so he's now building another home with the same plan. The Expanded Oxford has become a model of its own now—one of about twelve that WGB buyers can choose from. Like all designs and modifications, it has been captured in the company's computer-aided design (CAD) repository.

Unlike other suburban builders who construct the same designs over and over again, Burrill is always tinkering with and improving the house designs he builds. He initially hires an independent designer to create a CAD-based design, but thereafter the plan will constantly be revised based on feedback. Even when a house design sells well, Burrill and other WGB employees will talk to customers who live in the house, subcontractors, and anyone who sees the designs about what they think.

As with the Expanded Oxford, WGB will often make improvements to the designs and incorporate them into the CAD system. They are even willing to make changes for individual customers, although they think of themselves as production builders more than custom. "People are particular and want changes at this price level," Burrill notes. All changes are stored as CAD files, so they can be reused easily.

For example, one customer liked the overall design of a house, but didn't want a formal living room or dining room. So WGB accommodated the buyer, designing and building a big country kitchen and a bigger family room. Now that plan is available in the system for any other customers who want it. Further, the request and others like it have prompted the WGB team to deemphasize formal living rooms in general. In many of the available designs, what was formerly the living room has been downsized into a room that could be a library, study, or home office.

Another Group Judgment Call

Burrill doesn't only use the group consultation approach on design decisions. He tries to employ it on any topic on which others might have good insights. For example, a recent consultative decision involved setting a price for the resale of a condominium that WGB had built in the 1980s. Both Burrill's mother and his daughter Vanessa had lived in it at various times, and now it was on the market. An offer from a potential buyer had come in, but it was substantially below the asking price. Should Burrill accept, reject, or counter the offer?

Burrill had his own feelings about the offer, but he knew that others in the business were knowledgeable about the condo. Vanessa had both lived there and met the potential buyer. Joe, who handled sales at one point for WGB, had sold many of the condos when they were built. So Burrill convened a meeting with his daughters and Joe.

Burrill's consultation with his informal advisory panel revealed some differences of opinion. Vanessa and Erica wanted to keep the price high and reject the offer. Joe was inclined to sell it at the offering price. Greg Burrill was inclined to compromise a bit. "Maybe when we tell them about the improvements we've put in the unit, they'd be inclined to go a bit higher. We've put in new windows, new granite countertops, and new appliances. Let's invite them over to the unit and try to get them to raise their offer a bit."

Burrill had listened to the opinions of his colleague and daughters, but knew the final decision was his own. "Vanessa lived there and really loved it, so she may be a little sentimental about it. She and Erica, being in marketing and sales, want to make sure that the prices stay up at the complex. I understand that. But I don't want to have it stay on the market for six months."

There was certainly no rancor in the decision process. After Greg Burrill announced his intention to negotiate with the potential buyers in an e-mail to the consulted parties, the conciliatory response was rapid. Vanessa Burrill called her father a few minutes later, saying, "Dad, here's some text you might want to use in the e-mail to the buyers."

Reflections on WGB Homes's Organizational Judgment

As WGB Homes's story illustrates, even small, family-run businesses can benefit from activities to improve organizational judgment. In fact, when one bad decision can sink a company, good decisions are particularly critical.

The hallmark of decision making at WGB Homes is involvement by multiple knowledgeable parties. Greg Burrill, the CEO, has confidence in his own judgment, but he knows that better judgment derives from broader participation. It often makes sense to consult other expert sources in making a decision, and to build in processes and contexts for soliciting and discussing decision alternatives. Greg Burrill still makes the final decision, but he looks for insights and expertise in every place he can find it. A senior executive in an organization can and should listen to many opinions and sources of wisdom, but he or she still needs to make the call in the end.

The WGB story also illustrates a key aspect of decision process design: to delay decision making until more information is available, or to lower the cost of changing your mind if you decide your initial decision was suboptimal. This is, in effect, a way to minimize the cost of poor organizational judgment. It happened only rarely at WGB Homes, but the uncompleted home made it relatively easy to address.

WGB captures its design decisions in its CAD system. When a new or modified design is created, it's captured in digital form so that it can be used again—or serve as the basis for yet another modification. It's a form of knowledge management for house designs—and since WGB is a small firm, virtually any organization with design processes ought to be able to do something similar.

So Burrill's consultation with his informal advisory panel is a great example of building organizational judgment, and his late-configuration approach is a great way to lower the cost of decision making. The company's CAD system is a way to capture good design decisions so they can be reused with little effort. Think of all of the decisions in your company that might be improved if everyone with a good idea were consulted, if plans stayed flexible until the last minute, and if the firm's knowledge had been captured and stored for later reuse. It's a management approach that works for companies and organizations of any size.

3

McKinsey & Company

Should We Recruit from a Different Pool of Talent?

URING THE 1980S, the partners of the global professional
services firm McKinsey & Company struggled with an enviable problem: explosive growth of their consulting practice.
But for a professional services firm committed to competing on the basis
of distinctive talent, it was a fundamental strategic challenge: how to find
enough McKinsey-qualified associates to meet the demand.[1]

"We were at the beginning of the curve of some of the greatest thirst
for talent we had ever known," recalled Jerome Vascellaro, then director of personnel at the firm, adding with characteristic humor, "we had
so much work, we could almost have started hiring llamas." The idea of
hiring llamas brings a smile—but the joke had an edge beneath its comic
exaggeration. The problem was not finding quantity, but quality. For this
was, and continues to be, an organization whose worldwide reputation

has been built on having extraordinary people, known for their analytical skills, personal integrity, and leadership impact. "We realized we had a real problem," echoed Terry Williams, a retired director who led recruiting as the firm entered the 1990s. "We were hiring some 10 percent of each graduating class of the Harvard Business School—and even there, we weren't getting enough of the excellence we needed. We had to figure out some other sources."

In years prior, MBAs from Harvard and other top business schools (Stanford, the University of Chicago, and others) had been the traditional and most productive waters in which McKinsey recruiters had fished, usually pulling in the top performers for their firm. But now the effective yield was falling across all these sources, just as growth was exploding. Competition—both for clients and for talent—from other "best and brightest" consulting firms was also growing. Fred Gluck, managing director of McKinsey at the time, echoed more bluntly the same view of his partner, Terry Williams: "We had no choice. We were simply running out of human capital. It was inevitable that we would try something else."

But when pressed, Gluck acknowledged that if a new recruiting strategy was inevitable, its success was far from guaranteed. Other contemporaries remember the challenge as indeed a serious one. Thus Dominic Barton, today's managing director, saw the decision as "an iconic moment for the firm." Piecing together the history of those years, we see that Barton was not exaggerating. The story of how McKinsey found the right new talent strategy is as much about how the partners made the decision as what they did. It is also remarkable for how they both forged the new direction from, and also integrated it back into, the everyday working style of the firm. As a case study in organizational judgment, this tale reflects the power of an ongoing problem-solving process, embedded in a powerful set of values and deep organizational culture. The process yielded a multilayered transformation that successfully addressed the quest for the next generation of very special people.

Swimming Both With and Against the MBA Stream

The essence of the dilemma was whether McKinsey should start large-scale recruiting of new consultants without MBAs, as a complement to their traditional sourcing in top business schools. The question in those years was primarily a North American issue. Leaders in McKinsey European Union countries typically hired rising star managers from major national corporations; in Germany, there was an established practice, suited to their business environment, of hiring PhD's, especially in disciplines such as engineering. The London office had historically hired top academic performers out of nearby Oxford and Cambridge universities and helped support the recruiting of Rhodes and Marshall scholars by American colleagues in the United States.[2]

But the North American offices were still very much the center of gravity for the firm during the 1980s—especially the large and powerful New York office, with its close connections with Ivy League and other prestigious business schools. For this critical part of McKinsey, a shortage of top MBA recruits was a significant problem. In those days, the commonplace of suspender-wearing, analytically incandescent MBAs weighed dominantly in much of McKinsey's work—both for its clients and for its own sense of self. The tradition had been many years in the making, in fact. In the earliest days of the firm, McKinsey was known for its experienced hands, and the mature counsel that its industry-trained partners brought to bear in their gentlemanly but deep relationships with the CEOs of America. The legendary builder of the modern McKinsey, Marvin Bower, began to shift the focus of his firm, as early as the late 1950s, by experimenting with hiring not just accomplished industry executives but also younger MBAs from his Harvard alma mater. And over time, as the status of the business degree grew in U.S. professional education, McKinsey took on board more and more graduates of top-tier MBA programs.

The MBA subculture of McKinsey further intensified during the 1980s. The success of sophisticated analytical models for business problem solving, prominently exemplified by Bruce Henderson and the "learning curve" and "four-box growth matrix" approaches of the rival Boston Consulting Group (BCG), pushed McKinsey to focus even more on best-and-brightest analysts from leading MBA programs. Unlike earlier MBA hires, the new generation of recruits tended to be younger and less practically experienced, but razor sharp in the strategic tools and thinking that characterized business school curricula. Marvin Bower had, during the 1950s and '60s, shifted assumptions about talent in his firm by embracing the radical notion that generalist business skills and education were becoming more important than industry business experience. In the 1980s, as he moved toward retirement, his firm turned the volume dial on those beliefs to the max.

During those same years, consulting as an industry boomed. Technological innovation, globalization, and deregulation were forces of change as the economy grew. Envious detractors spoke of the new "punks in pinstripes" (as one business magazine branded them), the young super-smart MBAs that were reshaping how leaders were approaching their own businesses. BCG, Bain & Company, and other strategy firms became the darlings of the *Fortune* 500, driven by Michael Porter–style strategic thinking and approaches. McKinsey & Company spared no expense or effort to lead this pack, and competed vigorously to hire top graduates. For all players in the new game of consulting, success now depended on luring the most qualified MBA candidates into the fold.

Not surprisingly, many at McKinsey who went on to become partners perpetuated the profile of what made for a successful new hire—someone who could, to put a fine point on it, be just like them.

The Battle Between Future Strategy and Past History

But as awareness grew of the rising shortage of excellent MBA candidates, the crescendo of debate increased over what to do about the fact that there weren't unlimited new Rhodes Scholars to hire, and the success of "the German approach" was politely compartmentalized by many in the United States as "suited to them but not us." Finding real analytical stars at second-tier business schools was not impossible, but the cost and trouble to reach both the quantity and the quality desired were likely going to be prohibitive. In true McKinsey fashion, "someone ran the numbers and convinced us all it was not going to fly," remembers Dolf DiBiasio, a retired member of the firm who was active in recruiting in those days.

DiBiasio in fact remembers vividly a meeting in Stamford, Connecticut, with other partners with whom he served on the North American recruiting team: "We went around the room, and as we talked to one another, and looked at our data, we were hearing we weren't getting the quality out of the MBA schools in the numbers we needed."

So what to do? Complicating the question during this time were several "elephants in the room" about what makes for great talent and where to find it. As everyone in the meeting at Stamford knew, the North American offices had been experimenting in their recruiting off and on for years with so-called nontraditional hires. There was no debate that most of the Rhodes Scholars recruited were good choices, helped along by an innovative training program started during the 1980s, the mini-MBA (a pragmatic crash course in core tools and concepts offered to highly talented, incoming recruits who lacked the gold-standard business degree).

More problematic was the evolving effort in some parts of the firm to return to the earlier approach of hiring more industry-experienced people. During the 1980s, certain areas of the firm began to target specialists with a deep technical expertise, intended for work in the newly formalizing industry practice groups. In the vanguard of this recruiting strategy was the fast-growing energy practice of the firm, led by the iconoclastic director John Sawhill. A former U.S. Energy Department administrator, PhD in economics, and president of New York University (NYU), Sawhill understood keenly the need of McKinsey to develop more specialist knowledge on its teams, particularly for clients in the oil, gas, and utilities industry that he was developing actively. Similar efforts were also under way during the 1980s to bring in more specialized associates in other practice areas such as financial services, information technology, and the pharmaceuticals sector.

Although practice leaders and many of the firm's consulting teams appreciated the expertise of these new associates, more often than not these recruits would run aground on the sandbar of the strong generalist (read MBA) biases of the firm—especially when it came time for evaluations and promotion. Outside of their specialized opportunities, they often had trouble being accepted in other kinds of client engagements—a great disadvantage since diversity of client experience was a critical success factor to reach partnership. And on many more intangible dimensions— but still important dimensions in a firm built on its culture and personal relationships—these "experienced hires" had trouble fitting in. Bob Harvey, a Harvard MBA and now retired director who had himself been active in the energy practice, recalls many painful moments related to the would-be social and professional integration of specialized hires in the Texas office during the 1980s:

> There was always a question about what career track they were on, though some made the leap better than others. They tended to be older than many of us; we lived in the city centers, they lived in the suburbs. Their wives were different than ours; they were raising children, most of us were not. Many of them worked more with a corporate mind-set than a professional services one. And sometimes they seemed less interested than the rest of us in the all-out performance culture to excel at everything.

Because fit in the powerful McKinsey culture was so important, many non-MBAs had their tales of at least occasional feelings of second-class status. Many had trouble getting staffed on studies at first or ended up on projects with more marginal roles than MBAs on the team.

Dominic Barton himself—today's managing director, who was himself a nontraditional hire (he joined the Toronto office as a Rhodes Scholar in 1986)—recalls his early days in the firm as a little uncomfortable: "I did feel different at the beginning. When I arrived, I remember having the impression that there were partners who thought, 'Who is this guy? Can he really add?'" Rodney Zemmel, a molecular biologist hired during the early days of the program—and today a director with global oversight of all firm recruiting—remembers his first interview with the partner who hired him: "He started the discussion by telling me, 'This is very much an experiment for the firm.' He was encouraging me, but also setting some expectations." Luis Cunha, a director in today's McKinsey, offered a similar perspective: "These kinds of people represented their own form of cultural change, and it wasn't an easy ride for the firm to make the shift."

In fact, as the 1980s drew to a close, the track record for non-MBAs in North America reflected what many thought was in fact a deserved bias against nontraditional hires. "There was an aha moment in the room," remembers Dolf DiBiasio, again remembering the talent strategy decision he and his recruiting leaders wrestled with in the Stamford meeting. "We were running out of quality MBAs, but the numbers also showed that non-MBAs were not being elected partner to the same degree. It was something we were going to have to confront if we made a real move beyond the traditional pool."

Catalyzing the Decision for Change

At the center of the debate about the kind of talent needed in the firm was Fred Gluck, who became managing director of McKinsey & Company in 1988. Though the new talent strategy that ultimately evolved can rightly be said to have had many contributing hands along the way, most contemporary partners and subsequent observers credit Gluck as the real driving force in turning the flywheel of change.[3]

Gluck had a very personal stake in broadening the pool of talent for McKinsey recruiting. Raised in a large Catholic family in Brooklyn, he attended Manhattan College, got his master's at NYU, and later did postgraduate work at Columbia in operations research. As a young engineer at Bell Labs, he worked on guidance systems for missiles and was later program manager for the Spartan missile project—which allowed him, he later joked, "to claim I was in fact smart enough to do rocket science." In a somewhat unlikely career switch, Gluck ended up at McKinsey in 1967, though his hiring was yet another example of the firm's looking initially not for traditional associate work but rather for selected expertise that could be offered to technology company clients.

Soon after he started, Gluck ran into the ever-strengthening MBA bias. He recounts a series of early experiences in the firm in which he had to fight to actually meet with clients, and overcome the prejudice of some partners that kept him in the back room as a junior number cruncher. To the firm's credit (and demonstration of an overriding belief in meritocracy), Gluck's smarts and ability to achieve progressively impressive success with clients led to his eventual election to partner. In 1976 he was promoted again, to director.

Beyond his work with clients, Fred Gluck also made a name for himself by challenging the firm—and his predecessor as managing director, Ron Daniel—to step up more vigorously to the quest of the market for more analytically based strategy. A well-known memo he wrote to Daniel prodded McKinsey to answer the real competitive threat of Bruce Henderson and BCG. Daniel cleverly turned the challenge into a new assignment for the critic. During the late 1970s and early 1980s, Gluck led a series of initiatives to build McKinsey-specific knowledge by leading intellectual debate about strategy and its application. He also stimulated ongoing knowledge collaboration among multiple partners, later formalized as the first functional practice groups. By the time he was elected managing director, he was known across McKinsey as the partner who had changed the firm to compete much more explicitly on its distinctive ideas and knowledge, and he continued to work to make that a much more prominent part of its culture.

Not surprisingly, Gluck began to translate this new knowledge imperative into the firm's thinking about its talent. Though he had embraced the importance of strategic thinking now associated with the world of MBAs, as a proud non-MBA himself, he knew that business schools were not the only place where smart people could be found. Looking across the firm at many non-MBA colleagues (many European, in fact) and reflecting upon his own successful rise, he knew the essence of what McKinsey required was not this or that kind of degree—but, rather, distinctive people with superior analytical and creative intelligence. As the data began to show that McKinsey was reaching quality limits in its recruiting at the Harvard Business School and other such institutions, Gluck tasked his friend and member of the North American team Dolf DiBiasio to lead an initiative to figure out how to hire lots more very *smart* people—and indeed not necessarily more MBAs.

Mobilizing Judgment

If this sounds like "the decision" on which this case turns—the voice of the then managing director announcing what needed to happen—it would be a fundamental betrayal of what the McKinsey problem-solving approach and culture stand for. Gluck himself makes the point forcefully: "There was no single decision. We didn't all just get drunk one night and say, 'Hey, time for a new approach to talent.' Instead, there were a series of small decisions, interspersed with a series of trials, debates, and discussions—that finally led to the outcome that came to be."

Partner after partner when discussing these years—and the McKinsey culture in general—makes essentially the same point. Jon Katzenbach, a former director in the San Francisco office, office manager in New York, and a leader of the firm's organization practice, commented, "Decisions like this didn't come at a single moment in time. Our values as a firm encouraged debate and the 'obligation to dissent.' The partnership provided 'safe space' in which different ideas were voiced, challenged, and out of that a course of action emerged.[4] We used data, not ego or hierarchy, to find common ground." Vascellaro, with another comic metaphor, argued similarly: "You have to remember the DNA of this firm. A thousand small cells of experimentation going on in teams, in offices, all around the world. We had been doing this and that through the years, hiring lawyers, Rhodes Scholars, trying different kinds of backgrounds, the mini-MBA, all that. When the formal program of recruiting non-MBAs was developed, it was a Mr. Potato Head kind of thing—putting together lots of things that had already been proven and learned."

All that said, it would be wrong to assume that the new direction for recruiting happened impersonally and with no conscious leadership effort. Listening to Dolf DiBiasio, one hears about some of the critical micro-decisions made that, stitched together and tested in the crucible of the McKinsey and external market, ultimately prevailed. And it's clear he and Gluck were often the ones pushing those decisions. That said, the outcome that has made today's McKinsey the much more intellectually diverse place that it is was anything but guaranteed in 1991.

During that year, after analyzing—and then rejecting—the strategy of broadening the search for talent to a wider array of less prestigious business schools, Dolf DiBiasio and his recruiting colleagues fastened on the idea of focusing on PhD's, lawyers, doctors, and the like—people who were not trained in business per se, but who exhibited high intelligence, deep analytical skill, creative thinking, and the potential for "personal impact" with ever-more-demanding clients. In order to put real muscle into the effort, Dolf decided upon several key factors for success—developed and shaped through discussion and debate with Fred Gluck, Terry Williams, Jerome Vascellaro, and other partners, and the firm recruiting managers, especially its talented leader, Karen Kidder. There was never any single moment when this group proclaimed that an unambiguous decision had been made about pursuing this talent pool, but there was enough consensus to move forward with the approach, as the "internal market receptivity" for the idea began to build.

As a first step, they needed to change the language of what had been evolving and was now moving center stage; as Dolf DiBiasio recalls, "We got rid of the term 'nontraditional recruiting' and called it the 'natural athlete program.' We wanted to signal that this was like Michael Jordan playing any of a range of sports. Superior performance, whatever they do, even if not their current specialty."

The next step was classic McKinsey analysis put into process—a nationwide scan of the top PhD schools, medical schools, law schools, graduate and policy schools, and other professional education programs, followed up by DiBiasio and Kidder meeting, one by one, with their deans. The purpose was to understand the potential, size of appropriate pool, and viability for targeted recruiting on their campus, and the nature of work their graduates were doing. They also intended to sell the idea that for their graduates a career in McKinsey ought to be a fair option to consider. Again, Dolf DiBiasio: "All we were asking for was, 'Give us a shot.' A few resented us coming to their programs, but many were open to the idea, and we started to work with them." At the same time, Kidder and her recruiting managers began to design more specialized approaches to recruiting non-MBAs in their search for "natural athletes." These public policy types and PhD's in physics or history were often unfamiliar with the world of business, much less what McKinsey consulting was. The firm developed—and iteratively experimented with—different ways to engage would-be candidates, via specialized social events, intellectually challenging mock workshops, and outreach to anyone deemed promising by other successful McKinsey people who had a non-MBA background.

Dominic Barton recalls his own first approach by the McKinsey recruiters when he was still studying in Oxford: "I recall not being very impressed by the group presentation they made, feeling it was sort of mechanical and didn't really understand the kind of people we were. But that all changed when [McKinsey director] Ali Hanna took me aside for an informal chat. He simply said, 'I'm working on a kind of interesting client problem, and I'd love to get your ideas to help me out.' It was a fantastic conversation, and after that I knew this was the kind of place I could see myself working."

Building Support and Success

As the "natural athlete recruiting team" was working and learning how to succeed in the markets for talent, it was also working furiously internally within the firm to ensure the acceptance and success of the program. At every step of the process that evolved, there were problems and subproblems to be solved. Dolf DiBiasio called on long-standing colleagues who were office managers, securing commitments from a critical mass of established leaders that they would not only support the program but also promise to staff the new recruits on mainline, important McKinsey engagements. Vascellaro remembers, "Dolf went office to office and looked his buddies in the eye. He said, 'Look, I'll deliver these superstars and the talent you need, but you need to promise me you'll actually use them on your teams.'" Dolf himself remembers that he and his recruiting team took great care to lobby for the new recruits to be assigned to sympathetic engagement directors across the firm, and they diligently tracked the progress of all their precious hirelings, intervening when necessary to improve their chances of "fitting in."

And despite all the comments about the informality of the process, Dolf DiBiasio worked with others to brief—and sometimes jawbone—critical personnel committees across the firm, including the committees that evaluate candidates for partnership and perform the ongoing evaluations of partners in their work (the so-called PCEC and PRC). "Once again, all we wanted was a shot. We just asked the committees to give these new kind of recruits a chance in the evaluation process—but in the end not to be treated one bit differently once their performance could be fairly assessed."

As a measure of how decentralized and democratic the McKinsey culture was (and remains), it is interesting to note that major players in this decision process differ about whether and how the firm's shareholders committee (SHC) was engaged. The SHC is the firm committee that is the closest thing McKinsey has to a governing board, but given the strong and trusting culture of the partnership, it is more often met with for advice and counsel as opposed to outright yes-or-no permission to do something. Fred Gluck, looking back, insisted that "the decision was not made at the shareholders committee," and his lieutenant, Jim Goodrich, then chief operating officer of the firm, similarly concurred: "We didn't see the need for that." But Dolf DiBiasio remembers at least one important discussion with the committee about the program concept, and Terry Williams recounts how, indeed at an SHC meeting, "there was some pessimism about the idea until Fred Gluck went around the table and pointed out that half the partners at the table were themselves not MBAs. After that we had the backing we needed."

Institutionalizing the Decision

Dolf DiBiasio, Karen Kidder, and the other recruiters did their homework well, and most of the new talent flourished. As these "natural athletes" started to have success, more and more partners got on board to join the cause. Before long the program was rechristened with a more formal institutional name—Advanced Professional Degree program, which lives on at McKinsey today as APD. Dolf DiBiasio recalls how the recruiters and supporters diligently built up networks of support, as well as networks of advocates in graduate schools and other professional programs. With increased refinement and expansion of the mini-MBA program and the growth of a cohort of successful APD candidates, it became easier to attract and develop future waves of "nontraditionals." Once more, the McKinsey bent for analytical-based thinking also extended the success of the program, as the recruiting team rigorously tracked which institutions were providing the most successful candidates, and how new hires of the program in different offices with different kinds of supervising partners in different kinds of client work were performing. The model of what the firm was looking for, where to find such people, and how to make them successful got more refined every year.

It is a story of obvious organizational learning and continuous imp-rovement, following a disciplined—if not always predictable—problem-solving process. Recruiting efforts got smarter as the virtuous circle of try-learn-improve-focus became embedded in how the firm found and developed new kinds of talent. Today, estimates Michelle Jarrard, direc-tor of firm personnel, about 20–30 percent of North American associates are now classified as APD, compared to perhaps 10 percent during the early 1990s.[5] And though no one—starting with McKinsey the institution itself—would ever claim a causal relationship for the impact of this "nonde-cision decision," it is hard not to at least theorize that the financial success of the firm over the last twenty years (growth, by some external estimates, over sixfold) owes more than a little to this strategic talent strategy.[6] Terry Williams, the then director of firm recruiting, notes, "Our success as a firm has always been our ability to integrate new kinds of people and educate and develop them to perform."

Reflections on the More Diverse Talent Pool

Waves of incoming new associates with backgrounds as diverse as medical doctor, PhD in physics, or international policy maker are now accepted as normal at McKinsey, and there is no perceived difference in their over-all performance versus that of other associates. Though there are still plenty of Harvard MBAs in the ranks, few McKinsey people look askance at the idea of joining some high-flying former academic or scientist as a colleague on their team. The origins of this critical diversification are lost on some members of the current generation, though few doubt its impor-tance. Thus a director like Luis Cunha, himself active in recruiting for the firm, will say, "I have no idea who thought this up—but obviously some very smart guy." Michelle Jarrard notes, "I never have calls from partners about staffing problems like 'I can't deal with a physicist on my team.' This is commonly accepted as a strength of the firm now." She also noted, referring back to the comment of managing director Barton, "We have a lot of iconic moments around here, but we usually don't realize them at the time."

The more diverse pool of McKinsey talent also represents another installment in what has been a decades-long internal debate—and reflecting what all agree is a constructive tension—between generalist and specialist knowledge, and, similarly, MBA skills and other analytical and nonanalytical perspectives. What were once either-or debates about the necessary kind of background for success in McKinsey-style global consulting have evolved into much more nuanced discussion of both-and. As Brian Rolfes, administrative principal and director of firm recruiting, notes, "The diversity of background helps our problem solving, which is the heart of what we do." And at the same time, partners today similarly note that having, say, a PhD in molecular biology or a medical doctor on their teams serving a pharmaceutical client gives not only valuable content knowledge but "instant credibility with executives in that kind of industry."

For every case of a special edge that someone with a particular background brought to an industry-specific engagement, there is another story one can hear of how the unique complement of knowledge and thinking of a particular team—with no particular education keyed to the industry problem—created an unusually distinctive breakthrough for their client. Both Jarrard and Barton commented, in addition, how the diversity of the talent pool at McKinsey is increasingly defined in today's firm beyond educational background—including experience in different sectors (public, private, and civic) and now also race, gender, and sexual orientation.

Reflections on the Organizational Judgment of McKinsey & Company in This Case

The decision we have described emerged out of an extended process of problem solving, which was increasingly merged with actual "do it, try it" implementation—it was hardly made in one fell swoop. Market need, individual initiative, stakeholder debate, hustle to build institutional support, using analysis and trial to buttress the case—all came together over the course of a couple of years to build a strategic decision and make it work. No one seems to know exactly when the decision was made, and if early efforts to execute on it had failed, no doubt the decision would have been reversed. Since the initial decision to proceed was successful, however, it evolved into a formal strategy and program over time.

We see here a case (which we will see again in other stories of good organizational judgment) where the *what* and the *how* were inextricably blended. What made that successful was the combination of the process of problem solving with the backdrop of a powerful and enabling culture: the deep McKinsey values and its special way of working with its people.

Once seen as a marginal or fuzzy aspect of professional management, the concept of organizational culture in recent years has come into increasing focus as a critical aspect of high-impact enterprises, seen perhaps most prominently in the research of Ed Schein. Schein and other scholars have shown how the "behaviors, values, assumptions" that define organizational culture can exert such influence on the way both people and their organizations act and think.[7] It is culture that can help explain both how individuals pursue what they consider the path to success and what they teach others coming into the fold. It is also the beliefs and assumptions of culture that shape and—sometimes—constrain decision making. The culture of an organization cannot be separated from the collective judgment it manifests.

So many decisions at McKinsey, as is often pointed out, are not made but "develop over time." This is a consequence of multiple, interrelated dimensions that have come to be part of what founding father Marvin Bower simply called "the way we work around here." A look at some of the most important elements of this culture can put the "decision" of diversifying the talent pool in 1992 into valuable perspective.

Perhaps most important is the duality of self-governance and mutual accountability—which, as Michelle Jarrard noted, "often come into conflict—but the values give us a way to talk about that." Self-governance is the insistence of this firm not to be publically traded, and to manage affairs for itself. For individuals—and especially partners—it represents a freedom to do much of what one wants, how and when one wants. The counterpoint to this is the notion of everyone also accountable to everyone else—and the larger good of the firm overall.

That sense of mutual accountability has many behaviors, beliefs, and assumptions underlying it, as Ed Schein might note. These include several key McKinsey attributes:

- The way that partners share in a common pool of revenue, with strictures against outside sale or speculation in shares

- The intense "up or out culture," in which peers regularly assess the performance of their partners, including the most senior

- The relatively participative decision culture and lack of hierarchy of values such as the "obligation to dissent," which encourages even young analysts and associates to speak up when something wrong or ill-advised for a client or the firm is being advanced

The cultural glue that holds the various tensions together is an overriding sense of trust that is reinforced all the time. "We always operated in the belief that our colleagues were well intentioned and that disagreements were only about the right thing to do, not a personal agenda," as Fred Gluck noted. But this same culture is also about meritocracy and transparency, what Gluck himself always called "the marketplace of the best ideas," coupled with an expectation—here again mutual accountability—of transparency, openly demonstrating why something is being recommended, and laying out the facts of past experience.

Such an environment creates a fascinating balancing act between respect for tradition—"What would Marvin Bower have said?" and "Why do we believe this will work?"—and an embrace of innovation. Love of the firm encourages the A-types of McKinsey to both cherish the already successful and also search for new ways to make something better. Most new ideas start out as a conversation and then a debate—and risk tends to be leavened by first testing a pilot and then measuring what's working and not at every step of the way. So while the decision to pursue and implement a new talent strategy represented some degree of cultural change for the MBA-heavy McKinsey in those days, it was also the broader cultural tradition that allowed the firm to explore, test, and ultimately adapt to the change. McKinsey leaders today all agree the talent strategy decision was a very successful move. "Ultimately," commented director of firm personnel Michelle Jarrard, "we actually compete on judgment; that's what we bring to our clients. The talent diversity we have now—and continue to build—is simply making us better at that all the time."

Part Two

Stories About the Opportunities of Technology and Analytics

THIS NEXT PART OF OUR BOOK includes three stories that, each in its own way, showcase how organizational decision making is beginning to take systematic advantage of technology and analytics to create deeper and more sustainable judgment. The stories also include elements of other themes we have already explored (problem-solving processes, participative employee engagement) and others we'll explore in a more focused way later (e.g., the role of culture and leaders to set the right context); but these stand out in particular for the distinctive importance that strategic use of digital data and analysis makes to the challenges of difficult decision making.

We begin with a case study from the health-care industry—Partners HealthCare in Boston—and then, perhaps more predictably, move to a state-of-the-art systems integration firm, Cognizant, whose operating style is deeply imbued with the strategic use of the latest technological tools for the firm's own decision making. We round out the segment by jumping to yet another sector—public education—with a case study of a school system in Charlotte, North Carolina. This story is emblematic of the revolution sweeping schools now: using analytics to improve student academic performance.

4

Partners HealthCare System

How Should We Treat This Patient?

BLACKFORD MIDDLETON, MD, knew what was wrong with his patient before he even spoke. He'd heard the middle-aged male patient cough as he came into his office; he'd seen the color of the mucus on the patient's handkerchief as he sat down. He'd noticed the man's lethargic movement from the waiting room into the office. "Looks like a URI to me," he thought to himself. It seemed likely that the patient had an upper respiratory infection (URI), possibly a sinus infection or sinusitis.[1]

Middleton, who was, among other things, a physician at Partners HealthCare in Boston, of course examined the patient despite his suspicions. He confirmed that all the classic symptoms of a URI were present.

During his examination, the patient mentioned that he usually felt better "when he got an antibiotic for one of these."

Middleton winced to himself. It was well known that most URIs were viral in origin, and that treating them with antibiotics was effective only in increasing antibiotic resistance in the population. Yet he had found in the past that patients didn't find this a compelling reason not to want an antibiotic, and he disliked getting into arguments with his patients.

On this patient, however, he decided to try an approach he'd used a couple of times previously with success. Middleton, in his other job as head of Clinical Informatics Research and Development (CIRD) at Partners, had led the development of a new tool that was being piloted at Partners, and he was one of the pilot users in his own clinical practice. The Smart Form took a patient's electronic medical record (EMR) data, combined it with observations by the physician, and created both treatment suggestions and notes on the patient visit.

Middleton had found in the past that patients often found the system's treatment recommendations to be more persuasive than when the same ideas came from the mouths of their doctors. So he typed some information about the patient into the Smart Form and asked for treatment recommendations. As expected, the recommendations pointed out the low likelihood of the patient's URI being caused by bacteria, and explicitly noted that treatment with antibiotics was not recommended. Middleton showed the treatment recommendations on the screen to the patient. "I'd love to help you out by prescribing an antibiotic, but as you can see, I wouldn't actually be helping you," he commented.

As in the past, the combination of the Smart Form and his reinforcing comment did the trick, and the patient decided to tough out the virus, with the help of a cough syrup for symptom relief. Middleton reflected to himself that this benefit of the Smart Form wasn't something he and his colleagues had anticipated when they developed it, but he was nonetheless grateful to avoid an argument.

Improving Patient Care with Information
and Knowledge at Partners

Partners HealthCare System is a large academic medical center in the Boston area. It consists of twelve hospitals, with over seven thousand affiliated physicians. It has 4 million outpatient visits and 160,000 inpatient admissions a year. It is a nonprofit organization with almost $8 billion in revenues, and it spends over $1 billion per year on biomedical research. It is a major teaching affiliate of Harvard Medical School.

Blackford Middleton worked in both research and clinical roles, as did many Partners staff. His primary job at Partners was overseeing the CIRD group, which had a large staff of about eighty, and which was part of the Partners information systems organization. Many of CIRD's staff, like Middleton, had multiple advanced degrees; Middleton had an MD, a master of public health degree, and a master of science in health services research. The mission of CIRD was:

> ... to improve the quality and efficiency of care for patients
> at Partners HealthCare System by assuring that the most
> advanced current knowledge about medical informatics (clinical
> computing) is incorporated into clinical information systems at
> Partners HealthCare.[2]

It was CIRD's role to help create the strategy for how Partners used information systems in patient care, and to develop both some production systems capabilities and pilots such as the Smart Form. CIRD's work had played a substantial role in making Partners a worldwide leader in the use of data, analysis, and computerized knowledge to improve patient care. If that weren't enough, CIRD had several projects funded by U.S. government health agencies to adapt some of the same tools and approaches it had developed for Partners to the broader health-care system.

Blackford Middleton and his colleagues at CIRD were both advancing and benefitting from a couple of decades of work on systems in health care at Partners. The advanced capabilities of the Smart Form built on a whole series of projects and technologies that had been implemented over the years. Middleton and his very smart colleagues were undoubtedly giants of clinical informatics, but they stood on the shoulders of several other giants.

Boston is the home of many such giants in both the technology and the medical fields. Among the Bostonians whose work came together to drive the rise of clinical systems at Partners were Lucian Leape and Don Berwick, who provided the motivation for better clinical systems, and Dick Nesson and John Glaser, who began to create them.

Leape, a lanky and stern-looking white-haired New Englander, was, according to one editor:

> ... the father of the modern patient safety movement in the
> United States. A Harvard professor, Leape shifted his career
> two decades ago from his clinical practice as a pediatric surgeon
> to a focus on understanding how medical errors occur and how
> patient safety can be improved. The result was several ground-
> breaking studies and commentaries that helped shift the
> paradigm from "bad people" to "bad systems," and which paved
> the way for the Institute of Medicine report, "To Err is Human,"
> which he helped write.[3]

Berwick, a Boston-based pediatrician (and for a time the head of the Centers for Medicare and Medicaid Services for the U.S. government), developed a strong interest and deep expertise in procedures and pro-cesses to avoid medical error. He eventually founded the Institute for Healthcare Improvement, an organization that worked with many hospi-tals and health-care providers around the world to reduce medical errors and save lives.

Both Leape and Berwick advised the Institute of Medicine in the 1999 "To Err Is Human" study. It documented that about one hundred thou-sand deaths and a million injuries per year in the United States could be attributed to medical error.

Nesson, the head of Brigham and Women's Hospital ("the Brigham"), knew Leape and Berwick, and Brigham and Women's had participated in the research and quality improvement programs of both experts. Nesson had also sponsored research programs on medical errors of various types and inappropriate utilization of health-care services at the Brigham. Research there in 1995 suggested that more than 5 percent of patients had adverse reactions to prescribed drugs while under medical care; 43 percent of those inpatient reactions were serious, life-threatening, or fatal. Of the reactions that were preventable, more than half were caused by inappropriate drug prescriptions. About a third of the marginally abnormal pap smears and mammograms received insufficient follow-up. A study of the six most common lab tests ordered by physicians in the Brigham's surgical intensive care unit found that almost half of the tests ordered were clinically unnecessary. Another study there found that more than half of the prescriptions for a particular heart medicine were inappropriate. In short, just as the Great Man theory hasn't worked well for important corporate decisions, it also hasn't worked well in medical settings for individual physicians to employ their own intuition and judgment—even at one of the world's best hospitals.

The Role of Information Systems in Improving Care Quality at Partners

Several years before the Brigham combined forces with Massachusetts General Hospital (Mass General) and other hospitals to become Partners in 1994, Leape's and Berwick's work, and that of other researchers within Brigham and Women's, persuaded Nesson that something had to be done about medical errors. He knew that there were a variety of factors that affected the prevalence of medical errors—in particular, medication errors—but he was confident that one way to address the problem was through information systems. He began to discuss how that might happen with John Glaser, his chief information officer (CIO).[4]

Glaser had come to the Brigham as CIO in 1988. He had a PhD in health-care information systems and had also worked as an IT strategy consultant in the health-care industry. He was tall and bespectacled, and his personality radiated an unusual combination of braininess, intensity, sincerity, and easy good humor. Glaser's first hire at the Brigham, Mary Finlay, became his right-hand person for over twenty years. Finlay handled much of the day-to-day administration of the Brigham's (and later Partners') IT organization, freeing Glaser to think big thoughts and try to create big change.

The basis of any hospital's clinical information systems is the clinical data repository, which contains information on all patients, their conditions, and the treatments they have received. The inpatient clinical data repository had been implemented at the Brigham during the 1980s. Nesson and Glaser initiated an outpatient electronic medical record (EMR) at the Brigham in 1989.[5] This EMR contributed outpatient data to the clinical data repository. The hospital was one of the first to embark upon an EMR, though Mass General had begun to develop one of the first full-function EMRs as early as 1976. Still, by 2010 only about 8 percent of U.S. hospitals had a fully functional EMR in place.

A clinical data repository provides the basic data about patients, but in itself it didn't solve many medical error problems. Glaser and Nesson came to agree that in addition to a repository and an outpatient EMR, the Brigham—and Partners after 1994, when Glaser became its first CIO—needed facilities for doctors to input online orders for drugs, tests, and other treatments. Online ordering (called CPOE, or Computerized Provider Order Entry) not only would solve the time-honored problem of interpreting poor physician handwriting but also, if endowed with a bit of intelligence, could check whether a particular order made sense for a particular patient. Did a prescribed drug comply with best-known medical practice, and did the patient have any adverse reactions to it in the past? Had the same test been prescribed six times before with no apparent benefit? Was the specialist to whom a patient was being referred covered by her health plan? With this type of medical and administrative knowledge built into the system, dangerous and time-consuming errors could be prevented.

Although Nesson and Glaser were among the first to act to realize this vision, they were not the only observers of the health-care system to believe in its importance. For example, a National Academy of Sciences study described later in 2009 the roots of the problem:

> These persistent problems [of medical error] do not reflect incompetence on the part of health care professionals—rather, they are a consequence of the inherent intellectual complexity of health care taken as a whole and a medical care environment that has not been adequately structured to help clinicians avoid mistakes or to systematically improve their decision making and practice. Administrative and organizational fragmentation, together with complex, distributed, and unclear authority and responsibility, further complicates the health care environment.[6]

Nesson and Glaser knew that there were other approaches to reducing medical error than CPOE. Some provider institutions, such as Intermountain Healthcare in Utah, focused on close adherence by physicians to well-established medical protocols. Others, like Kaiser Permanente in California and the Cleveland Clinic, combined insurance and medical practices in ways that inspired all providers to work jointly on behalf of patients. Nesson and Glaser admired those approaches but felt that their impact would be less in an academic medical center such as Partners, where physicians were somewhat autonomous, and individual departments prided themselves on their separate reputations for research and practice innovations. Common, intelligent systems seemed like the best way to improve patient care at Partners. The Brigham embarked upon its CPOE system in 1989.

In 1994, when the Brigham and Mass General combined as Partners HealthCare System, there was still considerable autonomy for individual hospitals in the new "system." However, from the onset of the merger, the two hospitals agreed to use a common outpatient EMR called the Longitudinal Medical Record (LMR) and the intelligent order entry (CPOE) system developed at the Brigham. This was powerful testimony in favor of the CPOE system, since there was considerable rivalry between the two hospitals, and Mass General had its own EMR.

Perhaps the greatest challenge was in getting the extended network of Partners-affiliated physicians up on the LMR and CPOE. The physician network of over six thousand practicing generalist and specialist physician groups was scattered around the Boston metropolitan area and often operated out of their own private offices. Many lacked the IT or telecom infrastructures to implement the systems on their own, and implementation of an outpatient EMR cost about $25,000 per physician. Yet full use of the system across Partners-affiliated providers was critical to a seamless patient experience across the organization.

Glaser and the Partners IT organization worked diligently to spread the LMR and CPOE to the growing number of Partners hospitals and to Partners-affiliated physicians and medical practices. To assist in bringing physicians outside the hospitals on board, Partners negotiated payment schedules with insurance companies that rewarded physicians for supplying the kind of information available from the LMR and CPOE. By 2007, 90 percent of Partners-affiliated physicians were using the systems, and by 2009, 100 percent were. By 2009, over one thousand orders per hour were being entered through the CPOE system across Partners.

The combination of the LMR and the CPOE proved to be a powerful one in helping to avoid medical error. *Adverse drug events*, or the use of the wrong drug for the condition or one that caused an allergic reaction in the patient, typically were encountered by about fourteen of every one thousand inpatients. At the Brigham before the LMR and CPOE, the number was almost eleven. After the widespread implementation of these systems at Brigham and Women's, there were just above five adverse drug events per one thousand inpatients—a 55 percent reduction.

This approach to data-focused patient care was not only of interest to Partners. Many other health-care provider organizations—hospitals and physicians' offices—were beginning to adopt LMR and CPOE systems. In fact, the U.S. government had decided to sponsor implementation of these systems throughout the country, and was offering almost $40 billion in economic stimulus dollars to those organizations that both put them in place and used the systems in meaningful ways.[7] The government's National Coordinator of Health Information Technology for this initiative was Dr. David Blumenthal, a Mass General physician and research center director. John Glaser took a sabbatical year from his job at Partners to work with Blumenthal on these issues. Partners was thus an early and influential adopter of technologies that would soon become pervasive—and if things went well, the other health-care providers would achieve similar benefits.

Managing Clinical Knowledge at Partners

In addition to facilitating adoption of the LMR and CPOE, Partners faced a major challenge in getting control of the clinical knowledge that was made available to care providers through these and other systems. The "intelligent CPOE" strategy demanded that knowledge be online, accessible, and easily updated so that it could be referenced by and presented to care providers in real-time interactions with patients.

There were, of course, a variety of other online knowledge tools, such as medical literature searching, available to Partners personnel; in total they were referred to as the Partners Handbook. At one point after use of the CPOE had become widespread at Brigham and Women's, a comparison was made between online usage of the handbook and usage of the knowledge base from order entry. There were more 13,000 daily accesses through the CPOE system at the Brigham alone, and only 3,000 daily accesses of the handbook by all Partners personnel at all hospitals. Therefore, there was an ongoing effort to ensure that as much high-quality knowledge as possible made it into the CPOE.

The problem with knowledge at Partners wasn't that there wasn't enough of it; indeed, the various hospitals, labs, departments, and individuals were overflowing with knowledge. The problem was how to manage it. At one point, Tonya Hongsermeier, a physician with an MBA degree who was charged with managing knowledge at Partners, counted the number of places around Partners where there was some form of rule-based knowledge about clinical practice that was not centrally managed. She found about 23,000 of them. The knowledge was contained in a variety of formats: paper documents, computer screen shots, process flow diagrams, references, and data or reports on clinical outcomes—all in a variety of locations and only rarely shared.

Hongsermeier, who worked in Blackford Middleton's Clinical Informatics R&D organization, set out to create a *knowledge engineering and management* factory that would capture the knowledge at Partners, put it in a common format and a central repository, and make it available for CPOE and other online systems like the LMR. This required not only a new computer system for holding the thousands of rules that constituted the knowledge, but a very extensive human system for gathering, certifying, and maintaining the knowledge. It consisted of the following roles and organizations:

- A set of committees of senior physicians who oversaw clinical practice in various areas, such as the Partners Drug Therapy Committee, that reviewed and sanctioned the knowledge as correct or best-known practice

- A group of subject matter experts who, using online collaboration systems, debated and refined knowledge such as the best drug for treating high cholesterol under various conditions, or the best treatment protocol for diabetes patients

- A cadre of "knowledge editors" who took the approved knowledge from these groups and put it into a rule-based form that would be accepted by the online knowledge repository

With this human and technical infrastructure in place, Partners made great progress in organizing and updating its online knowledge environment.

High-Performance Medicine at Partners

Glaser and his Partners IT organization had always had the support of senior Partners executives, but for the most part their involvement in the activities designed to build Partners' organizational judgment was limited to some of the hospitals and those physician practices that wanted to be on the leading edge. Then Jim Mongan moved from being president of Mass General (a role he had occupied since 1996, shortly after the creation of Partners) to being CEO of Partners overall in January 2003. Not since Dick Nesson had Glaser had such a strong partner in the executive suite.

Mongan had come to appreciate the value of the LMR and CPOE, and other clinical systems, while he headed Mass General. But when he came into the Partners CEO role, with responsibility over a variety of diverse and autonomous institutions, he began to view it differently.

> So when I was preparing to make the move to Partners, I began to think about what makes a health system. One of the keys that would unite us was the electronic record. I saw it as the connective tissue, the thing we had in common, that could help us get a handle on utilization, quality, and other issues.[8]

Together, Mongan and Glaser agreed that while Partners already had strong clinical systems and knowledge management compared to other institutions, there were still a number of weaknesses that needed to be addressed (most importantly that the systems were not universally used across Partners care settings) and steps to be taken to get to the next level of capability. Working with other clinical leaders at Partners, they began to flesh out the vision for what came to be known as the High Performance Medicine (HPM) initiative, which took place between 2003 and 2009.

Glaser commented on the process the team followed to specify the details of the HPM initiative:

> Shortly after he took the reins at Partners, however, Jim had a clear idea on where he wanted this to go. To help refine that vision, several of us went on a road trip, to learn from other highly integrated health systems such as Kaiser, Intermountain Healthcare, and the Veterans Administration about ways we might bring the components of our system closer together.

Mongan concluded:

> We also were working with a core team of fifteen to twenty clinical leaders and eventually came up with a list of seven or eight initiatives, which then needed to be prioritized. We did a *Survivor*-style voting process, to determine which initiatives to "kick off the island." That narrowed down the list to five signature initiatives.

The five initiatives consisted of the following specific programs, each of which was addressed by its own team:

- *Creating an IT infrastructure.* Much of the initial work of this program had already been done; it consisted of the LMR and the CPOE, which were extended to the other hospitals and physician practices in the Partners network and maintained. This project also addressed patient data quality reporting, further enhancement of knowledge management processes, and a patient data portal to give patients access to their own health information.

- *Enhancing patient safety.* The team addressing patient safety issues focused on four specific projects: (1) providing decision support about what medications to administer in several key areas, including renal and geriatric dosing; (2) communicating "clinically significant test results," particularly to physicians after their patients have left the hospital; (3) ensuring effective flow of information during patient care transitions and handoffs in hospitals and after discharge; and (4) providing better decision support, patient education, and best practices and metrics for anticoagulation management.

- *Uniform high quality.* This team addressed quality improvement in the specific domains of hospital-based cardiac care, pneumonia, diabetes care, and smoking cessation; it employed both patient registries and decision support tools to do so. This team also took the lead in incorporating aspects of the Smart Form project into the LMR and CPOE systems.

- *Chronic disease management.* The team addressing disease management focused on prevention of hospital admission by identifying Partners patients who were at highest risk for hospitalization, and then developed health coaching programs to address patients with high levels of need—for example, heart failure patients; the team also pulled together a new database of information about patient wishes about end-of-life decisions.

- *Clinical resource management.* At Jim Mongan's suggestion, this team focused on how to lower the usage of high-cost drugs and high-cost imaging services; it employed both low-tech methods (e.g., chart reviews) and high-tech approaches (e.g., a data warehouse making transparent physicians' imaging behaviors relative to peers') to begin to make use of scarce resources more efficient.

Overall, Partners spent about $100 million on HPM and related clinical systems initiatives, most of which were ultimately paid for by the Partners hospitals and physician practices that used them. To track progress, a Partners-wide report, called the *HPM Close,* was developed that shows current and trend performance on the achievement of quality, efficiency, and structural goals. The report was published quarterly to ensure timely feedback for measuring performance and supporting accountability across Partners.

New Challenges for Partners

Partners had made substantial progress on many of the basic approaches to clinical information management, but there were many other areas at the intersection of health and information that it could still address. One was the area of *personalized genetic medicine*—the idea that patients would someday receive specific therapies based on their genomic, proteomic, and metabolic information. Partners had created the i2b2 (Informatics for Integrating Biology and the Bedside), a National Center for Biomedical Computing that was funded by the National Institutes of Health. John Glaser was codirector of i2b2 and developed the IT infrastructure for the Partners Center for Personalized Genetic Medicine. One of the many issues these efforts were addressing in personalized genetic medicine was how relevant genetic information would be included in the LMR.

Partners was also attempting to use clinical information for *postmarket surveillance*—the identification of problems with drugs and medical devices in patients after they have been released to the market. Some Partners researchers had identified dangerous side effects from certain drugs through analysis of LMR data. Specifically, research scientist John Brownstein's analyses suggested that the baseline expected level of patients with heart attack admissions to Mass General and the Brigham had increased 18 percent beginning in 2001 and returned to its baseline level in 2004, which coincided with the time frame for the beginning and end of Vioxx prescriptions. Thus far the identification of problems had taken place only after researchers from other institutions had identified them, but Partners executives believed it had the ability to identify them at an earlier stage. The institution was collaborating with the Food and Drug Administration and the Department of Defense to accelerate the surveillance process. John Glaser noted:

> There is serious potency here. We'll be better off in lots of ways because of our ability to leverage the data . . . What Partners is sure

of is the existence of a quicker and more focused, efficient, and cost-effective way to "getting a canary in the mine."

Partners was also focused on the use of communications technologies to improve patient care. Its Center for Connected Health, headed by Dr. Joe Kvedar, developed one of the first physician-to-physician online consultation services in an academic medical setting. The center was also exploring combinations of remote monitoring technologies, sensors (for example, pill boxes that know whether today's dosage has been taken), and online communications and intelligence to improve patient adherence to medication regimes, engagement in personal health, and clinical outcomes.

In the clinical knowledge management area, Partners had done an impressive job of organizing and maintaining the many rules and knowledge bases that informed its intelligent CPOE system. However, it was apparent to Glaser, Blackford Middleton, and Tonya Hongsermeier—and her successor as head of knowledge management, Roberto Rocha—that it made little sense for each medical institution to develop its own knowledge base. Therefore, Partners was actively engaged in helping other institutions with the management of clinical knowledge. Middleton (the principal investigator), Hongsermeier, Rocha, and at least thirteen other Partners employees were involved in a major Clinical Decision Support Consortium project funded by the U.S. Agency for Healthcare Research and Quality. The consortium involved a variety of other research institutions and health-care companies, and was primarily focused on finding ways to make clinical knowledge widely available to health-care providers through EMR and CPOE systems furnished by leading vendors.

Despite all these advances, not all Partners executives and physicians had fully bought into the vision of using smart information systems to improve patient care. Some found, for example, the LMR and CPOE to be invasive in the relationship of doctor and patient. A senior cardiologist at Brigham and Women's, for example, argued in an interview that:

I have a problem with the algorithmic approach to medicine. People end up making rote decisions that don't fit the patient, and it can also be medically quite wasteful. I don't have any choice here if I want to write prescriptions—virtually all of them are done online. But I must say that I am getting alert fatigue. Every time I write a prescription for nitroglycerine, I am given an alert that asks me to ensure that my patient isn't on Viagra. Don't you think I know that at this point? As for online treatment guidelines, I believe in them up to a point. But once something is in computerized guidelines, it's sacrosanct, whether or not the data are legitimate. Recommendations should be given with notification of how certain we are about them . . . Maybe these things are more useful to some doctors than others. If you're in a subspecialty like cardiology, you know it very well. But if you are an internist, you may have shallow knowledge, because you have to cover a wide variety of medical issues.

Many of the people involved in developing computer systems for patient care at Partners regarded these as valid concerns. "Alert fatigue," for example, had been recognized as a problem within Blackford Middleton's group for several years. They had tried to eliminate the more obvious alerts, and to make changes in the system to allow physicians to modify the types of alerts they received. There was a difficult line to draw, however, between saving physician attention and saving lives.

The Future of the Smart Form

The Smart Form pilot was successful by most measures. It had been piloted for use with upper respiratory infections, coronary artery disease, and diabetes. Most of the physicians in the pilot said they found it useful with their patients; some recommended changes that would make it even more useful.

Dr. Alan Cole, of Charles River Medical Associates, and chair of the Partners Diabetes Council, had this to say:

> The Smart Form is the easiest way to use the LMR. It provides
> access to vital signs and most labs and, in addition, permits
> entry of some data elements (e.g., vital signs and some Health
> Maintenance items) without screen changes or pop-ups.
> The Smart Form's decision support functionality assists
> compliance both by identifying deficits and streamlining most
> opportunities for correction. There are built-in individualized
> printouts that serve as teaching tools that are useful and
> appreciated. I find myself using the Smart Form 5–10 times
> every day.[9]

Dr. Elizabeth Mort, associate chief medical officer at Mass General, also used the Smart Form pilot for diabetes patients. She was also enthusiastic about the results:

> The Smart Form allows me to act on information rather than
> spending time pulling it together. The trend graphics have made
> it easier to show patients where they are and where they need
> to be. I had a very difficult to manage, noncompliant patient with
> an A1C [hemoglobin test used with diabetes patients] of 14.
> Showing the patient and her granddaughter the Patient View
> was critical in getting the whole family organized to support
> the patient. Her A1C came down to less than 9.

Despite these positive results, Middleton and his colleagues felt that the Smart Form needed more work, and more integration with existing Partners systems. In fact, they had identified several features of the Smart Form that could be incorporated into the LMR and CPOE systems. Middleton felt that the Smart Form was a successful experiment, but he was sure it should not be a stand-alone system. He viewed it as one of a series of innovations in clinical systems that would continue to improve health care at Partners and elsewhere.

Middleton was fond of quoting an article in the *New England Journal of Medicine* from 1976:

> I conclude that though the individual physician is not perfectible, the system of care is, and that the computer will play a major part in the perfection of future care systems.[10]

Reflections on Partners HealthCare's Organizational Judgment

It's clear from the experience of Partners and other health-care providers that decisions about patient care and many other issues can be made faster and more consistently through the use of information technology. The decisions made through systems can be either fully automated or—as in Partners' case—made through a combination of human and computerized judgment. Partners' early implementations of the clinical data repository, electronic medical record, and provider order entry capabilities are increasingly being followed by other care providers around the world; and in the United States, the federal government is heavily subsidizing these activities as a way to improve care quality and lower costs.

Of course, computer-assisted health care requires dramatic changes in the behaviors of health-care practitioners and in the overall culture of the organization, as well as strong leadership by senior executives and expert medical practitioners. Partners needed computers and software to achieve the advances it has made in care quality, but it also needed leaders like Dick Nesson, John Glaser, Jim Mongan, and Blackford Middleton. Systems that were just as capable as Partners' have failed in other institutions because of lack of leadership and effective change management approaches.

There are many ways to improve organizational judgment with respect to patient care, including care processes and treatment protocols that needn't involve computers at all. And there is still an important role for the individual intuition of caregivers. However, computers will inevitably play a major role in health care going forward. Any health-care provider that does not take advantage of its capabilities will eventually be justifiably charged with malpractice.

5

Cognizant

How Will All These Daily Decisions Get Made?

MPLOYEES AT COGNIZANT TECHNOLOGY SOLUTIONS, a large provider of information technology services, had a minor but annoying problem to solve on behalf of their client. It was the type of nagging issue often faced by multinational corporations. Cognizant's client, a global manufacturing company with its headquarters in the United States, had adopted a corporatewide system for logging, tracking, and resolving customer complaints. Most business units were using it successfully, but the client's Korean business unit was resisting use of the system. That unit had previously implemented a different application for complaint management. Corporate executives at the client, who wanted to monitor the frequency of customer complaints across the entire global firm, had insisted that the Korean business unit supply its complaint data for the corporate system. However, Korean managers felt that their local system was better suited to their unit's needs and customers, so they didn't want to give it up. In order to comply with the requirement from corporate, Korean personnel were entering the complaints into their own system and reentering them into the corporate system. This resulted, of course, in duplication of effort. Also, additional effort was spent on retrieving information when ad hoc inquiries on complaints were made by corporate management.[1]

Cognizant supplied not only consulting and systems integration services to this client, but also a system by which Cognizant employees could propose ideas and solutions to the client's problems. Called the Idea Management System (IMS), it was a component of a broader work management and idea-sharing system that Cognizant used internally called Cognizant 2.0 (C2). Cognizant used C2 for a variety of client service purposes, and it had recently been adopted for idea management purposes at this client. It is at the heart of the company's organizational judgment, allowing Cognizant people all over the world to share their knowledge with each other and communicate via social media, all within the context of performing the work they need to do. If the primary job of a consulting and professional services firm is to bring knowledge and experience to bear on solving client problems, C2 is an amazing tool to facilitate the task.

The particular problem at the Korean business unit was posted as an "idea campaign" in the C2 IMS platform, and associates at Cognizant who were familiar with the client's situation were invited to suggest ideas. From the list of ideas contributed, a proposal to integrate the local system with the corporate standard complaint management system was taken up for implementation. Thus, the Korean unit's system was integrated with the corporate system. This enabled a complaint logged in the Korean system to be automatically directed to the corporate system, and reentry of complaints was avoided. The actual complaint resolution workflow was managed in the corporate application, and the status on the complaint was updated in the Korean system. Thus, the goal of top management was achieved without disturbing the existing process at the Korean unit. Productivity was improved, manual reentry errors were eliminated, and two thousand users have benefited from the system interface. In all, $11,600 was saved.

Yes, this is small potatoes in a big company, but the idea is that such small decisions and judgments are identified and adopted on a continuous, frequent basis—it all adds up. IMS has been used to capture and track many other innovations by Cognizant associates at the same client. In total, the innovation efforts undertaken through IMS at that client have reaped rich business benefits. All 375 Cognizant associates on the account received information about innovation and the use of IMS, but 14 of them were trained extensively as idea champions. During the past year, IMS has provided a platform for 11 idea campaigns in which 310 associates contributed a total of 1,119 ideas. From this total, 124 idea proposals were identified as having the potential to be implemented, of which 75 were approved by the client and 70 eventually got implemented. All this ideation resulted in $1,643,536 of benefits for Cognizant and $1,585,880 worth of benefits to the client. And that's just one client in one year.

The implemented innovations range from improving software tool usage by the team, to creating efficiencies in business processes, to enabling the client to build better relationships with vendors and partners. The account scored an astounding 98 percent in the Cognizant Innovation Index (an internal measure of the extent of innovation) during 2010, which was the highest among Cognizant clients (out of 208 client accounts using IMS) and testifies to the innovation maturity of the account. Moreover, during the year, two Cognizant associates working with the client were given Best Innovation Champion and Best Idea Champion awards. The account continues to actively leverage IMS for launching idea campaigns to elicit ideas from teams both on-site and offshore as part of its innovation journey.

Cognizant's objective with IMS was to help its clients find solutions to many such small innovations, and some large ones. It uses other aspects of C2 internally to solve the daily technical problems resulting from the implementation of complex systems in large, global organizations.

A Typical Technical Problem at Cognizant

On a recent Microsoft client/server development project with a retail client, both onshore and offshore (India-based) Cognizant resources were working on the client system. However, software deployment had come to a halt because of a technical problem at the client site. The software system developed could not upload large documents. The key functionality implemented in the system was sharing design specifications for products to be sold across the client's geographical units. Since many of the documents shared within this organization were large files with graphics, it was imperative to solve this issue.

The onsite Cognizant project manager decided to use C2 to solve the problem. The first thing she did was to search the C2 software component database and locate a component that could potentially solve this problem. Upon further examination, however, she discovered that no existing component fit the unique needs of this situation, including dealing with multiple versions of Internet browsers and Web servers, handling multiple languages, and dealing effectively with constraints arising from very low bandwidth in some countries.

Since these issues required deep expertise, she decided to tap into the wisdom of the community to solve the problem. Using the process template defined within C2 for dealing with help requests, she opened a ticket by initiating a new request and wrote a short description of the problem. Since this problem had impacted the delivery schedule, she classified it as being of top priority. Based on the workflow defined in the system, C2 posted the problem on a Cognizant forum called AskGuru that aimed to address such issues. The question was tagged as dealing with retail, performance management, and Microsoft .NET (a framework for building Microsoft Windows applications) issues.

When this question was posed, no one responded initially because few developers had any experience working on projects that had to deal with such a requirement. Seeing that this was an urgent production issue with a client implementation and one that hadn't been answered in a day, C2 automatically escalated the problem to a moderator. The moderator, after understanding the requirement, helped connect the developer with the right .NET architects, who suggested specific modifications to the reusable component for multigeography support. The moderator also involved the performance engineering team to measure and suggest changes to the design of the component, and provided a solution involving mirroring and replication across servers. A set of retail business analysts were also consulted to ensure that the new approach would have no negative impact on the business process; they also identified aspects of the process that could be accommodated through background processing requiring no telecommunications. Each associate involved in answering the question collected WAH points (similar to frequent-flier points that can be redeemed for gifts).

The on-site team couldn't use the solution immediately, as they had some remaining questions regarding multilingual support. Since every posting on C2 has the associate's profile information, the on-site team was easily able to track down the Microsoft .NET architect and solve the problem. Once the problem was solved, the project manager answered a feedback survey and closed the ticket.

Cognizant Technology Solutions Background

Cognizant Technology Solutions was launched in 1994 out of a restructuring of Dun & Bradstreet Corporation. It was spun off as a publicly held company in 1998.[2] It listed its shares that year on the NASDAQ exchange and began an over ten-year period of rapid growth. Its 1998 revenues were $58 million; by the end of 2010, it had achieved over $4.5 billion in revenues and over $700 million in operating profit. Also by the end of 2010, it had more than one hundred thousand employees. Most were in

India, although Cognizant's headquarters was in Teaneck, New Jersey, and it had global delivery centers in over fifty locations, including Buenos Aires, Budapest, and Shanghai.

While the offshore outsourcing and systems integration industry had grown dramatically during this same period, Cognizant's growth in revenues, profits, and share price outshone all major competitors. In 2008, as the global recession took hold, Cognizant still managed strong revenue growth of 32 percent; by 2010, its growth rate was 40 percent.

Cognizant's strategy was distinguished by several distinctive capabilities, including the following:

- *A strong orientation to vertical industry client sectors.* Cognizant was one of the first offshore firms to organize vertically. In mid-2009, sectors included financial services; communications; consumer goods; health care; information, media, and entertainment; insurance; life sciences; manufacturing and logistics; retail; technology; and travel and hospitality. Most Cognizant employees were aligned to a particular industry grouping, and the firm did not seek—and often turned down—work outside its industry specialties.

- *Strong client relationship focus.* From its inception, Cognizant had focused on building and maintaining client satisfaction and relationships. Ninety percent of Cognizant's work came from existing clients. An extensive client satisfaction survey had yielded an average score between "satisfied" and "extremely satisfied" for nine consecutive years. Cognizant employed a *two-in-a-box* client relationship model, in which a client partner managed on-site client relationships, and a dedicated delivery manager ensured that off-site delivery resources were mobilized on behalf of the client.

- *An on-site/offshore global delivery model.* Unlike many of its India-based competitors, Cognizant was managed globally from its beginning, with a U.S. headquarters and major operations in Chennai, India. Virtually all client projects had components that were sourced from multiple global locations. Cognizant employees at the client site typically handled 25 to 30 percent of the project work; the remainder came from global delivery centers. A well-defined set of methods and tools ensured that project work moved seamlessly from client site to offshore delivery center. C2 was one of those tools; it enabled Cognizant to more effectively apply "intellectual arbitrage" and deliver in a globally seamless fashion. For instance, the platform helped Cognizant to divide delivery among nearshore locations like Budapest or Buenos Aires, in conjunction with global delivery from India or China. Cognizant could then leverage the best talent available worldwide to provide greater business value on a lower-cost basis for clients. This was done transparently to the client; the client saw the end result, not that a portion of the deliverable was built in China, India, Argentina, or elsewhere. It was delivered as if it were built in one location by one physically connected team.

- *A broad range of IT and business services.* Cognizant offered clients strong capabilities in many areas of IT development and infrastructure management, including system development, outsourcing, IT infrastructure management, data warehousing and business intelligence, and software testing and usability. In addition, the Cognizant business consulting unit addressed business topics related to IT, including business process design, change management, and analysis of what projects could be outsourced.

While other firms also possessed some or all of these attributes, the combination of their early, widespread adoption and disciplined execution at Cognizant had led to a successful and fast-growing firm—evidence of a good strategy and organizational design, and of effective day-to-day decision making and execution.

Knowledge Management at Cognizant

Knowledge management was a long-term focus of Cognizant.[3] Francisco (Frank) D'Souza, the company's CEO, and other company executives believed strongly that a global delivery model required global sharing of knowledge. Cognizant was one of the first firms with a major Indian presence to have a dedicated chief knowledge officer and be invested in knowledge managers and tools. Approximately 1 percent of Cognizant's annual revenues were invested in knowledge management activities.

The first major tool for Cognizant employees to share and access knowledge was the Cognizant 2.0 Knowledge Management (KM) Appliance (internally referred to as Channel One). It became the primary portal for accessing documents of various types—client proposals, presentations, technical papers, and so forth. However, unlike many firms, Cognizant was not satisfied with a document-based approach to knowledge management. Instead of a *repository* model, which involved constant problems of keeping the repository current and accurate, Cognizant's knowledge managers subscribed to a *router* model in which the goal of knowledge management and systems was to route people to the knowledge they needed. The knowledge might be in a centralized document repository, but it could just as easily be in an individual's head or disk drive, or in a decentralized repository. Therefore, Cognizant tried to provide search capabilities to make all such knowledge available to all employees.

Cognizant's knowledge management approach was also characterized by a *culture of participation*. Early on in the use of knowledge management, this meant the use of discussion boards and forums. More recently, as Web 2.0 tools came into wider use both inside and outside Cognizant, the firm relied on them as a major approach to knowledge management. These participative tools included blogs, wikis, and social tagging approaches. While conventional wisdom suggested that typically only 1 percent of online participants actively contributed content, Cognizant had much greater levels of participation. One analysis, for example, found almost eleven thousand employees had blogged; almost ten thousand had commented on blogs; more than five thousand queries had been posted to a business development forum; and there were over one hundred thousand queries to a technical forum.

Research by the knowledge management organization suggested that those employees who blogged had higher levels of satisfaction and engagement with their jobs. According to CEO Frank D'Souza, who wrote his own blog:

> Blogging has reinforced bonding among employees and helped us create an environment of honesty, openness, and progressiveness. We live in a naked knowledge economy where communication, collaboration, and collective ideation are indispensable for successful team leadership. My experience shows how blogging helps in achieving collective goals.[4]

There were several instances in which D'Souza had discussed strategic issues at Cognizant with entry-level employees in forums and blogs.

In addition to offering blogging and other participative tools, Cognizant had put various organizational structures in place to facilitate knowledge management. There were knowledge officers in each of the consulting practices. The Knowledge Management Office (KMO) at headquarters consisted of a KM central team and knowledge officers who reported to Sukumar Rajagopal, the firm's first chief knowledge officer (and now chief information officer and head of innovation). To facilitate social networks, Rajagopal created both *communities of practice* (CoP) and *network of practitioners* (NoP) structures. A CoP was organized within organizational (industry and practice area) boundaries, while an NoP operated across organizational boundaries. Each CoP had a knowledge officer who worked with knowledge champions within the business unit teams to document project-level expertise. The organizational structure for knowledge management was clearly effective at producing, capturing, and distributing knowledge, but to be certain it was being successfully applied to Cognizant's business, more work was necessary.

Cognizant 2.0

While the KM Appliance (Channel One) was very successful in terms of adoption and use of both stored documents and participative tools, the company's executives were concerned that the tools be used to support business goals. According to Sukumar Rajagopal, then Cognizant's chief knowledge officer:

> We felt that the participative and knowledge-oriented culture of Cognizant was a great asset. But we also wanted to combine it with the discipline of an organization equally focused on core process execution. That led us to the creation of Cognizant 2.0.

Malcolm Frank, the chief strategy and marketing officer for Cognizant, described the many attributes of C2:

> It's intended to be a common program management and knowledge-sharing platform for Cognizant, its clients, and its vendors. We want it to assist clients in leveraging the best delivery resources, regardless of location. C2 acts as a seamless platform for collaboration across geographically distributed project teams across Cognizant's extended enterprise. In addition, it needs to provide quality control over delivery at the most atomic, real-time levels. We have to create and control multiple projects at any given time. It should provide access to knowledge in the context of a particular work process, and ongoing process guidance. Finally, it should provide us with a consolidated view of key activities and measures across all projects. All of those attributes came together in C2.

The knowledge-oriented resources had been developed previously in the KM Appliance. What remained to be developed, however, was a set of structured work process guidelines and tasks for each major type of work that Cognizant performed for its clients or internally (for example, the idea management process mentioned at the beginning of this chapter). It was also necessary to establish predefined linkages between process steps and relevant knowledge, although Cognizant's employees could also supply such linkages through tagging. Together, these two capabilities would allow knowledge to be provided "just in time" on client projects.

By mid-2009, Cognizant had developed process workflows, with explicit task specifications, for three major client services, including systems delivery, systems management, and maintenance. Creating such processes was the responsibility of a dedicated process design group within Cognizant. The group's task was made much easier by the fact that Cognizant had long been a process-focused organization, and was one of the earlier firms to achieve Level 5 status in the Capability Maturity Model developed by Carnegie Mellon's Software Engineering Institute. This was a measure of an organization's use of process disciplines in building software.

The central process group was also working with different practices and communities on a variety of other process structures that could be used in Cognizant 2.0. Those under development included marketing campaign management, responses to client requests for proposals, and even strategy consulting. The developed processes were not rigid, but could be configured based on the size of the project and other circumstances. A quality manager on each project team certified that the process model was effective and valid.

In effect, C2 was a knowledge and process management portal, as well as a platform that managed Cognizant's work across a global delivery network. Although the placement of different items was configurable by the user, in figure 5-1 the left side of the screen is a series of tasks to be completed by the user in the context of his or her client project and work process. On the right are a set of potentially useful knowledge resources. The

FIGURE 5-1

Screen shot for Cognizant 2.0

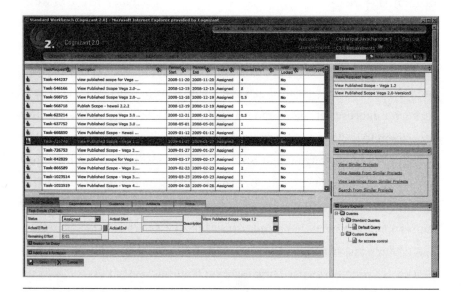

guidance and knowledge displayed are always shown in context. Some are focused on the context of the actual work, such as the guidance tab in the screen; others are more relevant to the project context, such as the links to view data from similar projects. For any task, there were guidance information, templates, artifacts, notes, and checklists. At any time, any project member could see what projects and tasks were assigned to him or her, and any dependencies with other projects and tasks.

C2 guided Cognizant project team members to collaborate with experts within the firm. It connected those seeking expertise to the right forums, posted their questions, and kept track of replies received. C2 also allowed the user to search for content from various issue, defect, or risk databases for relevant solutions, making past project information available to the current work environment.

C2 could also improve the delivery quality and productivity of information systems. It could integrate with various IT development environments to support automated execution of aspects of the development and support environment, such as automatic triggering of code review and automated unit testing, It could also integrate with version control and configuration management applications.

Rapid Take-Up

After the introduction of C2 in October 2007, new capabilities were rapidly deployed, and project teams rapidly adopted the platform (although usage was voluntary). By mid-2009, more than 3,200 project teams were using the platform. Most used it not as a collaborative platform, but as an individual knowledge and project management tool. There were, for example, over 5 million page views per month in the C2 *project delivery domain*—the primary source for viewing project information within the Cognizant 2.0 platform.

Although Cognizant employees seemed to find the system relatively easy to use, the Knowledge Management Office worked to make it even easier. It offered training sessions to on-board new employees and new users. The trainers found that Cognizant employees were used to the participative knowledge tools such as forums, blogs, and wikis, but they found the process structure and guidance somewhat less familiar. At the project team level, some projects used either the process side or the knowledge side of C2 well, but they didn't use them well in combination.

The Knowledge Management Office also encouraged competition in the use of Cognizant 2.0 and offered an annual award for the best project and employees in the use of the platform. An underlying objective of the awards was to try to make the most effective C2-using projects more visible to the entire Cognizant organization.

C2 and Organizational Judgment—Internally and at Clients

C2 had become one of Cognizant's key initiatives for improving the day-to-day decisions and actions of associates, and one upon which the company was depending heavily. When clients asked D'Souza at a conference about Cognizant's key initiatives, the first one he mentioned was C2:

> Cognizant 2.0 is a fundamental part of how we differentiate our global delivery model. We are just scratching the surface of what it is capable of, and we will continue to invest heavily in the platform.

Lakshmi Narayanan, vice chairman, told clients at the conference that:

> Using C2 we can deliver projects 20 percent more efficiently. It also allows us to increase productivity up to 70 percent in specific project management activities by efficient usage of the C2 delivery management functionalities.

Chandra Sekaran, Cognizant's president and managing director for global delivery, commented:

> Of all the projects we have started [recently], 89 percent of them are already on the Cognizant 2.0 platform. We recently launched the module to support the maintenance of projects and we see more and more maintenance products are getting on to the Cognizant 2.0 platform.

That "collective wisdom"—perhaps a synonym for organizational judgment—was well established at Cognizant, but the company's executives were equally excited about extending it into client organizations for their own use. Sukumar Rajagopal speculated on its ability to manage client knowledge:

> Customers are asking us to use these capabilities to structure their knowledge management. We're beginning to do some of that work, but they may not have the participative culture and process discipline to make a C2-like environment work as well for them as it has for us. This is something we need to learn more about.

Francisco D'Souza was particularly interested in the types of clients who would find Cognizant 2.0-like functionality useful in their businesses:

> We believe that some client processes would be particularly well suited for this, such as those involving regulation and compliance. Financial services clients see it as helping to deal with regulatory issues across geographies.

Cognizant had already begun to take Cognizant 2.0 to market as a service offering, as described in the case of the global manufacturing client at the beginning of this chapter. It was clear that C2 would be central to Cognizant's future—both internally and in client services. But just what would that future hold? There might, for example, be considerable benefits to giving Cognizant's clients real-time access to project status and the knowledge repository. For clients, this could lead to greater operational agility, unnecessary cost avoidance, and improved planning capabilities—as well as a closer relationship between Cognizant and clients. The key issue with C2, the management team felt, was simply not getting in its way, and determining which of its many potential contributions to exploit.

Reflections on Cognizant's Organizational Judgment

In a far-flung global organization like Cognizant, turning individual judgment into organizational judgment has to go beyond face-to-face interactions. Information technology is the only possible route to linking over one hundred thousand minds. C2 is one of the most innovative tools in any organization for creating that linkage.

Cognizant not only has employed social media and knowledge management tools to improve day-to-day decision making and organizational judgment, but has done so in a way that improves productivity and performance. Some of the most powerful aids to organizational judgment involve the combination of structured work process tools with social tools for knowledge sharing and collaboration; we call this combination "social + structure." Cognizant's C2 "platform" for knowledge workers is truly a platform; it is used for a variety of purposes that benefit both Cognizant and its clients.

Another key to the success of such tools is that their use is measured. Measurement of the success of these technologies and of the behaviors necessary for their effective use is critical to their successful implementation. It is quite useful, for example, to know that the greatest contributors to C2 are also the organization's highest-performing employees.

Of course, the usual warnings apply about the role of technology by itself. Social and collaboration technologies like Cognizant's are only successful when the organization already has a culture of participation. Senior managers have to support and model not only the culture, but also the direct use of these technologies, in order for both to be successful.

6

Charlotte-Mecklenburg Schools

How Can We Improve Student Performance?

MICHAEL ELLIS, a second-grader at David Cox Road Elementary in Charlotte, North Carolina, didn't notice the school's cheerful blue metal roof on a sunny Wednesday in May as he got off the bus and came in the front door.[1] He also didn't notice the new greetings painted on the three big rocks outside the school: "Happy 8th Birthday, Justin P.," "Lordy, Lordy, Somebody's Turning 40," or "Our Volunteers Rock!" The various cheerful signs and student portraits on the walls of the entry hall were wasted on Michael this day, because he was distracted. He knew that in a few minutes he would have his final *reading fluency* test of the year. This attribute of his student performance was measured by an oral reading speed test, although technically, in addition to speed, it included reading with expression and the automatic recognition of words.[2]

Michael, his teacher, and school support staff had been working diligently the entire school year on getting his fluency up. How did they do it? With data-based measurement, decisions, and actions. When Michael started the year, he was reading eighteen words correctly per minute—far below the benchmark of thirty to sixty for the beginning of second grade. Because of his below-benchmark assessment, he was pulled from his regular classroom every morning for the entire school year to work with a teaching assistant on fluency. He's sung songs—first slow ones, then faster ones—to help in sight-reading words. He particularly liked Miley Cyrus's "Party in the USA," and he now recognized many of the words in it.

Michael had also worked with his dad at home. His dad lost his job, so he had plenty of time to work with Michael on fluency improvement. Christa Olech, the reading facilitator for grades K–2 at David Cox, had sent Michael home one Friday with a packet about his fluency levels, and Chuck Nusinov, the school's principal, had called Michael's home to encourage his parents to help in addressing the issue. Michael's dad had ensured that Michael did all of his practice reading, and had signed the weekly log and returned it with Michael each Friday—ensuring that Michael got his weekly treat. Michael was one of one hundred David Cox students to be working on fluency with his parents.

Tameeka Wilson in Kindergarten

Tameeka Wilson, a David Cox kindergarten student, was already becoming restive in school after only a couple of months. In November, for example, she told her mom she was already bored with the instruction. "We're doing letters all the time and I already know them all!" Her mother asked about it at parents' night in October, and was told that the entire kindergarten curriculum involved letter recognition. That had been the primary focus for reading instruction in kindergarten for decades, and it would presumably continue to be for many more.

But not if Donna Helms had anything to say about it. She was Tameeka's teacher, and she wouldn't have been surprised at Tameeka's comment to her mother. Helms had thirty-three years of teaching experience, but she wasn't happy with the time-honored David Cox kindergarten curriculum. With that much experience and with exposure in other districts to other kindergarten curricula, she felt that the great majority of kindergarten students were capable of learning to read, and her own reading of a book called *Teaching in the New Kindergarten* supported her view. She felt that the standard curriculum for kindergartners was a waste of both time and learning opportunity. Instead of learning to recognize words, the children were asked to learn and discuss apples in October, pumpkins in November, Christmas trees in December, and so forth. Helms herself thought that the curriculum had outlived its usefulness, and she felt she was shortchanging her students.

At one of the regular kindergarten teachers' meetings in October, Helms brought up Tameeka and the many other children in her class who knew all the letters. With Chuck Nusinov's support for data-based decisions in the principal's office, she felt there might be an opening to change the curriculum. Nusinov was privately supportive of her ideas and encouraged her to bring them up with the other teachers. Most of the other teachers also said they had noticed that the children knew all their letters.

The David Cox Road Elementary School

The fluency work that Michael and his schoolmates had been doing and the possible change in curriculum for Tameeka and her kindergarten classmates are two manifestations of a major shift in how student performance decisions were made and executed at David Cox Road Elementary and other schools within the Charlotte-Mecklenburg Schools (CMS). For the past three or four years, the school's administration and teachers—led by Nusinov, the principal—have been embracing a data-based approach to student assessment and instruction. This school, of course, was not unique—there was a national, if not global, trend toward greater use of data in school decision making—but it was at the very least a good example of the movement.

David Cox was clearly a well-run school in the northeast suburbs of Charlotte, but it was no suburban paradise. It was racially mixed, with 60 percent African American students, 19 percent white students, and a variety of other ethnicities. Fifty-five percent of the students came from households considered to be living in poverty. But you'd never know it by looking at the school; it was bright, clean, and full of interesting visual stimuli. The administrative staff was outgoing and friendly, and students in the hallways were energetic, but focused.

Chuck Nusinov had been principal of David Cox for four years, and was assistant principal for a couple before that. Dressed in a golf shirt with a David Cox logo and khakis, he was energetic and extroverted. Nusinov had been pushing the culture in a more data-oriented direction since he arrived at the school, and it was beginning to take hold. Nusinov estimated that at least two or three teachers at each grade level (out of six to eight in total) had the data-based-decision religion, and he figured that if he were to be hit by a school bus one day, the movement would persist without him at the school.

Before becoming a teacher, Nusinov was a manager of a retail jewelry chain. "At age twenty-four, I had the American dream—a good salary, a company car, an expense account," he noted. "But my midlife crisis came early, and I decided to take a drastic salary cut and teach math." Nusinov remembered the value of the retail sales data he received in his previous job, however. "We basically knew at any time how we were doing for the week, the month, the quarter, whatever. Then when I got into education I realized we had no good data on how our students were doing at any given time. I've been working on it ever since. I even teach "Data Analysis in Education" to student teachers at UNC–Charlotte."

Nusinov had been slowly introducing data to the school in conjunction with a program called Data Wise that the CMS district had adopted in partnership with the Harvard Graduate School of Education.[3] Data Wise incorporated substantial training of teachers and staff on the effective use of data. But it was clear to both Nusinov and the Harvard faculty who created the program that it was a substantial cultural shift. Increased transparency would make some teachers appear less effective at teaching. The Harvard materials quoted one teacher from another district using Data Wise who commented, "Data can wound."

In order to address this issue, Nusinov phased in the data orientation slowly over four years. "When I came here," he reflected, "nobody shared scores, and we whited all the teachers' names out in the student performance reports." Then the next year, they shared average scores by teacher name. The year after, they shared data down to the student level with teacher names at every grade-level planning meeting. "After that, people were demanding the data," Nusinov recalled. "I'm sure some feelings were hurt initially," he said, "but we all got over it."

The Data Wise approach specified that each school adopting the program must create a "data team." It was run by the school's assistant principal, and included at least one teacher per grade and three to five facilitators. One purpose of the team was to train teachers in the interpretation of data along the lines of the Data Wise approach. The relatively new data team had begun to work with teachers to identify problems and use student performance data to address them. The data team had also made the decisions to employ teaching assistants to help with student reading fluency, and to add reading comprehension as a focus in the upcoming year.

Student performance data was also addressed in a variety of other school contexts. Each grade level's teachers met weekly, and data was a part of those meetings. Nusinov's staff also met weekly, and data was always a part of it. Nusinov and the staff and teachers had recently agreed to have data and assessment meetings for an hour every couple of weeks. Teachers wanted a separate time for that topic so that it didn't take away from the instructional planning in other meetings.

Because the state's and the CMS district's tests weren't yet suited to rapid decision making about student performance, Nusinov and the school's administration had to do a lot of testing on their own. On a shelf in the principal's office was a Scantron machine—which graded "bubble chart" tests—and piles of blank testing forms. In the quest for better assessments of student performance, David Cox students had been tested frequently in areas that the state and district didn't yet address, such as reading fluency and readers' understanding of the author's purpose, capability on fractions and decimals (in fourth grade), and teacher effectiveness. Close at hand on Nusinov's computer were spreadsheets on proficiency in a variety of topics, including reading, math, and science.

All this focus on data was beginning to yield results at David Cox despite factors that might have previously worsened performance. School boundaries, for example, had recently been redrawn, and more children from families of poverty had been assigned to David Cox (the percentage in poverty increased from 34 percent in 2006 to 56 percent in 2010). Some long-term, effective teachers had also been moved to a new school nearby. Nonetheless, the school had maintained an overall 65 percent proficiency level in both math and reading. Over the past two years, David Cox students had achieved, on average, a year's growth in learning over a year, which was a key component of state educational performance goals.

One goal of the school's administration was to close the "achievement gap" between white and African American or Hispanic students. For the 2009–2010 academic year, the goal was to close the gap by 2 percent. End-of-year tests revealed that the gap had been narrowed by between 6 and 18 percent for different ethnicities.

A North Carolina survey of teachers also suggested that the climate of the school was improving. In the 2007–2008 year, only 57 percent of David Cox teachers had even responded to the survey, but in 2009–2010, 92 percent responded. One hundred percent of the respondents agreed that "faculty and staff have a shared vision," compared to 92 percent two years previously. More than 90 percent of teachers agreed with several categories of questions stating, "School leadership makes a sustained effort to address teachers concerns about ..."

In short, data was clearly making a difference at David Cox Road Elementary. Nusinov and his staff felt they had made considerable progress in using data to judge and improve student performance. Of course, there was still considerable improvement to be addressed, and a sense of complacency was difficult to find in the schoolhouse halls.

Data-Based Decisions at Charlotte-Mecklenburg Schools

Nusinov, of course, was not alone in his pursuit of data-based student decision making. The Charlotte-Mecklenburg (the county in which Charlotte is located) Schools are also aggressively pursuing that approach at the same time David Cox Road Elementary does so. CMS's efforts were at the leading edge of a national trend toward data-based management of schools. As Arne Duncan, secretary of education in the Obama administration, put it:

> In other fields, we talk about success constantly, with statistics and other measures to demonstrate it ... Why, in education, are we scared to talk about what success looks like? What is there to hide? ... Every state and district should be collecting and sharing information about teacher effectiveness with teachers and—in the context of other important measures—with parents.[4]

CMS enrolled over 133,600 students, and was the second-largest district in North Carolina and the twentieth-largest in the United States. Like many urban school districts, it had struggled over the past several decades with issues of poverty, racial balance, and low student achievement. CMS was the subject of a busing initiative that was upheld by the Supreme Court in 1971, and the district was criticized by a county judge for committing "academic genocide" against students in poorly performing high schools in 2005.

A new superintendent, Peter Gorman, arrived at CMS in 2006. He brought a strong focus on academic achievement, measurement of performance, and accountability for teachers and administration. Gorman quickly developed a strategic plan that addressed those issues, and by 2010 progress was clearly being made. From the introduction to the 2014 strategic plan (developed in 2009):

> As 2010 approaches, CMS has accomplished many of the objectives identified in that plan, and is moving toward achieving others. The plan's overarching goal—to increase student achievement— has been met in many areas. In the 2008–2009 school year, student achievement increased in 24 of 25 areas measured by state and national tests. Equally strong gains have been made in the percentage of schools achieving one year's academic growth in one year's time. In 2006, 54.3 percent of schools in CMS averaged one year's growth or more in one year's time. By 2009, CMS had increased that percentage to 89.6 percent. That's a 35.3 percent increase in just three years.

Gorman's educational background was unusual for a school superintendent in that he had both a doctorate in education and an MBA. He described how he became so focused on data and measurement:

> When I got my PhD, I was frustrated with all the educational performance metrics being used at the time, because they didn't really address the customer—the individual students and their parents. When I went to business school, I saw that businesses were using customer metrics, balanced scorecards, and all sorts of performance measures, and I thought we could do that in schools. I was also influenced by Bill James, the great baseball sabermetrics guy. I used to read his *Baseball Abstract* every year, and at one point it hit me that we could apply the same approaches to students that he did to baseball players.

Under Gorman's leadership, CMS had established a variety of measurement and performance programs for students, teachers, and administrative functions. In addition to the Data Wise program being implemented at David Cox Road Elementary (and throughout the district), CMS subscribed to the DIBELS (Dynamic Indicators of Basic Early Literacy Skills) program from the University of Oregon, which was a set of procedures and measures for assessing the acquisition of early literacy skills, and a database of student and district performance with regard to literacy. CMS was also attempting to develop *professional learning communities* within each of its schools. According to Richard DuFour, who developed the concept:

> To create a professional learning community, focus on learning rather than teaching, work collaboratively, and hold yourself accountable for results.[5]

CMS had also received a $1.4 million grant from the Bill and Melinda Gates Foundation to support data-based decisions about student performance. The grant was particularly focused on the five CMS high schools in the Achievement Zone, a cluster of low-performing schools that were targeted to receive additional resources and intensive academic support to improve student achievement.

In order to pursue these and other data-intensive initiatives, Gorman had created a chief strategy and accountability officer role. This position, held by Robert Avossa, was responsible for performance measurement and management for the district. Avossa and his staff oversaw the Data Wise program as well as a variety of others related to data-based decision making. Members of Avossa's staff implemented new systems and processes, and trained schoolteachers and administrative staff on their use. For example, Farrah Santonato trained the staff and teachers at David Cox Road Elementary on the Data Wise program. In Avossa's office there were also four area support coordinators, one for each of the four regions of the district, who worked with schools in their area on data and performance-related initiatives.

Avossa's office was collaborating with those of the chief academic officer and the chief information officer to develop a student performance information portal. It would eventually include all the information about student performance that Chuck Nusinov had available at David Cox, plus a good deal more. When asked about Nusinov's school-based data, Gorman commented, "We love what he's doing, but we want to put him out of business. He shouldn't have to be spending time with databases and reporting tools. When the portal's ready, he won't have to." Eventually, CMS planned to build portals specifically designed for the needs of principals, area superintendents, and the district superintendent.

Gorman and Avossa had developed an overall architecture for the district's continued improvement in student performance called Cycle of Continuous Improvement (see Figure 6-1). It specified a virtuous cycle of transparent information availability, support in the use of the information, and pressure or motivation to drive usage. The two leaders hoped that these diverse mechanisms and tools would lead to persistent change in CMS's culture and processes.

With dramatic changes under a particular leader, there was always the danger that the changes would disappear under new leadership. But Gorman was confident that data-based decisions were at CMS for the long haul:

> The CMS board is on board with this. Using data to make decisions is part of their core beliefs. The head of the board is particularly supportive. In the formal policies of the board, we specify having data dashboards, school progress reports, and overall making decisions based on data. I believe I was recruited for this position in part because of my data orientation. People call me a data geek, but I view that as a badge of honor. However, most of the data we've had in the past serves others, not us—just as SAT scores serve colleges. Even the state exams we've had were too high-level to do anything with. They are like autopsies. But we want to give physicals, not autopsies. The data must be available while there is time to do something about it.

FIGURE 6-1

Cycle of Continuous Improvement

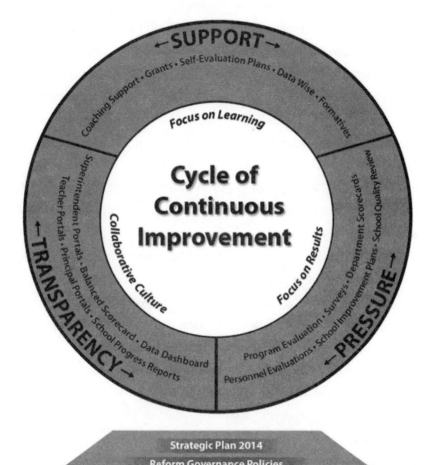

Gorman's predictions about the persistence of these data-based approaches would shortly thereafter be tested, as he, Avossa, and Nusinov all left CMS for other jobs in 2011.[6]

Back to David Cox Road Elementary

Michael Ellis, the David Cox Road Elementary second-grader with a reading fluency problem, took the final fluency test of the year in May, and the results were good news. He had gone from eighteen words to eighty-four in a year, which was certainly a dramatic improvement. He was still somewhat below the second-grade benchmark of ninety for end-of-grade testing in the Charlotte-Mecklenburg Schools, but he was just below the fiftieth percentile nationwide, and he was clearly coming up fast. His dad heard the news when he picked up Michael at the end of the day. He ran back to the office of Christa Olech, the reading facilitator for grades K–2, and gave her a hug. Both said that they couldn't believe what great progress Michael had made during the year.

Tameeka Wilson, the kindergarten student who was becoming bored with school because she already knew all her letters by November, also had a fulfilling year. Her teacher, Donna Helms, had advocated for a while that kindergarten teachers begin to teach reading skills. With principal Chuck Nusinov's approval, she had broached the issue with her fellow kindergarten teachers at a weekly meeting. Christa Olech had talked at length with Helms about the idea, and at the teachers meeting she proposed testing the students' letter recognition using a basic phonics skills test.

When the tests were completed at the end of November, the results showed that only 10 children (out of about 125 students in kindergarten) didn't know all their letters. In subsequent meetings, Olech and the teachers agreed to a new curriculum in which the kindergartners would track words in poetry, sort letters and sounds, and learn vocabulary. This was short of actually teaching reading, but it helped to build reading skills.

By the end of the school year, a lot of students were clearly able to read. This, of course, meant that the first-grade teachers needed to revise their curriculum, which they began to do.

For her part, Helms found the year in her kindergarten classroom to be perhaps the most fulfilling she'd ever had. While eligible for retirement after thirty-three years of teaching, she told Nusinov that she was having too much fun to leave David Cox Road Elementary. For the upcoming year, she was planning not only to start teaching the alphabet from the beginning, but also to use sign language as a way to teach letters and words. And by the end of her kindergarten year, Tameeka Wilson was already reading at a second-grade level.

Reflections on the Charlotte-Mecklenburg Schools' Organizational Judgment

The use of data-based decision making is a powerful way to improve organizational judgment, and it is being adopted in a variety of industries. The K–12 education industry is one of those. As in the health-care industry, U.S. federal government policies and funding are helping to drive the shift to data and analysis.

Strong leadership is typically necessary to transition to this approach to organizational judgment. At CMS, leadership from the superintendent down was an important factor in the introduction and spread of analytical approaches and tools. Leadership is also necessary in changing the culture to one in which fact-based decisions about student performance and other issues are appreciated—and even demanded. When data and analytics are the primary factors an organization employs to drive decisions, it often has the effect of pushing decisions closer to the front lines. Data-based decision making both requires and benefits from a culture of accountability.

The actual users of data and analysis tools—in schools, these tend to be teachers and administrators—often need assistance in finding the data they need, analyzing it correctly, and tying it to the decisions they need to make.

At CMS, administrators from the central district office, as well as those in regional organizations, provided facilitation services for these tasks.

While data-based student performance decisions are hardly the only answer to the many problems of urban schools, they are one avenue to improvement. They allow schools to direct resources to the students who need the most help and to their particular learning needs. There is little doubt that data has joined the pencil and the backpack as key tools for learning.

Part Three

Stories About the Power of Culture

T HE NEXT COLLECTION OF STORIES SHINES light particularly on the contribution of organizational culture—how, as the
famous shorthand goes, "the way we do things around here" can
enhance or even define the collective judgment of an enterprise. Our first
case is a historical retrospective, looking back across centuries at the question of how the world's first democratic culture created an organizational
capability for better decision making—in the world of ancient Athens.
Some principles of organizational judgment are not being newly invented,
but simply rediscovered. Our next case returns to contemporary times and
recounts a process of coming to a decision at the Vanguard Group, whose
cultural principles and values saved the firm from a disastrous investment.
The story is followed by another that in a different way emphasizes many
of the same lessons: how a technology company, EMC (a maker of digital
storage devices), used social media to help build some new cultural values
that dramatically increased the motivation and alignment of its employees
during a difficult economic climate.

7

Ancient Athenians

How Can We Defend Against Life-or-Death Invasion?

N THE LATE AFTERNOON OF THE JUNE SUN, in the summer of 480 BC, the sultry air that hung over the Pnyx was finally beginning to cool.[1] Here, where Athenian citizens gathered to debate and vote on matters of state, the mood was tense. The shadows of the limestone and brick civic buildings had begun to lengthen as some six thousand men clustered together on stone circular benches, facing one another. Some listened, others were shouting, and the president of the day overseeing the proceedings before them all was having difficulty keeping order. Everyone knew that the vote of their assembled democratic citizenry that had just been called would spell loss or preservation of their own lives, and the escape or enslavement of their families by the ravaging advance of a massive Persian army and navy headed their way. The oriental despot Xerxes, leading two hundred thousand soldiers and thirteen hundred ships from his vast eastern empire, had crossed the Hellespont to conquer the Greeks. Reports of his terrible movement through Hellenic lands—with slaughter, extorted submissions, beheadings, and other savagery—had been coming into the city day by day. The citizens faced a life-or-death vote about the defense of Athens—and indeed ultimately for all of Greece. What would the Athenians now elect to do?[2]

Democratic Decision Making in a Historical Context

It was a historically famous moment of decision making for a democratic organization. What can we learn from it? If, as we argue in this book, organizational judgment benefits from a participative problem-solving process and a culture that supports collective engagement of an enterprise, we would be wise to look back to what might be called "the Ur-case": the world's first true democracy, and the democratic culture formed by the ancient Athenians during the course of the sixth and fifth centuries BC. In our Internet-enabled age, with growing interest in open innovation sourcing and the "wisdom of crowds," what can be gleaned from the culture that invented debate and decision making by literally thousands of people?[3] Though truly "democratic" enterprises are still a rarity in today's modern economy, we have witnessed over the last few decades a growing recognition that more decentralized authority, collaborative problem solving, and team- and network-based approaches to doing work are becoming more mainstream assumptions about the culture and processes of contemporary organizations.[4] Ancient Athens can be a touchstone to understand how equality, freedom, and deliberative debate first came together to form a very early version of great judgment shaped by a culture of collective decision making.

Most historians narrate this "ancient golden age" as the rise of popular political power against kings and oligarchs, a radical new form of governance that gave birth to the cherished democratic values and institutions whose two thousand-year legacy embody western civilization. But much less often has the ancient democracy been studied or explained in terms of an organizational model that mobilized collective knowledge to make better decisions.[5] It is in fact just what this historical state did. If the ancient Athenians created true mass democracy, they also invented an approach to create a kind of organizational judgment—based on the notion that well-orchestrated processes of deliberation and debate among a wide range of accountable citizens could drive better decisions than the individual opinions of a single king or a small group of aristocratic leaders. We'll look at how their collective judgment was exercised in this case, and then probe more deeply into the culture, values, and processes that enabled that kind of capacity.

The Decision for Defense

In the days leading up to the fateful vote in the Athenian assembly that day, fear mingled with defiant anger in the dusty streets below the Acropolis. Xerxes, the emperor on the march, was hungry for revenge; soothsayers prophesied disaster for Athens. The previous generation of Athenians had supported an inflammatory revolt in the Asia Minor provinces ruled by Xerxes' father, and humiliated the father's earlier attempt to subjugate them. The son, Xerxes, now intended to honor his father by crushing Athens and whatever other Greeks dared to resist him. He vowed to at last swallow Hellas into the ever-growing Mede dominion: "to make the land of Persia border only on the sky that belongs to Zeus himself."

The Athenians gathered in assembly in their city center on that day understood that the decision before them was a grueling choice among difficult and potentially disastrous options. To stand with other Greek city-states—notoriously self-interested sometimes—or go it alone, in either case outmatched in numbers? To march north and meet the invaders or to attack by sea? Or to wait and hope that defending the city from the central citadel might thwart the advance?

Some believed that the specter of the huge Persian force would rally a majority of Greek city-states to stand with Athens and to oppose the oriental enemy as a unified front. But most suspected, from both rumor and experience, that under pressure many of their would-be allies wouldn't stand with Athens. They either would submit to the hostile king (as many had begun to do), hoping for tolerable treatment as new subjects, or would instead retreat south to take a stand at the isthmus of the Hellenic peninsula (near Corinth). This would leave the Athenians in Attica vulnerable to the brunt of the attack, coming from the north. Athenians knew they would have to take action to preserve the safety of their families while also positioning themselves to fight back on some kind of terms that they might pray would give them an advantage. What would that be? After days of debate and related investigations, the proposition now before the citizens of Athens was the call for a bold but wrenching strategy: totally abandon homeland and city, with women, children, and elders emigrating to offshore sanctuaries, while male citizens would man hundreds of recently built fighting ships to do battle against the Persians by sea.

As the herald called for silence, he began to read the terms of the decree being put to the vote. "Resolved by the Council and the People," he began, honoring the values and culture of democratic governance, and then went on to detail:

- How the city and homeland was to be evacuated and "entrusted to Athena"

- That women, children, and possessions be transported to nearby Troezen and Aegina (each about a half day's sail from Athens)

- That all men of military age now embark on the triremes of the Athenian navy, some to sail north and ready for battle at Artemesium and all others to make the adjacent island of Salamis their base to defend against subsequent attack

- That some key political exiles, sent away in earlier years ("ostracized"), were now called back to help with the cause

Across the throng of men who listened, a few glanced out at the surrounding ancient city hills, others further beyond, to Mount Hymettus or Pentele on the horizon. They briefly lifted their thoughts away from the bleeding, grunting, and claustrophobic rowing below decks of the naval fighting that they knew awaited them. Some, who had never rowed or fought in a trireme, wondered how they would do it, and whether it was foolish not to try to meet the Persians as armored soldiers on land. Many more turned to others around them, asking how on earth an entire population of women, children, and elders could be moved from ancestral homes, and wondering whether those loved ones would in fact find safety in nearby settlements like Troezen.

But most men stared at the cunning and eloquent statesman Themistocles at the front of the crowd, inspiring but not always so trustworthy, asking themselves whether the motion he had just authored was indeed a piece of patriotic brilliance or instead a wild "Hail Mary pass" destined for catastrophe. Should they adopt the arguments of this fleshy-faced and bearded man, sometimes described as the "subtle serpent of the Greeks?" Debate raged for another half hour, for and against the proposal, and then the vote was called again. Six thousand men suddenly fell silent. As the shadows lengthened further, all that could be heard were the distant sounds of a few animals in the market, the summer buzz of cicadas in nearby trees, and a low murmur of the crowd as hands went up. The resolution passed.

Toward the Battle of Salamis

In the coming weeks, as the heat of the summer intensified, Athenians made further plans and began to take action, as resolved by their own democratic assembly. Ships were prepared and a base at Salamis was established. Families began to gather belongings and set homes and livelihoods in order before evacuation; some started to leave soon thereafter. Meanwhile the Persian threat grew more real every day.

The Athenian decision to combine evacuation and wholly naval operations as the strategy for defense was then carried to a meeting of other Greek states at the Isthmus of Corinth, and made part of a more general plan to fight together. The allied cities would to try to stop the Persians by both land and sea to the north, beyond Boeotia. Further scouting of specific locales was done, and by August, as Xerxes advanced and various northern Greek cities defected to the emperor, the remaining allied Greek forces took up defense positions. By land, they mustered in the narrow—and later famous—pass of Thermopylae (between Boeotia and Locris), led by the Spartans; for sea battle they harbored nearby, off the northern Euboean port of Artemesium. The fleet was nominally also led by the Spartans (a recognition of their prestige in war), but heavily weighted with the substantial Athenian contingent of 180 ships.

At the end of August, the Persians finally clashed with the defending Greeks. At Thermopylae, in a difficult and bloody triumph, they overwhelmed the combined Hellenic forces, with the Spartans fighting to the last man—later to become the subject of heroic poetry, many books, and admiring monuments. But at the naval battle of Artemesium, Fortune smiled differently on the Greeks. In a series of contests punctuated by violent storms, and marked by bold surprise attacks and brilliant rowing maneuvers, the Hellenic forces fought the vastly larger imperial navy of the invader to a draw. Emboldened, the Greeks returned south, and the naval task force headed to its new strategic station on the island of Salamis. The Persian expedition force rolled on, and with its victorious army and still vast fleet of ships, set course for its next desired target: Athens.

Persian Surprise and Greek Victory

However, when the Persians finally arrived at Athens, in early September, they were shocked to find it all but empty. Following the assembly's decision, all the Athenian families had departed and all male citizens were manning ships, docked nearby on the island of Salamis, preparing for naval battle. What would this wily Greek enemy do next?

In the ensuing weeks, the Persians sacked the city. Meanwhile, the alliance of other Greek states, which had now also assembled with the Athenians at Salamis, quarreled among its members about where actually to engage the Persian fleet and army. Though the Athenians had themselves voted to make it a naval battle nearby their homeland, their general Themistocles—who had forged the resolution that authorized the strategy with his fellow citizens—now had to negotiate with generals from other Greek states. The question was whether to indeed fight close to Athens, in the narrow straits—which would give Greek ships an advantage—or instead retreat down south to the isthmus, preferring to bet on the land advantage of that position.

In the end, through a colorful combination of rhetoric and trickery reported by Herodotus, Themistocles' preference—the strategy first backed by his fellow Athenian citizens—prevailed. The Greeks would defend their homeland in the waters off of Salamis. It was the right decision. As was hoped, between the collective bravery, the daring of the Athenians, and the edge provided by the rocky but familiar straits well known to the locals, the Persians suffered a huge defeat. For all practical purposes, this became the turning point of the war and set in motion the collapse of the Persian expedition. It was also the beginning of a huge shift in power—for after Salamis, Persian control of the Aegean Sea passed to the Greeks, and the change ultimately ushered in a new age of particularly Athenian power and glory. The wisdom and bravery they had demonstrated, and exercised through a commanding new naval fleet, positioned the Athenians as the major force of Hellas; in later years they went on to steward a vast empire of tribute-paying allies, with their city the center of culture, art, and commerce the likes of which the world had never before seen.

Assessing Athenian Decision Making and Judgment in Action

In evaluating the impact of the strategic decision made by the Athenians, we should not underestimate the results it ultimately enabled. To quote one eminent historian of this period, "It is not too much to say that the decision really did set up the battle that saved Western civilization, and gave the Athenians the opportunity to create the empire and democracy that ultimately shaped it."[6] Though no single decision creates future inevitable success, the vote of the Athenians on that particular fateful day laid the foundation for a chain of further events (and comparably bold but good decisions) that boosted Athens' glory to grow to legendary proportions, and allowed them to establish a distinctive and unmatched way of life in the ancient world. Its legacy extended for centuries thereafter.

Historians make a living by debating such propositions, but in the good company of many of them, we can laud the democratic decision for the strategy that saved Athens and led to the Persian defeat. The more interesting question for our purposes is, How did the Athenians come to such a good decision? Both our sources and recent research into the nature of the ancient democracy suggest the successful course decided upon by the citizens was not simply luck, but rather an illustrative outcome of a revolutionary approach to creating collective judgment. To understand the origins and nature of that revolutionary approach, we must understand both its working in actual operation and how it came to be. To do that, we'll look at the context of this decision, the process by which it was arrived at, and the deeper cultural and institutional capability that enabled it.

Understanding the Culture of Collective Judgment of Ancient Athenian Democracy

The stakes on which this decision hinged in 480 BC were very high; it was unambiguous what the Persians intended as they marched through Greece, especially with a stated goal of "revenge on the Athenians." The consequences of their potential victory were understood by every Athenian man, woman, and child. Further, as the citizens worked through the options for what to do on that June day, they certainly saw that the choices in front of them were far from clear, and all had risks. Staying and fighting by land would pit a sturdy but much smaller army against the hordes of the invader. On the other hand, Athens' fighting capability on land had been tested and, though not at the standard of their fellow Greeks the Spartans, it had shown its mettle before in many battles. Fighting by sea had its pros and cons too. Yes, they had invested in and built an admirable fleet of ships; but this navy was relatively new, and most Greek cities did not see fighting on the water as a preferred way of defending the homeland.

Abandoning one's city and farms, to create both surprise for the attacker and safety for loved ones with no land army to defend them, was a bold but also troublesome idea. Deeply connected to their land and homes by religious and ancestral tradition, Athenians realized that a strategy to uproot themselves for evacuation would be not only emotionally jarring but also almost unprecedented in the Hellenic world.[7] Against the backdrop of these challenges, it is interesting how the Athenians finally made their strategic decision in 480 BC. Unfortunately, the ancient sources don't provide a lot of detail about what might called "parliamentary process," and the actual testimonies are problematic, with some clear fictional embellishment. Nonetheless, extrapolating a bit from other periods of the democracy and piecing together some different traditions about the event, we can reconstruct the picture of what likely happened: an increasingly confident body of citizens exercising rational decision making, against historical forces of religious counsel and tradition-bound advice. It is a small but significant portrait of the world's first democratic organization and the culture its members were creating all around them in real time. The Athenians took action, developing and exercising real collective judgment, overcoming prejudice and ambiguity, in the face of a terrible and difficult decision.

Sorting Through Religion and Reality

In the weeks prior to the final vote about Salamis, the Athenians had been meeting and debating what to do, as news filtered in about the Persian advance. According to Herodotus, the citizens took an initial step to seek advice by sending a mission to the famous oracle of Delphi.[8] Delphi was a religious sanctuary of Apollo, served by priestesses who spoke riddlelike prognostications about the future, for those who came seeking guidance (and bearing offerings to the god). The response that came back from the first inquiry of the Athenian mission was profoundly negative; the veiled suggestion was one of imminent Athenian destruction, "as the God of War, speeding in a Syrian chariot, shall bring you low."

The Athenian envoys were about to leave in despair, until at the suggestion of a local leader, they approached the oracle for a "second opinion." What came back (perhaps indicative of a priestess not wanting to alienate totally her Athenian "customers") was another ambiguous message—but one perhaps more optimistic. The critical lines of the dictum were:

> *That Zeus the all-seeing grants to Athena's prayer*
> *That the wooden wall only shall not fall, but help you and your children*
> *But await not the host of horse and foot coming from Asia*
> *Nor be still, but turn your backs and withdraw from the foe.*
> *Truly a day will come when you will meet him face to face*
> *Divine Salamis, you still bring death to the women's sons*
> *When the corn is scattered or the harvest gathered in.*

In the ensuing days, these words were debated for their meaning and significance among the Athenians in their citizen assembly. We can imagine a fully empowered group of citizens discussing the oracle and simultaneously formulating possible options for Athenian strategy. According to Herodotus, elders in the meetings advanced the point of view that "the wooden wall" that would not fall referred to a traditional hedgelike fence that surrounded the Acropolis, meaning that only the sacred citadel of Athens would survive. Others argued that the wooden wall referred to ships, the Athenian triremes that now made up the navy. But those advancing this contrary opinion took no comfort when a small group of "professional interpreters" pointed out that the lines about "divine Salamis, bringing death to the women's sons" suggested that reliance on ships as the wooden wall and fighting off the island offshore would be the demise of the nation.

Herodotus goes on to explain that the standoff was finally broken by the general Themistocles, who persuaded the Athenians—meeting as citizens in the assembly—that the riddle was in fact good news. Because Salamis was described as "divine" and not "hateful," the women's sons to die would be those of the enemy, not Athens. Salamis would be divine because it would save the day for the Athenians in their wall of wooden ships.

Whatever the actual sequence of events, Herodotus portrays a group of citizens continuously gathering news from events afar, and then deliberating and weighing a course of action based on differing interpretations of seemingly authoritative information provided. The ancient commentator notes how in the end "the Athenians found Themistocles' explanation of the oracle preferable to that of the professional interpreters"—essentially evaluating differing options and then overturning a group of experts whose judgment seemed more questionable in the end. Themistocles was a persuasive speaker—but he was also the advocate of an earlier strategic decision (as we know from various sources) in fact to build up the same Athenian navy that was now being called upon to "create the wooden wall." A few years before, when the city came into a large fortune from the discovery of silver in a nearby mine, Themistocles had persuaded the citizenry not just to distribute the wealth across the population, but instead to invest it on behalf of their collective defense—by building two hundred new ships. This earlier decision by the assembly had vaulted Athens into the status of a major Hellenic power, suddenly at the head of an unprecedentedly large navy. In the end, the assembly of citizens, having made a previous decision to build up their defenses by building a huge fleet of triremes, now came to the very logical conclusion that their best bet to fight against the coming Persians was to put the new asset into full use.

In the days before the final vote, the assembly of citizens listened, debated, and challenged the initial ideas of experts, and interpreted in a more rational and strategic way the prognostication of an esteemed religious voice. And then, with Themistocles' summary proposal put forward on that fateful afternoon, they finally decided to leverage their most strategic asset. They hoped not only to put up their own best defense, but also to rally other Greek states with their courage and what they distinctively could offer to the cause. By evacuating the city, they enabled—and even forced upon themselves—every man to serve in the emergency navy, ready for battle at Salamis. The decision was intimately linked to accountability to make it happen. No one doubted the immediate need to "vote with their feet" as soon as they had voted with their hands. Once the decision was made, what followed was totally engaged and immediate implementation. As later history shows, the overall strategy and mobilization turned out to be very smart moves.

Origins of the Democratic Culture for Judgment

We might hypothesize that these smart moves could have been simply thought up by one man—and in fact the ancient sources suggest that much of the "thought leadership" for the eventual winning strategy came from the hero Themistocles. But even if it were in Themistocles' power to simply dictate to all Athenians what the plan would be—which it was not, due to the democratic constitution then in place for this ancient polis—he would have still faced three problems whose generic form still plague any leader today faced with complex, high-stakes decisions.[9] First, how to assemble all the knowledge needed to inform a good decision? Second, how to align the interests and motivations of the collective mass, to leverage the action of not just a few but all the people? And third, how to create plans and processes so that collective decisions and alignment translate to action, and at the same time create some framework for continued decision making as conditions continued to evolve?

The traditional corporate or military answer to these kinds of organizational performance challenges in modern times is the hierarchical enterprise. Someone or some small group at the top comes up with the strategy and then informs and mandates others to execute, usually through some combination of fear and incentives. Buried in this traditional model is another taken-for-granted assumption: complex decisions require deep knowledge and experience that only a small coterie of experts can bring to bear. We know, however, that modern organizations are changing this paradigm—typically becoming "flatter," more engaging of their employees and a wider range of knowledge, and consisting of and/or increasingly linked to more flexible and open networks. The Athenian invention of democracy essentially pioneered this kind of thinking and action. Thanks to the political revolutions of the late sixth century BC, Themistocles in 480 BC was able to shape and steward a decisive strategy through a newly established process of collective problem solving based on pooled knowledge; alignment of interests in the service of a common goal; and the translation of planning into action and ongoing decision making, as needed. Looking a bit farther back into Athenian history, we can see how those capabilities and that cultural way of working—all critical elements of this story of organizational judgment—were first developed.

Historians have traced early sparks of democratic thinking into the remote history of Greece, but most agree that the major period of innovation came during the shadowy reforms of the Athenian statesman called Cleisthenes. In about 508 BC, Athens was riven by civil war among aristocrats, and also faced a mortal challenge to its freedom by a simultaneous invasion by hostile neighbors. With Athens' very survival in question, one of the aristocratic leaders—Cleisthenes—turned crisis into opportunity. Throwing convention aside, he desperately launched a democratic movement among the people. By leading a series of proposals that reshaped the society and laws of the state, he and his followers rather quickly established what became the foundation of popular democracy. The core of the reforms—which most Athenians apparently embraced in the heat of the crisis—was to create a new and all-embracing concept of democratic citizenship, extended to all adult males, empowered to vote and to make decisions for themselves. These revolutionary reforms were at the same time also coupled with a new organization of a full citizen army. The structure of the new citizenry both created a new structure for the military defense of the city and at the same time established an ingenious "architecture" for participation and decision making on behalf of public goals. In essence, the revolution was founded on a simple but deeply engaging principle: "we govern together, we fight together." The details of how all this was accomplished so quickly are lost—but we know it was both effective and motivating to allow the Athenians to rapidly come together and defeat the neighborly invaders; and it also created a culture and platform for deliberative decision making in coming years.

Part of the magic of this revolution was how it combined—through this pioneering concept of citizenship—a number of cultural values related to the common good (freedom, equality, commitment to the polis). It also included a series of practices and processes that both encouraged public participation and leveraged networks of different kinds of knowledge. The newly formalized "citizens" were grouped together in deliberately randomized combinations of families and geographical locale, and then engaged in ongoing random (selected by lot) rotational participation in the central city, to govern themselves. The reforms suddenly empowered all citizens as deciding all questions of their own destiny: setting the agenda for decision making, leading discussions and deliberations among themselves, and serving in the courts of justice. Everyone was artfully "mixed together" (as Aristotle notes) and took turns being important leaders in their own government—on a "learn-by-doing basis."[10]

The architecture of how people were combined in their civic groupings guaranteed that people who knew one another in some ways stayed with others they knew, but also had to work with others whom they did not. And in so mixing people, the arrangement also guaranteed that different people who knew different things—about social matters, farming, sailing and ships, mining, metallurgy, and so forth—were connected across boundaries to people with knowledge whom they might not otherwise get to know.

Under the rules of the new constitution, all worked together, rotationally, to solve problems through debate, deliberation, and decision making based on different perspectives brought forward. This was ensured by the regular and disciplined meetings of citizens in their assembly, and a series of protocols for structuring, limiting, and creating actionable proposals out of debate. This democratic process and culture had been evolving for decades and was now firmly in place in the Athens of 480 BC.

The system of interlocking processes and cultural values that evolved came to be deeply effective and motivating for all engaged. From scattered sources, we have a pretty good idea that over time most Athenian citizens did participate in their own democracy at some level and with some regularity; it offered an unprecedented model for aggregating many different kinds of experience and knowledge, and provided a forum and vehicle based on dialogue and shared commitment to allow for problem solving that made issues transparent. Debate and dialogue allowed the risks and rewards to be fully understood; innovation and learning, through citizens both listening to others' ideas and participating in the problem solving themselves, were intimately coupled. Because the citizens were both the decision makers and the implementers, accountability and implementation were also fully aligned. A vote for war was followed by leaving for home to collect one's armor or to bid farewell to loved ones before boarding a ship.

Similarly, because actions were codified in rules and laws, the people themselves created the means to expand implementation and also reopen deliberation as future conditions warranted. Laws of the people could be amended or undone by other laws of the people. The democratic process enabled decisions to be brought to scale or revised as conditions warranted.

Collective Judgment, Catalyzed by Leadership

Against this backdrop, we can now understand the real challenges Themistocles faced as he stood before some five or six thousand citizens in the late afternoon of the June day in 480. It was not whether he could tap into the collective wisdom of his fellow Athenians or force them to do something they may not really want to do. Nor was it to force some decision that would be once and forever. Themistocles in fact had a different challenge: how to stimulate and start the right conversation, and use his own powers of persuasion to start the right "democratic flywheel" of dialogue and deliberation moving.

In these final moments of decision making, let us imagine the scene. The citizens—some mixing with one another in the random groupings of the council that led the assembly, others simply standing and talking with one another in the open-air debates that raged on—listened and learned from one another and weighed the different arguments being made. As news filtered through the countryside—from friends, neighbors, and messengers—about the Persian advance, the understanding of "facts on the ground" informed and hastened the decision making. Experts had to be listened to, and oracles from religious voices had to be interpreted; these too were debated and put against what was known about armies, ships, impending weather in the waters off their coast, and the readiness and ability of families to abandon their homeland. These and thousands of other facts, interpreted and analyzed through smaller and larger conversations, became the raw material for the final "answer."

Eventually, with an eloquent leader shaping a proposal based on persuasive arguments, the people decided for themselves the best bet for the future that they could make, and for which they themselves would be life-or-death accountable. A culture of democratic deliberation and judgment flourished in the face of great danger, and in this famous case, it yielded the first of a series of decisions that spelled victory and a path to glory for this ancient state.

Reflections on the Organizational Judgment of the Ancient Athenian Case

This historical case offers insight into what repeatedly surface as critical elements of good decision making in modern organizations: reasoned deliberation that brings together differing viewpoints, informed by facts and a broad range of knowledge, and sharpened by constructive debate and challenge. The act of coming to a decision is guided by an explicit process that values equality, fairness, and transparency.[11]

We also note that this was not one single decision, but really a series of iterative decisions, each built upon new knowledge and the learnings coming out of the earlier stages of the process. Decision making was not a single moment, but rather a continuous-improvement kind of judgment that grew over time. Also, as also seen in modern best-practices cases, the decisions weighed were intimately linked to—and deliberated upon by—those accountable for implementing the decision. Leadership played a critical role, but more as helping to facilitate the formulation and debate about the best ideas; Themistocles had no power to decide on his own. Perhaps most important, the case is a story about the power of democratic culture—a set of values, assumptions, and a mind-set about the value of collective thinking, the right and obligation to participate, and an understanding that "together, we are wiser than any one of us."

8

Mabel Yu and
The Vanguard Group

Should We Recommend
This Bond to Investors?

FROM LATE 2005 to the summer of 2008, Mabel Yu was increasingly pushing herself over the edge, both physically and mentally. She'd been working until ridiculous hours night after night, poring over complex descriptions and analyses of structured finance securities, including mortgage-backed securities; commercial mortgage-backed securities; asset-backed securities for credit cards, car loans, and leases; and asset-backed commercial paper. Were they safe investments or too risky for Vanguard to buy on behalf of its customers? It was devilishly difficult to figure out the answer to this question. Even as she and the world began to realize the problems in the assets behind mortgage-backed securities, there were all these other complex asset types. Yu felt she was fighting fires from all sides.[1]

Yu's health was suffering—whether from lack of sleep or stress, she didn't know—and she had frequent migraine headaches. Her young daughter felt she was ignoring her in favor of her work, so Yu resolved to do the analyses after her daughter went to bed—at the expense of sleep, of course. She simply couldn't make sense of the risk levels of these bonds and the pools of mortgages behind them—in addition to all the other structured finance products she had to review.

In the spring of 2005, she had been in her investment job at Vanguard only a few months, but her previous experience, she thought, had qualified her to assess credit risk. She had an MBA, and had been a CPA, corporate controller, and financial analyst before joining Vanguard. Why was she having such difficulty with these securities? Was she simply too inexperienced or incompetent to get what everyone else seemed to understand? Or was there something seriously wrong with these investments?

It was Yu's job at The Vanguard Group to evaluate and make recommendations on fixed income investments. In her role as a relatively new fixed income credit analyst, she was to assess the underlying structure of the bonds, the quality of the assets (in this case, a pool of mortgage loans) behind them, and the risk of default. She was then expected to make recommendations to Vanguard's portfolio managers about whether they should buy the bonds or not. The category of mortgage-backed bonds was a relatively new one, but it had exploded in volume over the past several years.

All of the bonds Yu was evaluating had been rated AAA—the supposed "gold standard"—by the premier ratings agencies such as Standard & Poor's and Moody's. In addition, they were being offered to Vanguard by top-tier Wall Street firms—Lehman Brothers, Citi, Morgan Stanley, Goldman Sachs. How could such leading firms be selling a bad product? Even more ironically, Yu was given a supposedly easy assignment as a new analyst. What could be difficult about evaluating AAA-rated bonds? The advertised ease of the assignment only added to Yu's stress level. How could she be killing herself if it was supposed to be an easy assignment for a new analyst?

Yu's difficulties in assessing the bonds derived from both the volume of new issues—she was having to assess up to ten deals per week—as well as the complexity of the products, the lack of transparency of the underlying assets, and the short turnaround time in which these securities had to be reviewed. According to data from the Securities Industry and Financial Markets Association, the total global volume of securitized finance issues peaked in 2006 at $2.7 trillion, and the total volume of mortgage-backed security issues had increased from $684 billion in 2000 to over $2.2 trillion in 2005. Yu was concerned about the whole deteriorating trend of the structured finance industry, and she had particular concern about the deteriorating credit quality of the mortgages behind the deals. (The collapse of the mortgage-backed security was only the poster child of the whole government bailout of the structured finance industry.)

At this time, the "subprime" mortgage industry was in full flower. Many homeowners were receiving mortgages who would not previously have qualified for a mortgage at all, or who had furnished little documentation of their income and ability to repay. It was not just that the customers had subprime credit profiles, but also that a host of new mortgage products were being offered to subprime customers for the first time. The new exotic products included interest-only loans, negative amortization loans, no documentation loans, teaser rate loans, overblown appraisal values, no down payment, and virtually any other deal a creative mortgage finance person could dream up. Ratings agencies were using historical data to estimate future loss rates, but neither these borrowers nor these products were present in the past data, so their predictions were irrelevant.

Vanguard, a conservative firm, was immediately suspicious of these types of mortgages, and Robert Auwaerter, Vanguard's head of fixed income investments, had determined that Vanguard would avoid them— as well as the more complex "collateralized debt obligations" (CDOs) based upon them. But mortgage-backed securities with prime mortgage loans as assets were believed to be safe.

However, Mabel Yu's painstaking analyses of the mortgage-backed securities seemed to suggest that even AAA bonds had some subprime exposure and that the level was increasing over time. Yu's suspicion was that the banks were "camouflaging" the subprime loans by slicing and dicing them into complex securities. Yu felt uncomfortable with the securities for many reasons:

- The people rating them seemed very inexperienced.

- She wasn't sure they had taken enough time to do a thorough review.

- Untested, exotic mortgages were being pushed to subprime customers at unprecedented speeds and volumes.

- It was impossible to use past data to test the likelihood of default.

- It was very difficult to capture risks for the exotic securities, particularly the correlated risk if all assets fell in value at the same time.

- Sell-side firms and ratings agencies had conflicts in their business models, in that they both made a lot of money by pushing the products to the markets.

Whether the securities were a conscious subterfuge by the investment banks or not, it was extremely difficult to determine what the quality of the investments was.

When Yu began to reveal her concerns about the securities to other members of the credit analyst group and their portfolio manager partners, they supported her and gave her the benefit of the doubt when she substantiated her credit opinion with in-depth investigation. The portfolio managers could have overridden her recommendations, but they took them seriously.

In order to reinforce her conviction, Yu wanted to speak directly to the "sell-side" investment bankers who were offering these loans to Vanguard, and to the ratings agencies that had granted them AAA ratings.

These organizations themselves had undergone a recent transformation. Because the structured finance industry grew so rapidly, there were a lot of new employees with little experience reviewing the complex and high-risk products. Also, the demand for such expertise was so high that as soon as the analysts had some experience, they left for higher-paying jobs.

Yu, never one to shrink from a challenge, contacted them. In some cases the Wall Street bankers contacted Yu when they heard that she—a junior analyst—was standing in the way of their sales of AAA-rated mortgage-backed securities. But the direct contacts only increased Yu's stress level. They suggested that Yu's concerns were unfounded, to say the least. Yu was told, "We have a lot of very smart people who came up with these ideas," "There are very sophisticated mathematical models behind them," and "Why should you be concerned when there are so many firms and investors buying the products?"

The sell-side bankers and ratings analysts suggested—both to Yu herself and to her colleagues at Vanguard—that her doubts related more to her own inexperience and naïveté than to any deficiencies in the securities. In their impatient and condescending tones, they were effectively saying, "How can you be smarter than our whole troop of people with decades of experience?" When the market was red-hot and they had plenty of orders, they simply didn't answer Yu's questions at all.

The Vanguard Culture and Values

If she were making the decision about whether to recommend these securities on her own, Mabel Yu might have caved in to the growing amount of pressure from the external financial community. After all, the rest of the world seemed to think that these investments were fine. And they were providing higher returns for investors between 2005 and 2007 than other types of fixed income investments.

Yu, however, worked at Vanguard. The company had one of the stronger and more well-defined cultures in the financial services industry. Some of its relevant cultural values included:

- A belief that "get rich quick" financial schemes never pay off, and that investors and Vanguard itself should pursue long-run strategies. Wealth, in the Vanguard view, depends less on how much money we make, and more on how we save and invest wisely for the long term.

- A deep and constant focus on the individual investor. Vanguard employees are taught that it is a privilege and an awesome responsibility to be entrusted with the financial hopes and dreams of its customers.

- A view that every Vanguard "crew member" (the company is replete with nautical metaphors, and its brand symbol is a clipper ship) is capable of making a contribution to the organization and its customers. The saying goes that "one person can make a difference."

- A strong recommendation that Vanguard analysts and portfolio managers should not invest in financial products that they do not fully understand.

- The faith that hard work, an independent view, and due diligence in evaluating investments for clients will pay off for all parties in the end.

- The policy that Vanguard and its employees do not try to time the market, and they recommend the same advice to their investors. During the technology and Internet bubble of the early 2000s, then-CEO Jack Brennan refused to cave in to the market pressure of making quick money through technology investments, even when Vanguard experienced significant cash outflows. Hindsight, of course, proved that strategy correct.

Many of these values had been explicitly advocated since Vanguard's founding by John (Jack) Bogle, who started the company in 1974. The client-focused culture has been reinforced by successor Vanguard CEOs Jack Brennan and Bill McNabb. Bogle, now officially retired, remains active at Vanguard and is an object of veneration by many employees. Mabel Yu, for example, peppered her comments in interviews with admiring references to "Mr. Bogle" and quotations from him. She took comfort in her period of adversity, for example, from his comments such as, "The courage to press on regardless—regardless of whether we face calm seas or rough seas, and especially when the market storms howl around us—is the quintessential attribute of the successful investor."[2]

Bogle was well known in the investment industry for his advocacy of a straightforward, patient approach to investing. In a book he wrote in 1999 called *Common Sense on Mutual Funds*, he laid out this advice in eight maxims for investors:

- Select low-cost index funds.

- Consider carefully the added costs of advice.

- Do not overrate past fund performance.

- Use past performance to determine consistency and risk.

- Beware of stars (as in, star mutual fund managers).

- Beware of asset size.

- Don't own too many funds.

- Buy your fund portfolio—and hold it.[3]

Yu had internalized these investment approaches, but felt that Bogle's most important legacies were his values, priorities, and attitudes toward investment and clients. Yu felt that Bogle had instilled the values in every Vanguard crew member and even the public through his books and speeches. The title of one of his books, published in 2009, summarized his perspective on wealth accumulation: *Enough: True Measures of Money, Business, and Life*. Bogle gave a free copy of this and his other books to each Vanguard crew member. Mabel Yu adopted these values even though she was a relatively new employee; indeed, they were what attracted her to come to Vanguard. She said:

> I know Vanguard isn't perfect, but I love the company. I invested all my savings—$10,000—with Vanguard before I came to work here. They treated me like a queen. I wanted to work for an organization that would treat even its smaller customers that well.

While she felt that she was having to work much too hard to decipher the risk of the asset-backed securities she evaluated, she persisted in part because she wanted to protect the firm's clients, and because hard work and due diligence were expected at Vanguard. Also, she did not want to fail. She said:

> I am not a "quitter." Deep, deep, deep in my heart, I believed that I was doing the right thing even though the world doubted and questioned me. I also believed that the long-term result would prove that I was "right," even though no one may ever have known what I did. But that did not stop me from pressing on. I never thought of compromising the review standard [for the securities], but I thought of quitting or changing my profession often. I was afraid to be wrong, I was tired of being considered dumb, I was exhausted, and I felt I struggled for nothing. Very often I cried. However, I always managed to wipe my tears and keep doing what I believe is right. I didn't want to fail. I didn't want to disappoint my deceased father and God. I wanted to tell my daughter that "Your mother is never a quitter. That's why you should never quit or give up just because it is hard."

Yu had also come to respect another value that Bogle had instituted at the firm: helping out to serve customers in need. Bogle likened it to the "Swiss army," in which citizens take up arms when the country is threatened. At Vanguard, crew members are drafted into answering customer calls during peak seasons and when financial turmoil leads to high call volume. Yu has answered the call on a regular basis from December to April every year. She wasn't sure she liked the idea of leaving her regular job to answer phones when she first arrived at Vanguard, but now she feels it is beneficial in remembering that all crew members work for customers. When she was really tired from examining the mortgage-backed security deals, she thought of the customers she spoke with on the phone. She asked herself, "How could I not do a good job for them?"

Of course, Vanguard's values were not the only ones that influenced Yu; there is a limit to the influence of any organization on individuals. She pointed out that:

> It is certainly true that Vanguard encourages and allows the crew member to do the right thing. For me, however, that wasn't enough to keep me going during this difficult time. When the challenges become monumental, where does the person get the work ethic, courage, and moral fiber to do the right thing, especially when no one is recognizing it? Personally, I learned and internalized the right values from my parents. Also, my faith gives me the courage and the peace to hang tough, even when no one would ever know what I had done.

The Power of Dissent

The Vanguard culture was also one that encouraged dissent when crew members feel it is warranted. That came naturally to Yu, who said in our first conversation with her, "I am a very direct person." But she never felt any discouragement from Vanguard colleagues or executives when she clearly stated her views. She was teased a bit a couple of times by portfolio managers when she complained about the Wall Street brokers—"You put them through the mill for a couple of hours, and then you didn't buy from them"—but she never experienced direct criticism for her views, even though they went directly against the prevailing Wall Street wisdom, and even when Vanguard investors initially lost out on the high returns from mortgage-backed securities with hidden subprime loans.

Bob Auwaerter, the fixed income head at Vanguard, says that he often encourages dissent, even among junior employees:

> One of the principles here in fixed income is that superior investment decision making requires many different perspectives. Just because some of us have been here a long time doesn't mean we have all the answers. I remember when I was running the corporate bond fund, and we were looking at a utility bond. I thought it was too expensive and we shouldn't buy it. An analyst who had been there for six months pointed out something I missed about the company. He was right and I was wrong. Constructive conflict is important. We try to make people at the low end of the experience curve feel comfortable in challenging senior people.

There is considerable evidence in decision-making research that dissent is a powerful tool for making better decisions.[4] This is not a new idea; the Roman Catholic Church created the "devil's advocate" role in sainthood decisions in 1587. Unfortunately, it only continued the practice for a couple of centuries; one could argue it would still be useful now, and not only for calls on sainthood.

Since then, there has been research in a variety of domains that supports the value of dissent. The sociologist Irving Janis was perhaps the first to address the issue in social-scientific terms. He coined the term *groupthink* in 1972, using it to describe decisions by groups in which there was insufficient dissent. Such groups, even when consisting of talented and well-meaning members, tended to reach a premature consensus if no one disagreed with it.[5]

Much of the subsequent research on the value of dissent has been led by Charlan Nemeth, a psychologist at the University of California at

Berkeley. Her early work on dissent focused not on business, but on jury deliberations.[6] It turns out that the *Twelve Angry Men* notion—that dissent can yield a better verdict—is true not only in drama, but also in real life. Nemeth led a study in the 1970s that found smoother, fairer deliberations in juries when someone initiated dissent from the majority opinion. Nemeth's research has also demonstrated that while institutionalized dissenting roles—for example, the devil's advocate—are useful, dissenters who actually disagree with the majority direction are even more valuable to decision processes.[7]

Of course, it's often difficult to be a dissenter. There is also plenty of evidence that dissenters are shunned by and lose status in groups. Just as the other jurors in *Twelve Angry Men* attacked the lone "not guilty" voter, groups want to achieve consensus rapidly and easily. If an organization wants to facilitate dissent, it has to continually encourage it. Everyone we talked to at Vanguard brought it up, which is a very good sign.

Yu's Decision and Its Aftermath

Perhaps obviously, by this point, Yu recommended strongly that Vanguard's portfolio managers avoid these AAA-rated bonds. In 2006 and 2007, however, the suspect bonds rallied, and Vanguard's returns were a few points lower than those of some competitors. "Management didn't give me any trouble," Yu says. "I got only average reviews those years, but there was no big problem."

This same class of investment was, of course, a primary factor in the near collapse of the U.S. and world economies. One prominent seller (and buyer) of them, Lehman Brothers, went out of business as a result. Others involved in them, such as AIG Financial Products, were forced to take massive government bailouts. Vanguard, not surprisingly, needed no such emergency help, and its investors were not exposed to the massive losses from subprime-backed bonds.

Shortly after she argued that Vanguard should not buy the AAA-rated bonds, Yu received a request from the ratings agency Moody's to discuss—she thought—the overall relationship between Vanguard and the agency and her opinion about the mortgage-backed market. The call turned out to primarily address the bond ratings issue. Yu was characteristically direct. As one prominent media account described the conversation:

> In one agency internal memo noting a conference call, Mabel Yu, an executive with Vanguard Investments, felt that the downgrades in the summer of 2007 from S&P "came about 1½ years too late" and expressed "frustration" with the ratings agencies' willingness to "allow issuers to get away with murder." She is finding the phenomenon particular to RMBS [subprime securities] and CMBS [commercial mortgage-backed securities].
>
> The memo continued: She feels that, particularly in the area of subprime, too much credit is given to individuals who haven't had access to credit before. She felt that there wasn't enough historical data available to track the performance of these more aggressive loans. Yu said that over time, Vanguard bought less and less of this asset class and stopped investing in it entirely by early 2006. Vanguard has witnessed the deals "getting worse and worse" and Yu reported that the market has been screaming for a while, "look at sub-prime!" adding that "the agencies are giving issuers every benefit of the doubt." Yu added that "I feel that if Moody's doesn't give the rating, the issuer can simply go elsewhere and get it somewhere else."[8]

The content of the call had entered the public domain through a highly unusual series of events. For reasons unknown to Yu, Moody's transcribed the content of the call and saved it as a document in its repositories. After the economy declined precipitously in 2007 and 2008, the U.S. Congress held hearings about the causes of the financial crisis in October 2008. It subpoenaed a variety of documents from the rating agencies, one of which was the transcript of Mabel Yu's call with Moody's. Because of the publishing of Yu's objections, her stand against the mortgage-based securities briefly became a popular news story. A National Public Radio (NPR) segment, for example, summarized her objections:

David Kestenbaum (NPR reporter): Mabel Yu, yes, she worked at Vanguard, which manages $400 billion in bond investments. And every time a new structured finance deal came out, these deals, with their triple-A bonds would land on her desk, and on the desks of hundreds of people like her. And those deals looked great to a lot of investors, but they did not look great to Mabel Yu.

Mabel Yu: I got names of the rating agencies' analysts, and I asked them lots of questions. In the beginning, the questions would be fifteen minutes to half an hour, but then it turned into hours and many hours, for me to understand the risk profile of the deal.

David Kestenbaum: And what did they say to you?

Mabel Yu: I asked them, I said triple-A is supposed to be minimum risk, what triple-A really means, is even if things go bad simultaneously, at the same time, our investors would still be protected. That means if the economy goes down, if the housing price goes down, if interest rates go up, if all those things happen at the same time, what would happen to our investments? And I could not get a straight answer.

David Kestenbaum: Did they say, look, you worry too much, we have a lot of smart people working on this?

Mabel Yu: Many, many, many, many, many times I felt so dumb many times. And they asked me in many ways, they asked me, don't worry about it; have a life. Instead of staying up so late and preparing all those hours of questions for them, just go ahead and enjoy your life. I worry too much. Almost every day.

David Kestenbaum: Almost every day?

Mabel Yu: Yes. Yes. Yes.[9]

Vanguard's Reaction

Mabel Yu may have been a media celebrity, but the reaction to her decisions at Vanguard was typically muted—albeit supportive at all times. Her boss in fixed income analysis, Bill Roberts, was positive about Yu's story, and mentioned that Yu had been named Analyst of the Year in 2009. However, he deservedly gives some credit to the Vanguard culture:

> This was good for Mabel's career and her confidence level, and now she oversees analysis for the entire energy industry. She didn't report to me at the time, but we are proud of the decisions that she and others made during that period. We did realize that Mabel was working too hard; now we have four people doing the work that she was doing back in 2006, and there are many fewer new issues now. But her decision not to recommend these investments was not unusual at Vanguard. We go out of our way to make sure there is debate about these topics, to make sure we are not missing anything. And Mabel's decision was consistent with our belief that you have to understand what we're investing in. If there is extra yield there is probably a reason for it.

Bob Auwaerter, the head of fixed income investments at Vanguard, was similarly restrained:

> We're proud of Mabel, but I could point to a multitude of decisions like hers that didn't get so much visibility. There are two factors that drive them. We have an organizational philosophy that is very consistent with the approach Mabel took, and we try to hire the right kind of people. Our philosophy is to look at good, longer-term performance. We're not looking to hit the ball out of the park in any

particular year. We have an expense advantage relative to our competitors, and we are willing to give some of it away in order to have cleaner portfolios from a credit perspective.

When asked what kind of people Vanguard hired, Auwaerter contrasted Vanguard hires to those in some Wall Street firms:

> Our people are smart, hardworking, and ethical, and they have to have broad-based experience. Some Wall Street problems have occurred when they hired MBAs from top schools and put them on the trading floor, and they lacked experience. They had the attitude that they were "masters of the universe." We don't hire people who think they are masters of the universe. Maybe we don't pay enough to encourage them!

Even John Bogle recognized Yu by taking her to lunch, but in typical Bogle and Vanguard fashion. Their lunchtime venue was not an expensive bistro, but rather the Vanguard cafeteria. Yu ordered a salad and a drink, following the Vanguard $5 lunch coupon celebration tradition (the company gives out a $5 coupon for crew member birthdays and achievement of milestone asset levels). Bogle assured Yu that she could order more, but Yu stayed under the limit. "He is very frugal, so I wanted to do things his way," Yu reflected.

Yu has some higher values in common with Bogle:

> Money isn't what drives me. I just want to be good at what I do. I was already a confident person before all this, but I have become more so. Despite the financial crisis, I got a very good result for my company. I am not afraid to make calls different from the market. If they say, "Sell, sell, sell," I say, "Buy it," if I believe it is the right call. During the BP oil spill crisis in 2010, I made several difficult credit calls that were against the market consensus. It turned out that they were the right calls. The value of this is not that I make money because of these decisions, but that it will be a great story to tell my daughter. And I can go to bed and sleep well. If I worked on Wall

Street and made a hundred million dollars, I still couldn't sleep if I had lost so much of my clients' money or brought down the firm.

Yu says that eventually she wants to work in Asia—she came to the United States from Hong Kong—but right now she is happy in her job and with her company:

> I get to do what I really want—doing analysis for the whole energy sector. I thought they were kidding when they gave me the job. But I am very loyal to Vanguard. The company cultivates loyalty and commitment among crew members. Unlike Wall Street, Vanguard believes in a long-term commitment to its employees. They didn't lay anyone off in the recessions of 2001 and 2009. It was tough, bonuses were cut, but nobody was laid off. They are loyal to me, and I am loyal to them.

Reflections on Mabel Yu and The Vanguard Group's Organizational Judgment

The Mabel Yu story is also the Vanguard story. It is a tale not only of individual strength and leadership from Yu herself, but also of good organizational judgment arising from a distinctive culture. The strong Vanguard values and culture helped Mabel Yu resist external pressure and make the right decision for the company's investors.

The company's culture also facilitated dissent by employees such as Yu. Allowing and even encouraging dissent by stakeholders in decisions—whether the dissent is purely internal or, as with Yu, involving external influences—is an important factor in high-quality decision processes.

Vanguard's reluctance to make a public hero out of Mabel Yu is consistent with its culture that all employees can make heroic decisions and take heroic actions on behalf of customers. They are clearly proud of her actions, but treat her as just another brave member of the "Swiss army."

The Yu–Vanguard story, with all its press visibility, also illustrates that it is more important than ever to use good judgment and decision-making processes in the current transparent world. There is a good chance that both good and bad examples of individual and organizational judgment may be captured and reviewed by the public—so be careful how you make and discuss decisions!

9

EMC

How Can We Cut Our Costs in Tough Times?

A S THOUSANDS of employees at a $17 billion high-tech company called EMC came to work on April 23, 2009, they were expecting the worst. It was the day for the company's quarterly financial announcement for the first quarter of 2009, and everyone knew that things were not going well in the global economy for EMC—or virtually any other large company, for that matter. A global recession was in full flower, and customers weren't buying EMC's products at the rate they had been. Would there be massive layoffs and expense cuts? Would plants or facilities be closed? Some employees would hear directly how bad things were from Joe Tucci, the company's chairman and CEO, in a large auditorium in Hopkinton, Massachusetts. Others expected that they would find out soon enough.[1]

That morning, when EMC employees sat down at their desks and opened their e-mail inboxes, they saw an e-mail from Tucci. Excerpts from it follow:

To: EMC All

Date: April 23, 2009

Subject: *Keeping EMC Strong*

I am committed to communicating with all of you about exactly what's going on with our company in the most straightforward way possible. So, here's where we stand. This morning we reported our first-quarter financial results. We pride ourselves on consistently strong execution—even in the midst of the toughest overall market since the Great Depression . . .

Given the synchronized global downturn and the significant pressure on customers' budgets and IT spending, our Q1 performance, while not up to our own expectations, was still pretty solid. As always, you put in very long hours and made tremendous efforts to execute our strategy and give customers the best possible total experience. Thank you very, very much for your dedication.

The resilience of our business during Q1 reinforces my long-term view of our company's prospects. I am convinced that we are operating from strength with a winning strategy and vision, the strongest product cycle in our history, a very large and loyal customer franchise, a vital set of strategic alliance partners, and, best of all, thousands of the industry's most talented people around the world.

At the same time, I know—as do all of you—that the global economy is experiencing its most severe recession in decades. The latest consensus forecast from economists is that the global economy will actually shrink this year (by 1.6%) for the first time since the mid-1940s. We now expect global IT spending to decline by a high-single-digit to low-double-digit percentage this year compared with last year. In addition, many of our customers are practicing what I call "just-in-time, just-enough" IT spending.

Having anticipated most of these developments, we've been working for more than a year to carefully reduce our non-people-related costs. In early January, we announced a far-reaching restructuring program, part of which involved reducing our global information infrastructure workforce by about 2,400 people. We are now about halfway through this workforce reduction and will complete the balance later this year.

But in light of everything we know today, we now need to take additional steps to further align our costs with our revenue. I have been hearing from hundreds of you across our great company who have offered constructive and creative ideas for how we can continue to drive EMC's costs down. The most common theme is this: Let's do whatever it takes to best serve our customers while preserving EMC jobs. I couldn't agree more. Clearly, our people are the heart and soul of EMC, the engine of our growth, and the key to delivering the best total customer experience in the industry. I appreciate your dedication to our colleagues and our customers around the world.

After examining many different what-if scenarios and thinking long and hard about what to do, we have come up with an approach—guided by suggestions from EMC people around the world—that we believe will preserve jobs while helping us save EMC an additional $100 million this year. These savings, when added to our original plan of lowering our costs by $350 million, should enable us to reduce EMC's 2009 Information Infrastructure cost base by about $450 million this year, increasing to about $500 million in 2010.

Our plan is to institute a *temporary base pay reduction of 5 percent* that will apply to our employees around the world. This pay reduction will take effect on May 1 in the U.S. and on June 1 internationally, and will remain in place until December 31, 2009. Where local law requires, this pay reduction will be voluntary . . .

Please recognize that a global company facing an economic environment that is difficult across the world needs *everyone, from every geography*, to participate and make a sacrifice. We are all in this together. This reduction in pay applies to me and my entire staff and is in addition to the pay cuts (ranging from 5% to more than 20%) that the senior management team and I signed up for in January. In an expression of unity, our fully engaged and supportive Board members, who reduced their pay by 10% in January, have also signed up for this new 5% reduction.

I want you all to know that the 5 percent reduction in base pay plus all of the other actions we are taking to reduce costs will translate into *saving more than 2,000 jobs* at EMC this year. That's how important this action is.

I understand that even a modest cut in pay can create a real hardship. I recognize the significance of that sacrifice. As an accommodation we have decided to grant every EMC employee affected by this pay cut five days (or 40 hours' worth) of additional paid time off ...

I also want you to know that your management team and I are very serious about our commitment to stay close, listen carefully to your ideas, and communicate fully and frequently. We've learned a great deal, for example, by following the cost saving discussions on EMC|One ...

I'm charged up about our future and very proud of all of you.

Joe

Neither Tucci nor any other executive anticipated the employees' reactions, both virtual and face-to-face. When Tucci delivered similar content in a speech to employees that day, there was loud and long applause. E-mailed responses to Tucci were similarly positive. One Boston-based employee wrote:

Joe,

Hi. Just a quick note to pass on one employee's support for your efforts. Tough times call for tough decisions and it is clear that you are making every effort to set EMC up for strong growth when economic conditions improve. No one wants to take a pay cut, but by spreading the burden across all employees, it is made clear that we are all in this together, through thick and thin.

This is a strong move and one that not everyone is going to like. But these are the times where true leaders show their stuff and I am proud to work for a company that is transparent, open, and willing to do whatever it takes to succeed long-term, not just quarter to quarter. Thanks for letting us all know the details that went into these recent decisions.

Best,

(An EMC employee)

Another employee based in California responded to Tucci:

Joe

I am sure that you will get many replies to this message, but I wish to thank you for this strong decision and leadership stance. It is the right thing to do to maintain our workforce, to keep us going through these hard times, but also to ensure that we are ready when the turnaround does happen.

Thank you.

Perhaps these employees had been expecting worse cuts. Perhaps they were simply grateful to still have jobs. Perhaps they appreciated the shared sacrifice the policy employed. However, Tucci and his senior management colleagues were confident of one thing: EMC had a new culture, and social media had helped to bring it about—and that had everything to do, as it turned out, with how certain decisions would start to be made.

The Old EMC

EMC—the name is derived from the founders' initials and not the formula for atomic energy—is a company based in the Boston suburbs, sometimes called "Route 128," though EMC's headquarters is really near Interstate 495. Its primary business is computer data storage systems and software, and it is the market leader in that category, with more than double the market share of its closest competitor.

EMC's corporate culture traditionally reflected the personality of its founder Dick Egan, who was described in obituaries as "hard-charging" and "hypercompetitive." The direct sales force at EMC, in particular, was known for its aggressive sales tactics. One aspect of the sales force's new hire training was walking (quickly, one presumes) over blazing hot coals; as EMC's newsletter put it in 2001, "Fire walking helps [the staff] prepare for intimidating sales situations. Overcome self-doubt, and everything is possible."

Like most companies, EMC was managed in a hierarchical fashion. Leaders had strong personalities and in general didn't ask for much input or brook much disagreement. No one would describe them (at least the company's more recent leaders) as "dictatorial," but they held the reins of command firmly. In short, although the company manufactures and sells information infrastructure technologies, it was not the place to look for bottom-up use of technology to enhance employee participation in decision making.

The Unlikely Rise of Social Media

So it's surprising that EMC has become an enthusiastic adopter of social media and participative decision making. But that is indeed the case. Social media has been either the catalyst or the result—probably both—of a substantial evolution in decision making and corporate culture at EMC. Decisions that would previously have been made behind closed doors by senior managers were influenced by and discussed over online chats. Policies that would previously have been announced by memo were announced online, and clarified or evolved based on online reactions. EMC has drafted many of its 49,000 employees worldwide into improving its organizational judgment and decision-making capabilities, and they have responded enthusiastically.

The big shift at EMC began slowly in 2007. Chuck Hollis was asked to lead an effort to think strategically about social media use in the company. Hollis is an EMC vice president who had been at the company for thirteen years in a variety of functions including engineering, marketing, sales, and corporate management. He's a sort of middle senior management type who is assigned to projects and roles that are important and need further definition. He's also quite loquacious, both in person and online. Hollis started a blog in August 2006, created a blog purely to discuss EMC's adoption of social media in August 2007, and wrote a white paper in 2008 describing the company's "journey in social media."[2] So we'll quote him liberally in this chapter (and how could one avoid excerpting blog posts in a chapter about social media?).

Hollis confirmed in his blog the fact that exploring social media was a somewhat countercultural act at EMC:

> I knew I was working within a company that was more comfortable with command-and-control . . . information sharing wasn't one of our key corporate tenets. We thought we had unique IP [intellectual property]. Even letting people know what we were thinking about was considered an important corporate secret. Everything was on a need-to-know basis. And, strangely, the behavior was reinforcing, because once you were "in the loop," you didn't want to buck the system that had given you privileged access to information.

Nonetheless, EMC's senior management team—specifically, B. J. Jenkins, the head of global marketing at the time—asked Hollis to plan and implement technologies, policies, and processes for social media use at EMC. Other executives had asked Hollis informally to play the role. Hollis noted, "I made darn sure I had the backing of the executive team before I went out."

There had been some previous activity at EMC in this area—but it resulted in almost all private discussions, and they didn't lead to widespread, open information exchange across the company. This time, Hollis and his executive colleagues hoped for a more transformative impact.

Hollis quickly formed a team, and they had a social media platform up and running before the end of September 2007—a little more than a month after the initiative began. The team named it EMC|One, in part because it was intended to help create "One EMC." Hollis decided that all postings would be viewable by all employees within EMC. He wrote in his blog:

> Since the company has lots of ways of sharing confidential and private information (physical doc distribution, email, eRooms, private file shares, etc.) I felt we didn't need yet another way to do this ... We want people to be curious and nose around ... We want people to get comfortable having open discussions about real problems and collaborative outcomes—that's the behavior. And it won't happen in a walled garden. So, from day one, we've got a simple rule: *no private spaces*. Period.

The early uses of EMC|One were primarily by various employee affinity groups and hobbyists. Many of the early discussions were devoted to "pets, photography, and painting," as one EMC|One user put it. There were also some discussions by technical groups of various technologies and competitive initiatives. It was expected that the technical workforce would be the primary users—not just R&D, but technical people in the field. It would give them a channel for feedback on product requirements, installation, and field implementation issues. Before long, however, EMC|One would be commandeered for other purposes.

"Cost Transformation" at EMC

Like many companies, EMC was beginning to worry a bit in the latter half of 2008. The financial services sector—a big customer for EMC's storage devices—was imploding, and IT buyers in other industries were beginning to cut their spending. EMC had a great fourth quarter in 2008, but as David Goulden, EMC's executive vice president and chief financial officer (CFO), said in an end-of-year press release, "Through 2009 we will continue to streamline operations, reduce costs and strengthen the efficiencies of our global operations." Goulden and EMC estimated that global IT spending in 2009 would decline as a percentage in the mid to high single digits, compared with 2008. The company wanted to be ready, so it had embarked upon a Cost Transformation Program halfway through 2008.

The Cost Transformation Program was intended to permanently remove cost from EMC. A number of companywide task forces, led by program managers from the company's finance, IT, and other business functions, were created to look at people costs, indirect costs, and product costs. Indirect expense received a high degree of focus, including costs from travel, real estate, contractors, consultants, and so forth. People costs were also examined closely: did EMC need major layoffs? Could it afford the same benefits, vacation policies, and so forth? Given the sensitive nature of these issues, the task forces' deliberations were largely secret until their conclusions were announced—at least at the beginning.

However, EMC's traditional culture and decision approaches were changing—in part because its business had changed dramatically. As David Goulden, the company's CFO, put it in an interview:

> When I started here in 2002, EMC was a single-product company—our Symmetrix storage system was it. We had a direct sales model, selling only to large enterprises. Any software and services were attached to Symmetrix. With that kind of organization, you could be very top down from a decision-making standpoint.
>
> EMC today is in the storage market in multiple classes of technology, selling to large enterprises, small businesses, and even consumers. Channel partners are a major part of business. We've got software and services groups. We're based on the East Coast and the

West Coast, and international is a much bigger piece of the business. Our many acquisitions—more than fifty—have brought multiple approaches and styles together. Given all that, there had to be an evolution and maturing of decision styles.

Given all those changes, Joe Tucci, EMC's chairman and CEO, led a "One EMC" initiative to further unite the company's products, processes, and cultures. That was, of course, the inspiration for the name of the EMC|One social media platform. Hollis described the reasoning in his blog:

> EMC acquires dozens of companies. EMC establishes clear leader-ship in most of its chosen markets. It all gets wonderfully diverse and complicated and ... well, it's a very different game, isn't it? Hint: in any company that has 45,000+ employees, they're all going to be working on different aspects of The Problem—and they're going to need to work with others that aren't in their group, aren't they? The new business challenges aren't at the product/BU level—it's getting people to work together cross-functionally. The DNA that made us successful is now getting in the way of our most fundamental busi-ness problem—acting like one company, rather than an aggrega-tion of many. Joe Tucci and the exec management even sent a clear message—"ONE EMC"—just to reinforce the problem and the need to solve it ...
>
> We had a quick discussion in our community about what to call this platform. Clearly, it needed a name. I offered the sugges-tion that—whatever we called it—it ought to reflect a Big Honkin' Corporate Priority. Someone (I think it was [EMC employee] Len Devanna) came up with EMC|One—a clear derivative of the "ONE EMC" corporate priority. I think we intend it to mean "EMC One Network of Employees" or some such thing, but the interpretation of the acronym is far less important than the message the name sends—this is all about working together in very different (and concrete) ways.

Cost Transformation and EMC|One Converge

By mid-2008, the topics discussed on EMC|One started to change. Michelle Lavoie, an EMC employee working in the technical certification area in the company's professional services business unit, described the mood at the time:

> In 2008 there was anxiety and nervousness among employees thanks to the macro-economy—there had been a layoff, and people weren't certain about their jobs. The economy was turning. Just when people were feeling very anxious about their jobs, EMC|One was a way to talk about it.

One of the first big cost-related issues to be discussed on EMC|One was a change in EMC's vacation policy. It specified that employees with leftover vacation time in one year had to use it by March of the next year. Michelle Lavoie didn't think it was a big deal. Neither did Chuck Hollis. However, as Hollis reported on his blog, it galvanized a major response on EMC|One:

> The first memo came out in a traditional way—there was a minor change to our vacation policy to keep the amount of carryover vacation down to a manageable number. Not a big deal in the broader scheme of things, at least the way I think about these things.
>
> But a couple of spontaneous discussions emerged on the internal platform, right out there for everyone to see. A few people were (ahem) rather *pointed* in their thoughts about this particular change in vacation policy. Some people were quite upset regarding the inconvenience involved—they had made plans far in advance, which were now impacted. Others had particular work-related situations that didn't make it easy to burn off enough vacation in time—they were concerned about losing a valuable benefit. Still others felt free to spout off a bit—ill-advised in any public setting, but there you had it.
>
> *All very valid concerns.*

Before too long, we had over 10,000 views on the threads, and hundreds of comments. Over time, though, more moderate voices joined the discussion, and softly rebuked some of the more vocal participants.

These more moderate people said that the economy was getting tough, and the company needed to look at every reasonable avenue for lowering expenses. If this meant a small change in the vacation policy, fine—better than some of the alternatives.

Fine, came back the collective response—then the communication should have been worded with this in mind. Be open and transparent, they said—don't try to whitewash the situation. The executives in charge of the policy (formation and communication) got to see this all unfold in real time before their eyes—warts and all.

Very useful feedback, I might offer . . .

Michelle Lavoie also believed that the change in vacation policy was a minor issue. She felt it really indicated a broader set of concerns:

People need clarity and they had a lot of questions. It turned into this very long discussion on EMC|One. People were asking whether this was the first step toward massive layoffs. And there were the details, like how do I get my vacation in before the time it would expire.

In the online discussion, Lavoie tried to counter the negative tone of the discussion with some positive contributions. She said in one post that she thought EMC people should be happy to have jobs at all. A few days later, she was thinking in the shower that morning about how EMC|One could have a positive effect on the "cost transformation" process. So on November 17, 2008, at 2:45 p.m., she posted her 430th contribution on EMC|One under the heading of "Constructive Ideas to Save Money":

And not one word about the vacation policy, please.

Maybe we could consider:

- Optional week-long (unpaid) furloughs
- Incentives for retirement or leaving the company
- Holiday week shutdowns (as business units permit); unpaid
- Across-the-board pay freezes through 2009
- Options for employees to voluntarily go to 4-day weeks with 20% pay cut

Don't get me wrong; I'm not "in" for any of these things . . . but you never know who might find one or many of these options desirable.

Other ideas?

That discussion took off. More than a year and a half later, it had over 26,000 views, and 364 responses—and new ones were still coming in. As the discussion thread lengthened, senior executives joined the discussion, including Chuck Hollis and Jack Mollen, executive vice president of human resources. Members of the cost transformation task force participated as well. The focus of the suggestions was, like Lavoie's, primarily different ways to cut costs. Some were, according to Lavoie, "crazy and off the wall," but many were quite practical, and EMC took notice.

For example, there were several suggestions about working from home and saving energy, and Mollen soon announced a flexible and remote work program called WorkWise. All printers throughout the company were set to double-sided printing. There were many suggestions about travel policy, and EMC made updates to it. Employees suggested a variety of ways to save on telecommunications costs, and EMC announced a new program to replace employee reimbursement of mobile phone charges with direct payments to carriers, saving more than $3 million.

The mobile phone reimbursement change was indicative of the ways in which EMC|One was impacting the EMC culture. According to Goulden:

It just led to a lot of positive back-and-forth discussion. First there were suggestions on EMC|One that we might save money with new cell phone policies. The cost transformation team looked at it, and we announced the new policy. In addition to the likely cost savings, we announced how many jobs it would save. The policy change got a very positive reaction—I got more letters from employees on that than any other topic. But there were many questions about the ramifications—what happens to personal lines, how to deal with cancellation fees, and so forth. We'd sent out the memo on December 17 (2008), but by December 19 I sent out a clarifying memo. EMC|One helped us realize that we had to do a Q&A on our initial Q&A. Overall it's been very helpful.

But perhaps the greatest impact on both costs and company culture was the 5 percent salary cut, which was accompanied by an extra week of vacation for employees. Goulden described the difficulty of the message, and how it was communicated:

> We had to get 40,000-plus people to understand what we're doing, why we're doing it, and what role they can play. Sometimes, it means getting them to buy into difficult situations—for example, we instituted a temporary base pay reduction of 5 percent that applied to our employees around the world (Joe Tucci and his leadership team also took additional percentage salary cuts). We explained how by doing that, we were able to make a smaller reduction in jobs when our competitors were making much larger reductions. In many countries around the world where EMC operates, a company can't mandate a pay cut like here in the US. Local laws mandate that employees volunteer, and more than 85 percent of our employees in those countries did so. We explained to employees that salary levels would be reinstated, provided that the company recovers, and we did so on January 1 of this year. But the sign-up percentage, I think, reflects that the message was communicated correctly.[3]

Lavoie seconded that perspective and described the personal implications of the online discussions:

When in the April meeting the 5% pay cut was announced, along with the addition of five days of paid vacation for the year, a lot of people understood that they made a difference, and that the discussions were being heard. The pay cut was difficult for some people but we were proud and happy to do it because we'd been discussing it all along ... from my perspective, it was the proudest moment for EMC|One. It had moved from being just a social interaction tool to a business tool.

For me, my cost comments were a turning point. I'm an individual contributor, sitting in a cubicle in Franklin [Massachusetts]. David Goulden, the CFO, sent something out saying that if you have an idea to save money, click here—and it went directly to my post. I could see the influence I had.

Putting the Change in Perspective

In an interview with Goulden, he suggested that the change from EMC|One was more about communication, culture, and participation than specific ideas for cost reduction.

After the second of my over a dozen memos it became clear that EMC|One would be a great channel for communicating with the organization. I wish I were insightful enough to have planned it that way; it was just very fortunate. Every time we put out a policy communication we pointed to EMC|One for discussion. We got subject matter experts involved, and we made it a team sport to identify areas to save money.

Ultimately we distilled about 200 different ideas coming from employees on EMC|One. There was nothing huge that hadn't been discussed in the Cost Transformation Project teams, which themselves involved a lot of people across eight different work streams. But it's clear that the feeling of participation and morale issues were the most important contribution from EMC|One. People had a sense of being part of the process, as opposed to receiving memos about it. And we tried to show graphically on EMC|One how these approaches saved money. The more we saved through indirect expenses, the less we had to do through people.

The positive reactions that we had to the cost reduction were more about the culture and sense of identification with the company than just EMC|One. Employees understood the leadership team was doing everything possible to avoid employee cuts. EMC|One discussions and communications just made that clear, and gave a voice to employees.

Michelle Lavoie agreed with Goulden from the perspective of how EMC|One supported attributes of the company that already existed:

In my group—and, I think, EMC as a whole—we've always been very collaborative. My colleagues were always hard-working, technically savvy, and very innovative. EMC|One was a place to facilitate that collaboration.

Chuck Hollis reflected on the value of EMC|One during the cost transformation period in his blog:

Look, any time you have to share disruptive news with your workforce, there's an inherent disruption. People want to ask questions, discuss among themselves, share perspectives. It's a natural human reaction—you have to process things a bit before you can get back to work. Well, using the online platform, we seem to be getting through that introspection phase far faster than before. Anyone can see the memo, and what everyone else has already said about it. Anyone can leave their thoughts and concerns as well—all in about 3 minutes flat. No need to wander around the building, finding people to talk to. Or getting on the phone to discuss this with your friends. Or to immediately schedule a meeting with your manager to discuss pronto.

Sure, there are people who are going to want to do some of this traditional processing, but—as of today—the online platform is where people appear to be doing the majority of this "processing"—and it's all there for everyone to see—including our executive management.

Finally, executive communications is not a precise art. Getting real-time feedback on how you did in crafting the message is valuable feedback for any executive. And you can find out pretty quickly just how well you did, and how to do better next time.

Going Forward with Social Media at EMC

EMC|One continues to be a channel for all sorts of communications to and among EMC people, although by 2010 the company's business had returned to growth and profitability. Social media has become a general business tool, used for a wide range of communications and collaboration purposes. For example, Michelle Lavoie used it to advance her ends with regard to education programs. She posted new courses, addressed certification issues, and answered questions that her peer employees posed to her online. Her manager insisted that her social media activities become part of her formal responsibilities—"So now it's on my goal sheet," she commented.

Would she make suggestions again if tough times returned? "You betcha," she replied, although she adds, "We don't wait for hard times anymore. That's the kind of culture you want, and I have seen proof that people listen."

EMC is heavily engaged with other dimensions of social media. Lavoie, for example, had both Twitter and Facebook accounts, both EMC-branded. The company also had a set of external EMC|One-like networks (called EMC Community Networks, or ECNs) that it used for engaging EMC customers, partners, and employees worldwide for collaboration, communication, and innovation. From EMC's perspective, they provided a number of benefits, including customer engagement and additional support.

David Goulden, who previously headed customer relationships before becoming CFO, noted that they have been very successful:

> We thought about them partly as a cost reduction opportunity, but we have found that customer satisfaction is higher for support interactions through online chat or community forums than for call center calls. It's counterintuitive, but the satisfaction is higher online.

Social media has transformed EMC in a variety of other ways as well. In his last blog post for "A Journey in Social Media," Chuck Hollis summarized some of them:

> At the start, I was asked to put a strategy and several efforts in motion to get this whole social media proficiency thing off the ground and moving in the right direction. I did that. Thanks to the efforts of many passionate people at my company, I can honestly say *"mission accomplished."* Sure, there's always more to do—in some ways we've only just begun.
>
> But there's no denying that my company is a fundamentally different place in April 2009 than it was in August 2007 when it comes to being a "2.0" company. We've got many thousands of people actively collaborating and sharing on our internal platform. Not only is it successful beyond our wildest imagination, we can't imagine getting business done without it.
>
> We've graduated dozens of external bloggers and literally hundreds of "unofficial brand managers" from this platform. You can see them out there—in force—every day of the week. No one could ask for anything more.
>
> We've taken that momentum and created our external community platform initiative, and it too has enjoyed great success so far. But that's just the surface stuff. When you really look closely, there's far more interesting things starting to happen.

Subtle—But Profound—Changes Abound

When most people at our company think about process, or collaboration, or engagement—they're now starting to think about things in 2.0 ways. It shows up in just about every conversation these days. As we look at different staffing plans across the company, we're starting to see more job descriptions for "community developer" and "community evangelist." To me, this represents a structural change in how people are thinking about resources—and strategies—going forward. Our new "community college" (coursework regarding how to design and build a community) is now extremely popular internally. I think the people teaching this material will be busy for quite a while! Our investment pattern in marketing and other business functions has significantly shifted. There's far less spent on traditional collaboration and process, and far more effort invested into learning how to do things the new way.

One small (large?) example: we're a product company, so it's all about the launch. You wouldn't try to accomplish a major launch at my company anymore without a detailed "social plan." As I write this, we're planning a humongous product launch tomorrow, April 14th [2010]. About 50% of the total launch effort went into 2.0 stuff. That's big, if you think about it.

I'm very proud of the fact that our executive management has learned to become very comfortable with the 2.0 management ethic. People are now quite comfortable publicly disagreeing with each other without being disagreeable.

Communications and engagement have become much more transparent and open. The org chart isn't what it used to be! And when we have the inevitable "issues," there's a willingness to work through various pros and cons, rather than the instinctive "shut it down" from yesteryear. There's no valid excuse anymore to not knowing what's going on across the company. In the past, many people felt it was the company's job to make sure that they knew what was going on; now that responsibility has been shifted to the individual.

Our efforts in social media proficiency have started to transform our corporate culture and leadership style in an extremely positive and progressive way. That's very cool when you think about it.

Reflections on EMC's Organizational Judgment

The comments of Hollis, Goulden, and Lavoie all suggest that there has been a dramatic change in EMC's culture and approach to decision making. No longer is it an environment where a Great Man can make pronouncements from on high without any comment or involvement by the other 49,000 employees. Cost saving and other ideas no longer must come only from handpicked experts. No longer does EMC speak with only one voice. It is a big and complex company, and that is reflected in its public and private voices.

Of course, executives still make decisions at EMC, and some employees still know more than others about particular business problems and objectives. We don't want to imply that there is no longer any hierarchy of power or expertise at the company. Sometimes, as in the case of M&A planning, senior management will have to keep important decisions to themselves. Sometimes, as with new product R&D, deliberations and decisions won't be democratic.

But the EMC story shows that a previously top-down and buttoned-up culture can begin to accommodate new voices and influences in its organizational judgment. If a company this big and successful can change to involve more people and their perspectives in its organizational judgment, perhaps any organization can. We're confident that EMC's expanded judgment capabilities will enable it to make great decisions in the future, and that the broader participation in those decisions will make employees feel much more engaged in the execution of them.

Part Four

Stories About Leaders Setting the Right Context

THIS BOOK BEGAN BY INSISTING THAT the era of the Great Man as decision maker is now over, and is being replaced by new paradigm focusing on the judgment of the organization more broadly—more participative, problem-solving oriented, and technologically advanced. But we were careful not to write out the role of leaders entirely vis-à-vis decision making. Indeed, leaders can play an all critical role to set the right context, mind-set, and "organizational permission" (if it doesn't already exist) to allow for a more participative and fact-based approach to finding solutions. The stories in this part are about three such leaders—people who deliberately turned away from what had been decision making primarily as their own prerogative, and coupled the problem-solving process of a particular difficult decision with building a new culture and capability among a deliberately wider circle of people. The first case highlights that transformation through a business model overhaul of a major regional news organization, Media General. It is followed by the story of change leadership combined with strategy setting in educational reform by the president of the New York–based philanthropy, The Wallace Foundation. And we conclude with a story of an entrepreneur's successful launch, expansion, and final cash-out of an innovative beauty products company, Tweezerman—which hinged on his personal transformation about sharing decision making for the first time in his life.

10

Media General

Should We Restructure for a New Strategy?

A S THE digital revolution of the 1990s rippled and reshaped the global economy, Media General, like so many mainstream media companies, watched its advertising-based businesses come under increasing pressure. By the time the Great Recession of 2008 hit, and advertising budgets all around began to collapse, this $700 million newspaper and broadcasting company, focused primarily in the southeastern United States, knew that media business models were about to change forever. As it struggled with declining revenues, new members of the board were demanding more value and calling for different approaches. CEO Marshall Morton and his senior executives wrestled mightily with what to do: Was it time to reinvent this historically successful company? What was the right way to bring together—or create mutual reinforcing advantage among—Internet, publishing, and broadcasting businesses? How should they do that?[1]

Unlike many rivals, Media General had not been running away from the digital revolution, but instead doing its best to embrace it. It had launched a few successful Web properties and was actively experimenting in selected markets about how to take greater advantage of the fast-developing convergence of different kinds of content development and delivery. But its overall strategy, organizational structure, and general way of doing business were still driven by a traditional media company approach—aligned around *platforms*—business units organized by product or delivery: a print newspaper division, a broadcasting division, and a separate (and much smaller) Internet division. With each passing year, however, the new "digital convergence" thinking and the old way of working were increasingly coming into conflict. As a traditional, southern family-owned business, Media General was not easily given over to any kind of abrupt change. Like all successful enterprises, it was cautious about rash action that might undermine something carefully built up over years.

The dilemma was very real, but during 2008 pressure for change became absolutely urgent. The story that follows explains how the leadership of this company came to terms with the challenges and turned them into real opportunity, moving decisively to transform Media General amid some substantial risks. In the process of reaching for a new strategy and a new way of working, CEO Marshall Morton went through his own quiet revolution—in the process, building a new kind of organizational judgment based on a different kind of leadership.

The Challenge of Transformation

If ever there was a corporation that embraced tradition, it was this one. With pre–Civil War roots, and a long history of control by the distinguished Bryan family of Virginia, the company over time built an operating culture of southern gentility, journalistic integrity, and community service. The culture was consistent with its business, focused primarily on local and engaging metropolitan newspapers. But, beginning in the 1950s, like other newspaper companies, Media General also expanded into the fast-growing broadcast television business. It later also went through the then fashionable "conglomerate" approach, buying up newspaper, cable, and communications-related businesses in other parts of the country, even including a paper mill. In 1994, it was one of the first media companies to start a community-based Internet information service in one of its major markets, Tampa. The digital revolution added further complexity to the mix. Though not nearly as resistant to its potential transformational force as many other media companies, Media General continued to wrestle with the real long-term impact that Internet and other digital technologies would have on publishers and broadcasters.

As the digital revolution gathered more force, traditional local media were pressured to deliver more value for less cost. After 2000, then-chairman and CEO of the company J. Stewart Bryan III led an effort to consolidate Media General's assets and strategy around its three core businesses of newspapers, television, and Internet, focused more tightly in the southeastern United States. The consolidation and greater focus made huge business sense, but the new "tighter model" had its own, more subtle disadvantages. The organizational structure based now on the three separate platforms—newspapers, broadcast, Internet—did everything to reinforce and even exacerbate three professional subcultures seen in any multiproperty media company. As one vice president wryly described the years following the consolidation, "You had the journalists with their reverence for the print cathedral; the TV people, emphasizing visuals and immediacy, always accused of no depth of content; and the young digerati, impatient and irreverent about everything."

The diverse divisional operating cultures were more than just friendly and clichéd rivalries, however. They became stumbling blocks to performance. This organizational model had been developed originally to address some of the fundamental and seismic changes in the media business, particularly newspapers. The development and distribution of content had been for years fragmenting among more sources—in the video world, from broadcasting to an increasing array of cable and satellite channels, and in the journalism world, across an exploding set of Web sites, online services, and electronic portals. The digital technology revolution had similarly put more power into the hands of users and consumers—breaking up historical monopolies, and increasing viewer and reader choice that in turn created shorter attention spans and more fickle interest in advertising. The landscape was further complicated by changing federal regulation that ended up accelerating competition among different sources of news and other content.

As audiences shifted their tastes and viewing across different platforms for information, Media General content providers in each of the three divisions began competing with one another for different angles or timeliness of the same local news stories. "Every time there was a big fire when I worked in Tampa, the TV trucks and the print people would both be showing up, each trying to scoop the other, " remembered Jim Zimmerman, who now oversees the markets of the Virginia and Tennessee regions. "We were losing margin, and it was just crazy." The same competitiveness was both confusing advertising customers and losing opportunities. As Marilyn Hammond, vice president of sales operations, recalls, "Each of our divisions would be calling on the same auto dealer in a city, basically tripping over each other, and more interested in making the sale for their units instead of really figuring out how to help him sell more cars. The division mind-set was hugely frustrating. And we were leaving money on the table because of it."

In earlier times, when newspapers and broadcasters enjoyed near monopolies in their markets, competing and less customer-centric divisions were a luxury Media General could afford. There was plenty of money for everyone, and the company continued to grow quickly. But the internal competitiveness and lack of operating efficiency still goaded many managers, especially against the backdrop of a largely harmonious company culture and a growing sense of bigger missed opportunities. Jim Zimmerman, again looking back to his earlier days in Tampa as the local broadcast leader, remembered bumping into his newspaper colleague—and sometimes rival—Doyle Harvill at a major charity event: "We saw each other across the room and realized each of our divisions had bought a table for the cause. Why didn't we just have one Media General table? And why wouldn't our broadcast and print people just sit together?"

Early Steps

In fact, across the company, some initiatives grew to find more serious ways to bridge the traditional gaps between divisions. After the charity event, Zimmerman and Harvill embarked on a few projects to try more collaborative selling to advertisers, and in various parts of the Media General organization, there were efforts to bring closer together diverse news-gathering and commercial operations. One of the more successful collaborations, in fact, went on to develop in Tampa, when Zimmerman and Harvill took advantage of a technology transition from analog to digital transmission to colocate journalists and broadcasters in a new single building. As Harvill recalls: "The print and the TV people kept seeing each other in the elevator, and they actually started to work together more. And later they both started to appreciate the value of the Internet." Print journalists began to appear on the television news, promoting their stories, and TV reporters found opportunities to participate more substantively and productively in their colleagues' print products. The local newspaper and TV station showed gains from the crossover, and the local Internet portal rose to prominence as an early example of community news gathered from all over.

Chairman and CEO Bryan had since the early 1990s repeatedly declared that the company would not shun the digital revolution but instead embrace it. A few markets, like Tampa, had begun to demonstrate the real potential of doing that. But the divisional structure still posed significant barriers; supported by the mostly good economic times in those years, the company treated Bryan's rallying cry more as aspirational vision than operating reality. Chief operating officer (COO) Reid Ashe recalled a cross-divisional working group of leaders set up during the same period to facilitate "convergence collaboration" across the divisions. One of their first accomplishments was to charter for themselves "Standards of Respect"—which they swore to honor whenever the internal negotiations about working more closely together became too heated. It happened frequently.

Nonetheless, as the years passed, and despite the occasional tension among the divisions, most forward-looking leaders in the company knew the digital convergence was coming. The real question was whether and how Media General could more deliberately take advantage of it, particularly in its business model. The crisis of 2008 forced the issue—big-time.

The Perfect Storm—and the Search for Opportunity

The year 2008 was indeed a perfect storm of multiple challenges pressuring the company at the same time. Like other media companies dependent on classifieds and traditional cost-per-thousand advertising, Media General was on the losing end of the click-through advertising revolution of online information businesses. Despite heroic efforts at Web portals and the like, the company's culture and center of gravity was still heavily based on the traditional media approaches. Its divisional structure was not nimble enough to pivot toward needed new directions. Into the mix roared the catastrophic 2008 recession, which ravaged all forms of media spending. Contributing to the collective stress during that same year was the addition of some poker-faced new directors on the board, put forward by an activist major shareholder (and hedge fund manager). "Is it not possible," the hedge fund manager asked as he cast the vote for the new directors' election, "that some venture capital experience might make for a helpful contribution to Media General's strategy?"

Though Media General remained firmly in the Bryan family hands, due to a dual stock ownership structure, there was no doubt that the shadow of the "dissident investors" began to threaten the focus inside the company. With each passing day, the new board members were, in the words of vice president George Mahoney, "becoming a major internal distraction," especially amid the free fall of the U.S. economy.

The new board members were asking demanding performance-oriented questions, exacerbated by the fast-eroding economy and advertising markets. Earlier in the spring, Mario Gabelli, another longtime investor, had invited the hedge fund manager and Marshall Morton—now CEO, after a transition into the role with Bryan's support in 2005—to join in an open debate about shareholder value at a meeting at the Harvard Club in New York. By all reports, CEO Morton acquitted himself very well that morning and outargued his adversary. But when the dissident directors were nonetheless voted onto the board, Morton knew, debates under Ivy League banners aside, that the only real—and appropriate—defense was to create more value across the company. What was the right way to move the company forward amid the new digital revolution?

After the annual meeting in April, Morton began a series of conversations with his direct reports and others around the company. He shared with them all the challenge he had been living for the last several months: what are the real opportunities to increase value, given both the new world of media and a collapsing U.S. economy?

How Best to Change the Game?

In style and manner, Marshall Morton is a refined but unassuming leader. Courteous and soft-spoken, silver-haired and with an understated dignity, he has been widely respected for his long experience in the operational and business planning of the company. Stewart Bryan had hand-selected and mentored Marshall Morton to be his CFO in 1990, and then helped steer his promotion to CEO fifteen years later. The two had always worked well together, with Bryan, "a newspaper's newspaperman with a deep love of journalism," appreciating and respecting the more substantial business and operating skills of Morton. Morton, in fact, came into Media General from the textiles industry.

Marshall Morton respected the world of journalism—"I had always thought about it primarily as a valuable public service"—but held no pretensions about an editorial career. He knew that he had been recruited into the company for his experience as a businessman. In his early years at Media General, he was surprised at how loosely revenue was tracked, and how few operational processes and structures were actually in place. He worked diligently to build up a disciplined reporting and planning framework at both the corporate and the divisional level. After some initial concern about his lack of media experience, he came to appreciate how much his perspective, coming from a nonmedia business, could be helpful to his new company. As the competitive pressures and economic challenges became more intense during the digital revolution, he saw how much value could be created by an enhanced professional and streamlined operational approach. At the same time, well aware of how such things can threaten or disrupt a journalistic culture, he consistently worked changes quietly, behind the scenes, and in such a way as to gently nudge rather than convulse the Media General organization.

But the speed with which digital change was affecting all media companies in 2008 now called for more than gentle nudging. It was also clear to Morton that his traditional way of managing—private, one-on-one or small conversations with relevant colleagues—would not be able to accelerate the new solutions and new thinking that the situation now called for. He had built a strong group of vice presidents who comprised his five direct reports—but he rarely gathered them together for formal meetings. He realized now that without more collective thinking and problem solving, Media General would never be able to take the leap required. In the weeks following his Harvard Club debate, he decided it was time to change that.

Establishing the R&R Group

On the morning of May 13, Marshall Morton sent a short memo, titled "R&R," asking his leadership group to come together more formally and to help him with a process of necessary change—to "Rework" internal inefficiencies and "Remove" external barriers to performance:

> It's clear that, as a corporation, we recognize the need [to] adapt to a changing customer. It's equally clear that, even though recognizing the need for change, our divisions are still, in part, so heavily invested in their past and current heritage that they are not always fully able to achieve it. As a group, we have a role to play there. In fact, we *have* to play a role there.
>
> Naturally enough, there continue to be instances where old-time thinking crops up in our divisions and there are pockets of resistance even to the need for change. Complicating it further, some of our customers resist any change while those who comprise the real value of our future are demanding that we either change or lose them ...[2]

The memo included a list of topics under each of the Rs, which would become the starting agenda for the group's work, including such issues as operating improvements, selling assets, staff efficiencies, transitions to mobile phone advertising, capital allocation, innovation, and so forth. In traditional terms, one might have characterized it as an overall strategy rethink and the beginning of a formal planning process. But the style and process of the engagement that followed was very different—and thus begins the real story of building a particular, culturally attuned form of organizational decision making. It laid the foundation for not just a reorganization but a new way of exercising judgment more broadly about their business.

As Morton and his team recount how they worked together in the R&R group, a picture emerges of a deliberate effort by the company leader to open up new thinking and eliminate traditional boundaries for solutions. From the very first, the tone set was informal and conversational. As Jim Woodward, then head of HR and one of the members of these planning meetings, recalls, "Marshall made it instantly clear that we were going to work together as total peers. The tone was one of shared problem solving, conversation, and open dialogue. Marshall spoke simply and directly, no ego, no hidden politics, and no consulting-ese. It set a tone that prevailed through all the work." George Mahoney echoed the same: "Informal, collaborative, and inclusive. There were no presentations expected or even allowed." Lou Anne Nabhan, Media General's vice president of corporate communications and a member of the R&R group, added a further note: "You have to understand that we all share a background and values of the southern culture: courtesy, civility, and respect. It was another part of the secret sauce for those meetings."

But the informality and civility of the conversations did not imply a lack of discipline, hard problem solving, or forward momentum. The group felt a sense of urgency. As the meetings progressed, the group members developed an increasing focus of inquiry and built their own form of process discipline as a working team. The original list of topics from the first R&R memo was winnowed down early on, and as the collective learning proceeded, the group devised a brief charter to enhance even further the focus of their work together. Proposed changes and refinements to the status quo had to address one of five themes, or they were discarded: speed to market, product development improvement, getting closer to the customer, "Web-first" business integration, or increased efficiency and flow of information across the corporation. As thinking advanced, the group took steps to structure their progress—documenting decisions made, highlighting points of disagreement or requiring more inquiry, and establishing a working agenda for the kickoff of the next meeting. Under the surface of the discussion, there was a quiet codification of interim decisions, and a drawing and redrawing of the course for the continuing journey in search of solutions.

Marshall Morton's style, low-key and even self-effacing, perfectly suited the tone of the meetings, and he created a culture of peers working together on different ideas that evolved into answers; it was a conversation moving slowly but deliberately to greater and greater clarity about performance-critical issues, the opposite of a leader simply "getting feedback on his ideas" or the formalistic strategic planning that many leadership teams engage in.

Designing for Good Judgment

Like many seemingly effortless activities, the working engagement of the R&R team in fact had more than a little conscious design surrounding it. First was the membership of the group. Though a CEO gathering his direct reports for enhanced performance planning hardly seems revolutionary, Morton thought carefully about each person before starting R&R, seeking a good balance between cultural compatibility and diversity of thought:[3] "These people had different backgrounds but the same agenda—making Media General successful. They were good thinkers, and had complementary skills: some financial, some operational, and most of them had done a range of different things in the company before. They were all honest and had shown themselves as highly ethical professionals, which was critical in order to create the climate we needed in the room." Because Morton had actually not worked with them before as a formal team, bringing them together was its own new step with a particular intent: "I realized we needed more of a group dynamic for the problem solving we had to do. I wanted to avoid the danger of 'one-dimensional decision making.' I knew I couldn't dream up all the ideas myself. I just needed help."

A second aspect of the design was the trust and personal motivation built into the process. As Morton remarked, "One of the very first things I said, is 'Whatever comes out of this, you will all have a job here. It might be different than today, but you will still be working for Media General.'" (In the ultimate changes that resulted from the reorganization, careful efforts were made to redeploy rather than lay off people in management positions—signaling evolution and the embrace of change.) From the get-go, the CEO set a tone of constructive debate and deliberation: "I encouraged them at every step of their responsibility to disagree and debate as we worked through the issues. Which they certainly did." Morton felt comfortable promoting this kind of approach, having grown up with a father who was a business academic at the University of Virginia: "Debate and analysis have been in my blood since childhood. Every night at dinner, we had discussions that were like debates about case studies."

Morton further energized the work of the group by artfully tapping into the specific interests and preferences of his team around the table. As George Mahoney, vice president and general counsel, recalls, "As new issues arose in the conversations, each of us had opportunities to work on and think through particular areas that we found professionally interesting. We shared the problem solving based on what was attractive for each of us. There was an excitement in the room to think we were reinventing the company."

A third dimension of the design was the mobilization of knowledge and experience brought to bear. From the start of the process, the group was divided into subteams of two to pursue particular issues (e.g., innovation, staffing efficiencies). The subteams were chosen with deliberate cross-staffing, combining one leader with direct functional expertise and another who was relatively inexperienced in the chosen topic. "There's great value," Morton noted, "in the contribution of what might be called 'informed ignorance.'" This approach had proved very useful to the corporation through the extensive learning and implementation process of new technology during a huge Y2K project in 1999, and the group retooled many of the same principles and approaches for the R&R problem solving.

In fact, the R&R meetings really stood at the top of a pyramid of organizational input and an aggregation of learning from their businesses and customers through the years. The different organizational roles played by the members around the table through their careers at Media General ensured a richness of perspective from different parts of the business. The subteams of two, and their ongoing outreach to other leaders and experts in the corporation, ensured a tapping of relevant experience for every strategic issue examined. Division leaders were notified of the information gathering and openly invited to support the effort.

The R&R group also benefited from various background learning processes. The corporation had been running a selective high-potentials leadership development program over the last few years, which became another source of input. The program's workshops and role-playing learning exercises had repeatedly surfaced tensions about working in division silos; members of the program also freely voiced suggestions about changing the company to a market-based model. Kirk Read, formerly division leader for Internet services and now head of cross-market digital partnerships and new product development, recalls how "the leadership program made visible all the tension points and generated lots of brainstorming about how to fix those. Senior leaders of the company were part of those conversations, so the new direction had actually been percolating among a wide range of people for some time."

The sales organization across Media General also provided an ongoing intelligence system about changes in the market, another set of inputs for what became the new strategy. As one of the market sales managers noted, "We were listening to customers, and they kept talking to us about what needed to change about how we were serving them. They were frustrated, and we listened to the frustrations about how we weren't serving their real needs. More suggestions kept bubbling up from our best customers, and as they came to a crescendo, we made sure our leadership heard loud and clear. We also had launched a lot of products that fizzled in execution. But we learned from those experiences."

The Tampa market, in fact, was an epicenter of learning that directly informed R&R. Through the 1990s, the harsh competition from a large rival newspaper and rival broadcasting stations accelerated the need for more integrated content and sales efforts in that important market; some of that had in fact begun to blossom though the colocation of newspaper and broadcast staff in the same building, and a few additional collaborative initiatives promoted by Zimmerman and Harvill. Certain efforts to share content development among platforms moved ahead, and a few joint sales calls were undertaken, looking for ways to serve customers who were increasingly trying to reach many of the same audiences. But a substantive and truly integrated market approach never took root. Incentives were not fully aligned, and the commission structure did not encourage any significantly new approaches to the traditional media sales models.

Meanwhile, the ongoing success of the local Media General Internet service (Tampa Bay Online) tended to confuse more than strengthen the company's overall strategy in the region. As Kirk Read, then the leader of the digital division, remembers, "We were both the victims and perpetrators of changes in the market." But over the years, the lessons and the struggles of the Tampa "convergence experience" were front and center for the company, given the size of the market. The urgency of making substantial change burned even more brightly in Tampa, after its overbuilt real estate economy became an agonizing bellwether for the broader recession of 2008. CEO Morton reflected, "We always saw Tampa as a laboratory. It's where we first experimented with what to do about convergence, and through the years we watched it closely, including through some staff layoffs there that the down economy forced upon us. The Tampa experience—lessons about the difficulty of merging different media cultures on the content side, and getting the right sales processes and incentives for a whole new way of work—all of that was a major factor in our thinking by the time we started our work with the R&R group."

Moving Toward a Decision for Change

Members of the R&R group recall, as Marshall Morton's first memo hinted, that the process started out without any preordained outcome; the initial hypotheses were that various operational and incremental improvements could be found to enhance the overall performance of Media General. But with each passing meeting, and the aggregation of learning and ongoing debates about various courses of action, the elephant of overall reorganization entered the room. Members of the group began to talk about it informally, and the idea was kicked around in smaller conversations between the meetings. After while a consensus emerged that this kind of decision was really the best option. By mid-November, all understood that the real truth of action was now before them. One more meeting was convened, and as the R&R group entered the room and settled themselves in their conference room chairs, there was more than a little anticipation in the air.

"I think we're ready." Marshall Morton spoke quietly to his colleagues across the table. His announcement—to now start reorganizing the entire corporation—was not surprising after so many hints and tentative suggestions in previous meetings. But the short and direct statement imposed a momentary silence in the room. Jim Woodward glanced quickly out at the shadowy November afternoon and then quickly across to his colleague COO Reid Ashe. Jim broke the silence—and the sudden seriousness of the occasion—with a characteristic exclamation: "Daaaaamn! We're going to do this." Everyone laughed and then looked back at Marshall who was also smiling. They all knew they were about to begin to completely overhaul Media General—setting sails to catch the wind unleashed by the gales of the digital revolution.

By now they also understood what they really had not in the beginning: that the process initiated by Marshall Morton would also start a whole new way of working—not just for the company, but how the leadership of the company would start making decisions together. The R&R meetings had been building a more collaborative approach to strategic problem solving, a more open embrace of differing views, and gave new, special emphasis to learning from market feedback and experiments in innovation in different business units across the corporation. They were working together in a new way, and all felt the excitement of what this new kind of judgment promised for each of them and their company.

Taking the Leap

As the meeting got under way, it was also clear to the assembled members in the room that this would be no simple redrawing of a few boxes on an organization chart, or a token effort to bolt on some new form of

Web-based journalism to an old-fashioned business model. This team also sensed that the change implied would bruise some egos, create stressful personnel shifts, and start a cascading effect that would touch thousands of loyal employees. But what they embarked upon would turn out to be worth all that—a strategically shrewd and industry-pacing decision by a multi-property media company. Indeed, with the decision they took, the company, as COO Reid Ashe smiled and remarked, "went for the touchdown pass": choosing to embrace rather than simply "manage" the new digital convergence of traditional and new channels of information, and structure its business model (and particularly sales efforts) around the embrace. It was a bold and pioneering move, which other media companies are only now beginning to pursue for themselves.

From Platforms to Markets

The essence of the decision is simply told: a corporation of twenty-one daily newspapers, eighteen network-affiliated TV stations, and over two hundred specialty publications and Web sites abandoned its long-standing organizational and strategic approach of different divisions based on platforms—television, print journalism, and Internet-based information—and transitioned to a higher-performing operating model organized wholly by local markets. Thereafter, content would be provided to audiences in whatever form they wanted to receive it. Journalists began to contribute and cross-promote their information across all media channels. Advertising customers were served holistically on the basis of business and media need in their locale, rather than the form of technology delivering the content. George Mahoney, vice president and general counsel, summarized the change succinctly: "We moved our business to serving customers in market regions. Other media companies still see themselves as collections of platforms."

Here again, the process by which the Media General team got there is its own intriguing story. The R&R group quickly realized that the real work was not just the concept but the details of exactly how it would work: what would the new structure, the necessary processes, and all the needed supporting changes be? Each of the leaders, having done serious time in operational roles and become familiar with all the different dimensions of the business, knew that the promise of new value would really come in so many small changes in the nuts and bolts of the machine, and not in just the announcement of some brand-new vision about the glory of digital convergence.

In fact, the most important deliberations of the R&R group began after the decision to reorganize the company around customers and markets. A few minutes after the laughter of Jim Woodward's initial humorous exclamation in the all-critical November meeting, Marshall Morton called out the challenge: "So if this is going to work, what would it look like?" Woodward jumped to his feet, grabbed some paper, and started drawing some simple variations of a new organizational structure for the group to react to. His colleagues looked over the paper, and the simple sketch started a whole new conversation—friendly, experimental, full of "What about this?" or "What about that?", with others lifting pencils to suggest different ways the divisions could be replaced with market groupings. In subsequent meetings, the "map of the company," as it came to be known, became the central problem-solving artifact of the conversations—a safe and open exhibit for different ideas to be explored, tried out, and debated; after each meeting, Woodward and Morton redrew the models, readying material for the next round of brainstorming and "pros and cons arguments." As the overall concept solidified, problem solving shifted to more and more nuanced debates about specific geographic boundaries for markets, and the details of new roles focused on preserving the best elements from the divisional structure (e.g., various kinds of best-practice sharing, operational improvements, and digital entrepreneurialism) while still eliminating the costly elements of the former organizational silos.

By March of that year, the overall new model had been detailed and agreed upon—but the process of learning and input gathering did not stop there. CFO John Schauss, a member of R&R, gathered all the financial officers of Media General businesses and tested iteratively the evolving new direction with them to surface any additional ideas or problems with the new direction from an operational perspective. As the R&R process moved toward conclusion, Morton also brought the division heads—whose jobs and organizational units were about to go away—into the R&R meeting. He presented them with the new direction, probing them for issues and details that might have been overlooked—and then engaged them in helping to lead the transition to the market structure.

Key managers from all across the company were also engaged. The CEO also sent an explanatory letter to all Media General staff about the forthcoming changes; Lou Anne Nabhan's team set up a feature on the Media General intranet for comments, questions, and reactions from across the company—"and in fact we got some really good suggestions about different things which we incorporated in the final solution." Jim Woodward recalled, "At every step we were talking to and learning from our people. We knew we couldn't come up with all the ideas ourselves."

On March 23, 2009, Media General publicly announced its new operating structure and its full and integrated approach of digital convergence, leveraging aggressively content production and distribution across all platforms. Even more important, the market-centric model created a new sales organizational structure and a 100 percent commission plan that reinforced and rewarded customer-centric solution selling for the first time, and more generally supported new entrepreneurial approaches across the company. By the time of the official rollout, it had been thoroughly vetted, underpinned with operational support, and stress-tested from all different directions by a range of different stakeholders. The size of the leap being taken was surprising—but by the summer of 2009, as the new plan moved into full implementation, the strategy itself was not a surprise.

Initial Indicators of Success

Media General's degree of integration and embrace of digital convergence across print, broadcasting, and Internet platforms was pioneering. At the date of this writing, no other company had so fully integrated crossover content creation and advertising business development, though others are quickly doing what they can to follow Media General's lead. After the new model was announced, sales results in many markets began to outpace competitors'.[4] Digital sales postrestructuring rose fourfold across the company, with quotas met months earlier in the financial year. Visitors to the digital media local Web sites over the last years have risen substantially, as have the revenues attributable to those markets; and the new strategy has also opened up a host of unexpected opportunities for Media General people to work with new segments of third parties in the consolidated markets, including radio stations, coupon companies, and the like. All that said, the real assessment of the strategy will require a longer-term perspective, looking beyond the volatility of the persisting recession, and must also wait until better measurements are in place to track the consolidated sales of different media in industry markets.

Equally important, the Media General market-based strategy, shaped in large part by how the decision was made and developed across the organization, has also had many intangible benefits. Kirk Read voiced how the new model has wiped away years of frustration he and other colleagues felt during the "battles of the silos": "For the first time, we've created full alignment across the entire organization. Everyone knows what's expected and is now translating that clarity of focus into real competitive performance." His enthusiasm was echoed by Marilyn Hammond: "The new structure creates real incentives for our salespeople to work together to serve advertising customers holistically in a region. The accountability has shifted from serving the platform and the division to serving the customer in his local market. It's also opened up much more entrepreneurial and creative thinking about media selling among our people."

With the new model, salespeople have incentives to create cross-platform solutions for individual customers, working more collaboratively for their needs and not just "posting numbers on the scoreboard for the division." New sales partnerships have also blossomed, tapping into the experience and innovation of companies such as Yahoo!, Monster, Zillow, and others. And content development now also increasingly leverages multiple platforms and resources in each market, providing different vantage points and views on local issues while still drawing from a core of underlying facts. Overall, the new strategy increases content efficiency and advertising placement while also aggregating audience growth more effectively.

Reflections on Organizational Judgment at Media General

On the surface, Media General's leap into the new strategy—essentially "from product to market"—might seem relatively simple and even predictable. But no one should underestimate how challenging it really was. This was not a risk-seeking company with a historically well-structured decision-making process, nor can it be held up as a model of carefully constructed analytical frameworks and methodical gathering and application of knowledge applied to big strategic moves. It had evolved mostly organically, for many years buttressed by the healthy economics of media properties and the guiding hand of a journalistically inclined and protective family management.

What the story does tell of, instead, is a company that summoned up some greater collective wisdom in the face of a sudden crisis—major recession, difficult board dynamics, and a declining business model. The tale of Media General that began in 2008 was of a leader who quickly, if informally, constructed a system of greater organizational judgment that brought together diverse and distributed problem solving in a climate of open-ended deliberation. The relative ease with which Marshall Morton, working with his colleagues, did so benefited from the openness to learning embedded in its culture. That culture combined with an appreciation for civility and dignity of the individual that is characteristic of a business owned by a family and historically governed for "the public good."

CEO Marshall Morton, triggered to action by external challenges, went through his own minor transformation as a leader—from a collegial but often solitary decision-making executive, to one understanding and building shared commitment among many other professionals to find new solutions together for the ever-harsher new operating environment. The process he led and the context that he slowly shaped around him reflected some of the same almost paradoxical dimensions of his own background— deep experience and familiarity of the Media General business coupled with a challenging perspective carried over from a nonnewspaper industry; comfort with the value of intellectual debate coupled with a consistent insistence on operational grounding and process; a sense of mission to lead the company through a difficult time, coupled with a ready listening to the ideas of others, even including those who challenged him directly. When Jim Woodward described the overall process of the R&R work as "organized messy," he was in fact reflecting the broader culture and leadership of Media General overall in recent years: following a strong compass, but often in unpredictable and even nonlinear ways. Members of the R&R team report that the new approach that evolved out of their strategy making has been institutionalized, with new initiatives launched to accelerate innovation and new product ideas, and an expanded leadership council that brings a wider range of executives together for planning and deliberations, following the more open culture first pioneered by R&R.

Researchers have long recognized how important a leader can be in making a group or team work together and get to better decisions collectively. Whether it is helping with "sense making," establishing a safe environment for constructive debate and dissent, assembling the right players at the table, or simply encouraging the best ideas to come forward in the course of discussion and deliberation, leaders can make all the difference in building and leveraging judgment across a wider group.[5] Great leaders are well aware of how many cognitive traps and biases any single person—including him- or herself—brings to a decision, and the egoless leader recognizes that he or she must authentically depend on and mobilize others as a counterbalance to those traps.[6]

Over the past few years, leadership research and practice has increasingly moved away from the Great Man theory to models that are in certain ways more "democratic" and certainly understand and embrace more collaborative and even "servant" or "leading from behind" mind-sets.[7] These more contemporary models of leadership, consistent with the overall theme of this book, implicitly recognize the power of leveraging colleagues, partners, and "networks of knowing," trading away absolute power and hierarchy for more facilitative leadership that engages a broader and diverse mind for the challenges of today's more complex business environments. CEO Marshall Morton's approach to making the new strategy and organizational structure for Media General is a small case study of this kind of shift, and has had a positive impact on the judgment capability of his company.

11

The Wallace Foundation

How Can We Focus a Strategy for More Mission Impact?

SINCE ITS ORIGINS (in the multimillion-dollar family philanthropies of DeWitt and Lila Wallace, founders of *Reader's Digest*), the New York–based Wallace Foundation had always funded a wide range of cultural and educational programs. During the 1990s, however, its president, Christine DeVita, was increasingly bothered that its charitable giving wasn't making a real difference in society: "We were making a lot of grants to a lot of organizations, but it just wasn't creating any long-term change. We were dealing more with symptoms than root causes." After presiding over hundreds of grants totaling nearly $1 billion, she found that her concerns continued to grow. She began a series of conversations with board members, which culminated, in 1999, in a series of challenges that the board addressed to themselves: How could they concentrate the efforts of the foundation much more, to drive more sustainable impact over time? How could the foundation develop an overall mission and strategy that took them beyond "just distributing money?"[1]

That year, the board answered their own challenges with a new direction for the institution. Guided by DeVita's urging, they moved away from making small grants to hundreds of worthy causes, and vowed instead to focus on a much more limited set of issues. In so doing, the foundation would drive for more measurable and sustainable impact, concentrating its effort to make more of a collective difference in its mission.

In that same meeting, one of the focal areas that the board selected for programs in the future was decided to be—public school leadership. "Looking back," reflected DeVita, "it might have been something we could have guessed. The board members were all interested in education, and they were all CEOs or similar senior positions in their own organizations. Leadership was a natural thing for them to want us to pursue."[2]

But the mandate from the foundation directors left quite a wide berth for interpretation and actual implementation. In a complex socioeconomic system like public education, "leadership" is everywhere, at multiple levels—how were they to understand what kind of leadership really mattered, how to intervene to do something about it, and indeed what "meaningful intervention" was even required? What had at first seemed like a decision about a difficult dilemma suddenly became many smaller dilemmas—and posed even more difficult choices for the executives charged with carrying out the mission. For indeed, the board not only had left somewhat ambiguous the *what* but had been even less specific about the *how*. Greater focus made all the sense in the world—but how would Christine DeVita turn that directional guidance into something real and measurable?

This case is the story of how Christine DeVita and her team at The Wallace Foundation answered those questions—and made the kind of decisions implied by the new mandate of the board. In getting to those decisions, DeVita had to set a new context for better judgment. She had to change the way they worked—how they were structured, how they operated together. And in so doing, DeVita herself had to change her own way of leading, as did members of her executive team at the foundation. The creation of new organizational judgment at The Wallace Foundation was born of both structural and cultural change, and transformation of the foundation leadership itself.

Shining New Light . . . on School Principals

In the years after the 1999 board meeting, DeVita and her educational team gave greater focus to their grant making. They conducted a series of experiments, research probes, and policy engagements related to different aspects of public school leadership. Although there were a few other foundations that had started to explore opportunities to enhance school leadership, this early work of The Wallace Foundation raised the visibility of its fundamental importance. In time, their efforts focused even more, specifically highlighting the criticality of school principals.

Before then, most educational reform efforts were focused on other things, such as improving teachers or raising specific academic standards. The landmark 1983 study *A Nation at Risk* barely mentioned public school leadership as a source of potential leverage; in the 1990s, great attention was focused on voucher programs and charter schools—the latter of which grew into a nationwide movement—as reform advocates sought to lessen or circumvent the role of teachers' unions.[3] The Bill and Melinda Gates Foundation, in its early years of programming after 2000, bet big on creating smaller schools as the "theory of change." And throughout the last thirty years, there have been ongoing efforts by multiple reformers to revolutionize learning with technology. In all cases, forward progress has been frustratingly elusive.

To be clear, it's not that improving teachers, sponsoring charters, or using technology was ever wrong; rather, it was that all the reform efforts seemed to miss what in retrospect was a hugely obvious piece of also needed change—the leader in charge in the organizations where children were every day trying to learn: the school principal. Looking back, Chris DeVita marveled at everyone's (including, at first, her and her own team's) relative naïveté: "In all other sectors—military, corporate, governmental—we all just assume that leadership matters. But somehow it wasn't supposed to be important for schools. It was, on its face, a really ridiculous assumption. But as a result, nobody was really paying any attention to it."

Today, it is generally agreed how ridiculous the omission really was. The Wallace Foundation strategy has positively influenced multiple other efforts. State and district policy makers and supervisors now emphasize selecting and training school principals; and other reform-minded institutions (e.g., the Broad Foundation) have dedicated strategies to support principals and other public school leaders. And though there is notorious complexity in demonstrating a definitive source of change in any multivariable environment, there is growing evidence that school leadership really does matter. In 2004, researcher Kenneth Leithwood (with others) demonstrated that it influences some 25 percent of the overall "effects" of a school environment; similarly, in evaluating dozens of cases and quantitative studies, his team also found that "there are virtually no documented instances of a troubled school being turned around absent the intervention by a powerful leader."[4] Since then, evidence has continued to mount. A recent study by researchers from universities in Minnesota and Toronto, which analyzed thousands of students in 180 different schools, showed the impact on student achievement based on "the collective and individual efficacy of their principals."[5]

Chris DeVita, with characteristic modesty, believes, "we still need to keep tracking the evidence-based research to fully understand how leadership actually makes the difference"—but also notes it is now firmly on the nationwide education reform agenda. In addition to language in new federal legislation about leadership importance, secretary of education Arne Duncan now insists that federal aid to failing schools must include raising the performance of principals: "If, at the end of the day, our 95,000 schools each had a great principal, this thing [creating high-performing schools] would take care of itself."[6] This new thinking continues to ripple through the sector. Business and educational graduate schools have revised their school leadership development programs, in light of the best practices and standards resulting from Wallace work.

Building the "Culture of Inquiry"

But if DeVita and her team can rightly be proud of building much-needed momentum around school leadership for educational reform, it was not a strategy easily developed or simply just "decided." They arrived at this field-changing perspective after years of study, trial and error with grant making, and continuous learning—and, in parallel, some significant and stressful organizational change in their own institution. Alongside—and indeed in service to—the game-changing decision to shift educational reform toward leadership, DeVita reinvented The Wallace Foundation. The strategic decision-making process was embedded in an internal organizational transformation of the foundation: from a siloed, fragmented philanthropic institution to a more unified organization devoted to public engagement and impact, based on what DeVita calls "creating a culture of inquiry."

The essence of the change was shifting a philanthropic institution away from "giving money" to instead generating and disseminating knowledge aimed at creating real and measurable difference on the ground, across America. To do this, The Wallace Foundation built a new decision-making and problem-solving organizational culture. It created a new and more robust capability of organizational judgment.

This transformational journey had many detours and bumps in the road—just like the foundation's ultimate strategic decision itself: to focus on school leadership. One decision-making moment that tells the story of both came in the afternoon of a summer day in 2005, a pivotal moment in shaping the new strategy, when the criticality of school principals came to the fore.[7]

Preparing the Next Chapter of Strategy
for the Board

"It was an unusually bright and sunny afternoon," Edward Pauly, The Wallace Foundation's director of research and evaluation, recalled. "Our interdisciplinary team that was focused on education was meeting in one of the smaller windowed rooms in the foundation. The sun was just streaming in." Pauly, looking back at this critical meeting, hinted that the glaring light only added to the intensity of the occasion: "We all knew it was going to be an important discussion, and we were coming in with different points of view about the right strategy. We all believed that somebody was going to have to give something up. How would we get to a final answer?"

Edward Pauly is a tall, silver-haired man with the polish and demeanor reflecting the Yale professor and professional researcher he had previously been. Joining Wallace in 1996, he was a respected and senior voice in planning and problem-solving sessions. Pauly was known for "honoring the data" and not jumping too quickly to conclusions; DeVita joked that "he knows so much, he almost talks in footnotes." But in the heat of debate, others sometimes saw Pauly's academic discipline and skepticism as a brake on the urgent progress that national education reform required. The interdisciplinary team working on the topic brought strong and passionate voices to the table. For every objection of someone like Pauly, there were other calls for action, colleagues looking for faster forward progress, even if the data was not 100 percent in place to endorse it.

Opposite Pauly sat Richard Laine, the younger and articulate foundation program director of education, who joined Wallace in 2002 after major roles at the Illinois State Board of Education and with advanced business and policy degrees from the University of Chicago. "Strong personality, politically very savvy, and a real big-picture guy," as DeVita briefly sketched him. Also in the meeting, opposite Laine, sat Lucas Held, the quick-witted director of communications, with plenty of his own educational experience from his days of public affairs leadership at

Columbia's Barnard College. The group included a few others too, with still other perspectives. Laine was accompanied by senior program officer Jody Spiro, brought into the foundation not only for her multiple successes in different educationally oriented nonprofits, but also for professional experience in change management and leadership development. Senior communications officer Jessica Schwartz added some right-brain thinking to the mix. An art historian by training and a skilled public relations executive, she had spent her earlier career working with artists and critics at the Museum of Modern Art and the Guggenheim. An attractive, auburn-haired woman, Schwartz speaks with the style of New Yorkers at their best, peppering her direct, to-the-point comments with sardonic humor.

The purpose of the meeting was to revise overall strategy about Wallace Foundation programming and investment in educational reform, for presentation at another upcoming board meeting. The meeting would present to the directors the latest incarnation of the executive team's thinking, the next iteration of strategy that had continued to evolve since the board's focusing mandate in 1999. Such looming occasions, as Richard Laine wryly noted, "always seemed to force more clarification about our thinking." What now was "requiring more clarification" was how exactly the foundation should go about promoting and enhancing the quality of school leadership as part of its ever-evolving work; the strategy, as was said, still had a lot of "sprawl" and needed even further focus. Looking back, Chris DeVita noted that "each constituency on our team—program, evaluation, communications—had their own oar in the water about how the boat should go forward." The details of program development, implementation, and measurement can be subtle, but in broad strokes the debate in this meeting was about where to invest grant dollars in the future. Laine and Spiro had been steadily working with their partner states and districts, building educational programs, looking for systemic change. Their strategies had some emphasis on principal leadership, but in 2005 they were also wrestling with whether to pursue other levers for improving school leadership, such as with teachers' unions and school boards. Laine acknowledged that there had been various disappointments in initial implementation of the different state and district-level programs. Nonetheless, given his own experience in Illinois and his firm belief in the need to reach for greater scale, he and his team still wanted to emphasize the state role in the leadership strategy.

Finding a Stronger Solution in the Scribbles

Pauly, true to form, was skeptical. He felt that state leaders were too often ineffectual, and not the right focus for change: "We had been looking at the data, including especially where the Wallace money was ending up. The empirical story was about school principals as the key point of leverage, and where skills and support were most needed. They seemed to be the only ones making a difference." As the meeting got under way, the debate was at first not so neatly parsed. In the first thirty minutes, people listened patiently to one another, and many issues were talked around, knowledgeably but without clear agreement. Eventually, frustration in the room rising, the proceedings became more intense. The discussion began to center on a drawing one of them first sketched on the whiteboard in the room. Members of the team started to add to the graphical representations, with different people scribbling to interpret somewhat differently how the different players in the ever-complicated system of public education were either fostering or hindering change. The strategy question was where in the overall system Wallace should now intervene. As Pauly recalls, "We all came into the meeting with our own version of what the picture should be. After a while, we were drawing back and forth on the whiteboard, trying to get to a common map of what we all could agree to."

But as Held and Schwartz watched—also adding their own comments along the way—what struck each of them, as communications professionals, was how complicated the whole picture was. And the consensus-building efforts on the drawing were making the story less clear with each passing minute. Laine and Spiro gave some ground but still hammered away, making strong arguments based on all that had been learned in states and districts. Ed Pauly was polite but firm. He just didn't want to trade away what he felt the data was telling them.

Schwartz glanced at her boss, Held. How could they explain it more simply? The conversation and debate and the whiteboard drawing continued. Yet, after about ninety minutes, and some not always restrained emotion, a sense of consensus started to emerge. Schwartz stood up and asked for the marker, having listened carefully for the last few minutes. She spoke with her characteristic New York style: "Look, I'm just hearing it over and over now. The conversation keeps coming back here—," and with that she drew a big red circle around the word *principals* on the whiteboard map that the group was all staring at.

It crystallized a sudden sense of solution. Pauly's insistence on the data implications had been gaining traction, and Laine and Spiro respected the spirit of give-and-take that had honestly aired opposing views. Pauly in turn acknowledged, which his program colleagues had been arguing, that effective leadership at the school principal level still needed "supporting systems"—standards, training, and overall conditions—to ensure that leaders in individual schools could be successful. What began as a debate evolved into a stronger and ultimately agreed-upon solution. Wallace-supported work would now focus even more on school principals—as the main lever of change—but do so in the context of creating an overall "leadership system" at all levels, aligning training, standards, and other forms of support (e.g., access to increasingly more refined versions of student achievement data) to increase the chances of individual success. As Chris DeVita later reflected, "The team understood that they couldn't just create 'islands of excellence' in this or that school while everything else in the broader sea of reform was floundering."

Though this decision-making meeting had been heated, it had not become personal. As participants reflected on the occasion, it was clear that it had been one more installment in their development of Christine DeVita's culture of inquiry. Richard Laine recalled that when Schwartz stood up and drew the circle, "the light bulb went on for all of us." Tough but honest deliberation had moved the conversation toward closure, and within days the strategy was drafted for presentation to the board, emphasizing investment in focusing on and building capability of school principals, complemented by a broader system of support at the district and state levels. The decision also focused Wallace work by eliminating other areas of possible reform that had previously been considered—"We make strategy as much by what we don't do as what we do do," commented DeVita.

Later, the next month, the board roundly endorsed the principal and leadership system proposal. The executive team moved forward and continued to build on the strategy, increasing the success of the intervention year after year. And in so doing, they also continued to refine and further shape the culture of inquiry within their own organization.

Origins and Early Development of the Culture of Inquiry

To appreciate this new culture and the change it engendered, we must look back again to the earlier days of The Wallace Foundation; and we must also understand the normal approach to structure and responsibilities found in most philanthropic foundations. For many foundations—and so was the case for The Wallace Foundation in the years surrounding the critical 1999 board meeting—the "core business units" are the grant-making program officers, who decide what kind of issues and organizations to fund in the sectors of their interest (arts, education, human services, etc.). The evaluation people are typically a separate function, though they usually report up to the program staff.[8] As the title suggests, it is their job to evaluate the progress and/or variances of how and whether grants given are actually working. However, they are normally not called upon to offer up a lot of strategy about what it all means. Communications is also typically a separate "corporate" function, whose main job is to issue press releases, create brochures and reports, and provide information to interested audiences about the work of the institution. At the risk of overstatement, they, too, are tasked more with dissemination and execution than with any kind of strategic thinking. In sum, the program people do the hard analysis and make the strategic decisions, while evaluation keeps track of the progress, and communications disseminates the (hopefully) good news.

Over time, Christine DeVita saw the limitations of this standard model for The Wallace Foundation. Trained as a corporate lawyer, she had always understood the importance of evidence and fact-based argument. When, after the 1999 board meeting, the decision was made to focus one major part of the foundation work on educational leadership, DeVita sensed that what was called for was not just a change of content for their work but now also a change of process of *how they would work* to pursue that strategy. After a year or two of "business as usual" grant making in the general direction of building up different kinds of school leadership across the country (establishment of the State Action for Educational Leadership project, funding for executive training for school superintendents at the Harvard Kennedy School, and other such activities), she realized that, though helpful, the work of her organization was "still not doing what we needed." She was less bothered by the ambiguous results of the first investments—inevitable in any early-stage experimentation—than by the lack of collective problem solving and learning among her then team: "The silos were getting in the way, and we were not taking full advantage of what evaluation was learning, or the kind of constructive feedback that the field and market were telling us. We weren't engaging enough with people who weren't our grantees. And we also suffered internally from the typical foundation disease of everybody being superficially nice to one another, and never wanting to disagree about anything."

Getting Hard on Ideas

In 2001–2002, DeVita restructured her organization, bringing in some new program leaders (notably Richard Laine and Jody Spiro). Most important, she also started to build a new culture of working within and beyond the foundation. This new culture of inquiry began initially in various initiatives to break down silos, create more collaboration, and increase expectations of regular debate and challenge that was "hard on the ideas while still being soft on people." DeVita's belief was that The Wallace Foundation had to take much fuller advantage of the diversity of perspective afforded by the three key areas of contact with the field, and indeed insights from across the field per se. She also wanted to empower more than ever before her evaluation and communications teams and make them integral members of the problem-solving processes of strategy development for the organization: "Instead of seeing these people as simple evaluators of progress or disseminators of foundation work, I wanted them to play a broader role."

The new operating structure became a cross-functional, interdisciplinary team of peers—program, evaluation, and communications—all now equally on the hook for making and implementing strategy, and doing so with deeper understanding of learning both from one another and from the field. And being on the hook together began with making decisions together, such as that seen in the group meeting on that particular day in the summer of 2005.

But like all organizational changes, this one was neither quick nor painless. Traditional prerogatives and role identities persisted at first, and the group had to practice over time how to become, as Ed Pauly remembered the phrase, "critical friends." DeVita was blunt in her assessment: "I was taking away turf and it was really hard on people." She insisted that the cross-functional team go head-to-head in problem-solving sessions, which semiaffectionately became known as the "duke-it-out meetings." At every step of the way, DeVita played her role as president to reinforce the value of knowledge and learning and the culture of inquiry—and hard-on-ideas, soft-on-people debate—for the greater good of the foundation, and for what she and her team were trying to accomplish in educational reform. As she recounts the process of transformation:

> We had to learn how to do this together. We did a lot of
> organizational development work as a team, and we had to learn

about how not to "raise the white flag" when the going got rough—giving up on expressing our idea because there was opposition. Instead, we had to essentially signal to one another that "I'm not feeling that my point of view is being heard." It was about respecting one another without taking challenge personally. We had to go from disagreement meaning "you're wrong and I'm right" to "we need to check our assumptions and bring more facts to the discussion to be sure."

At first we had various tools—decision rights matrices, those kinds of things—but they were really just "training wheels" for the new bicycle of how we would work together and make decisions. Over time, like a child who masters the bike, the training wheels were taken off for the organization, no longer needed. It just became part of the culture.

Pauly and Laine both agreed with their president's impressions in a separate accounting of those years. "The key theme," as one of them recalled in a conversation about recent Wallace history, "was a constant call to 'how do we actually know?' It came to define everything we did as a team." DeVita later noted with amusement how at meetings with other foundations, executives would often express surprise: "In my foundation, people would never disagree with one another the way I just saw your team doing!"

Learning by Trial and Error

Building the culture of inquiry did not follow a carefully designed blueprint, as one might imagine in hearing after-the-fact accounts. In actual fact, there was a lot of trial and error and "learning by doing" through the years. Changing the way the foundation operated externally followed a process of test-learn-and-revise. This emerged from ongoing contact with grantees in Wallace's partner states and districts, what the research efforts were finding, and what the broader educational market was focusing on. As the strategy and cultural change progressed in tandem, DeVita continued to tinker with her team's roles and responsibilities. She continued to move, often against some real pushback, toward an organizational model indeed different from traditional foundation approaches. Over time, the team focused on making strategy that more closely followed the synthesized collective perspectives of program, evaluation, and communications, based on actual progress in the marketplace. Budget allocations came to be made following strategy needs, in step with learning from the field (as opposed to being "owned" by one function and their impressions of "the best way forward").

The new approach now also included working with public entities (policy makers, other institutions) that were engaged as both partners and challengers to the efforts of the Wallace programs. In this model, the communications group was expected to engage key decision makers and to disseminate knowledge, not for "PR points," but rather to advance the boundaries of understanding and collective learning. Similarly, evaluation staff no longer simply assessed program metrics, but was also charged to collect useful lessons from both grantees and nongrantees working in the same general field. Their new mission became to continuously identify knowledge gaps, and design evaluations to produce insights and, yes, also challenges, from a broad audience across the field. Consistent with the more outward-facing and learning-intensive approach of the culture of inquiry, the foundation also launched a regularly updated Knowledge Center on its Web site.[9] Here new advances were posted, and linked to e-mail, Twitter, and Facebook, with the goal of enabling broader learning and debate among readers and other followers of the foundation's work.

As the culture of inquiry was built through the years, so was the overall strategy of public school leadership and the eventual focus on school principals. In fact, looking back through the telescope of time, it would be unfair to emphasize disproportionately the summer afternoon meeting of 2005 and the drama-filled moment of one brave executive drawing a circle on what was then a very important diagram. Yes, it was a critical moment in a knowledge-intensive struggle to define a clear strategy; and yes, it exemplified an organization also struggling internally to come to terms with cross-functional teaming. It also symbolized the difficult cultural transformation in which no single expert could expect to prevail in his or her decision unilaterally, no matter how much experience she or he brought to bear. But faithful retelling of the story really requires a broader context and understanding of a long series of ongoing choices and progressively refined organizational learning resulting from their effects.

The new house of judgment was built slowly, one brick at a time.

The Leader Looks Back

Christine DeVita, who announced her retirement from the foundation in 2011, looked back on the change she led, and commented on what it had meant for all of them:

> It was a long process for us and a long process for the field ... There's still a lot more to do, but now, as never before, the leadership of individual schools is firmly on the public agenda, and we have appropriately elevated the importance of principals who used to be known only for things like budgets, buildings, and buses ... But in focusing on leadership in public schools and a more holistic system of thinking about it, we also had to reform our own leadership as an institution, at the same time. In the end, in so many ways, I and my team had to transform ourselves, too.

Reflections on Organizational Judgment at The Wallace Foundation

This case combines many of the same elements seen in other chapters of our book: the building of a new kind of "facts-friendly" culture, the introduction of deliberative process that encourages diversity of opinion and constructive debate, and the shift of leadership to a role that is less about wielding power than creating a climate and encouragement of marshaling and refining knowledge—from wherever it may come.

It is also worth, however, calling out the contribution of organizational structure, for that was a critical ingredient in the story, about which we have not said too much in other chapters. It is another part of the overall context that this leader built to enhance the collective judgment of her organization. Researchers and practitioners increasingly focus on finding the elusive golden mean between the organizing principle of deeper expertise that comes from aligning around functional groups on the one hand, and the more integrative value of so-called horizontal processes that focus on the creation of a product, or service, or project outcomes on the other.[10] Not surprisingly, in the new world of faster economies and rising complexities, much attention is being paid to various forms of "collaborating across the silos."[11]

There is, of course, no easy answer, but the best approaches seem to be found in organizations with the flexibility and values to somehow create a world of "both-and." The change in The Wallace Foundation took a few critical steps in this direction—raising the profile and responsibility of multiple functions needed for problem solving to the same peer level (program, communications, and evaluation); changing some key roles and responsibilities; and then instituting a new deliberative process—the duke-it-out meetings. Those meetings forced, against a set of values that embraced constructive conflict, an expectation of cross-functional analysis and synthesis of facts and beliefs. The judgment resident in the organization thrives, at its best, when professionals can both build and continue to sharpen their functional expertise but also have an explicit mechanism to exercise it in an integrated way with others who share in the same performance aspiration. Leadership that cultivates this both-and mind-set and way of working will further enhance the collective judgment of any complex organization.

12

Tweezerman

Should We Take the Business to the Next Level of Growth?

N THE LATE 1990s, the small but successful women's beauty products enterprise Tweezerman faced the dilemma that every entrepreneurial growth company eventually confronts: "How much bigger can we get—can we handle the risk, the scale, the exposure, and the demands on our capacity—if we now 'really swing for the fences'?" The particular challenge the company faced was about selling its line of prestigious, professional beauty tools to chain drugstores—risking dilution of the brand, losing existing core customers, and taking on financial commitments way beyond anything it had known before. That everything built over years of blood and hustle might come crashing down was a nontrivial possibility. But so was an increase in revenue that would elevate the company to a whole new league of wealth and market share.[1]

Founder and CEO Dal LaMagna chafed at the potential decision, and regularly paced the floor of his Long Island industrial location, talking and asking about the question with the nervous energy for which his team had always known him. By his own words, LaMagna was "a risk addict and . . . a compulsive capitalist," and deep down knew that he wanted to take his company to this next, bigger level. But he also wanted to avoid turning Tweezerman into one more failure in what had been a previous career of multiple entrepreneurial misfires. What if this last and greatest airplane, which had finally begun to fly—and fly high—now crashed and burned like so many other LaMagna ventures before? Besides, LaMagna had a lot of other interests too—humanitarian, political—and he had almost sold his company a few years before, thinking of pursuing something completely different. His leadership team reflected some of the same ambivalence. A few members continued to believe that widely expanded distribution and growth had always been the Tweezerman destiny, while others saw very clearly the risks and headaches that would come with trying to sell their distinctively branded professional products to the likes of CVS or Walgreens.

Earlier in his career, Dal LaMagna had always made such decisions alone. For many of his earlier ventures, he had de facto operated as a solo entrepreneur, so any kind of collaborative decision making was not even an option. In the early days of Tweezerman, things started out the same. But with the evolving success of the company, and the growth that followed, he began to see things differently. Over time, he had established a group of trusted executives around him, which formed a "steering committee." And they all had their own points of view, which they regularly voiced. The tension of the big-growth decision was always before them. "For years, I was a like a horse champing at the bit to do this, and the steering committee held me in the corral so we could really think it through," recalled LaMagna with a smile. "I know how reckless and impatient I can be, and these people kept me in check." In the end, the CEO and the leadership team made the final decision together—in fact, a series of interrelated and difficult decisions leading to the all-important outcome. What follows is the story of how the collective judgment they called upon was built and embedded in the entrepreneurial soul of this company, enabling what ultimately became a multimillion-dollar enterprise—and wealth for all of them beyond their wildest dreams. Of particular note is the context for better judgment that LaMagna built around him: the cultural values and sense of mutual accountability within this company that he, as founder, encouraged and reinforced steadily.

Early "Compulsive Capitalism"

Dal LaMagna's early personal and professional life—recently chronicled in his entertaining autobiography, *Raising Eyebrows: A Failed Entrepreneur Finally Gets It Right*—would not have suggested he was slated to make millions on the basis of building a special kind of beauty products company.[2] From a young age, he had tried this and that clever angle for a quick buck, most of which either fell short or utterly failed, whether selling church raffle tickets in local bars, starting a computer dating service (almost before there were computers), selling and installing waterbeds, launching discotheques in drive-in movies, trying to invent a new kind of lasagna pan, producing a just-miss Hollywood movie, or running a restaurant, which taught him, among other things, that this kind of enterprise "is the worst business in the world. Period. The end." He was smart and ambitious enough as a young man to get himself into the Harvard Business School—though he also managed to lose his student loan on the first day of class by gambling it away on a bogus stock tip (and thus becoming the only student ever to owe Harvard twice as much as it cost to attend the school!). But, ever buoyant, Dal LaMagna soldiered on year after year, relentlessly trying this or that new business idea, and steadily learning—albeit the hard way—with every new lap around the entrepreneurial track. Finally, in 1980, he launched Tweezerman—that went on to disprove the rule that Dal LaMagna always struck out.

Like so many of his other ideas, Tweezerman was an idea that grew out of an accidental insight. Thanks to an adventurous romantic frolic on a wooden deck one day in the mid-1970s, young Dal ended up with a backside full of splinters. His penance, as he searched for a pair of tweezers with needle points to pull out the painful shards of wood, was to discover the difficulty of finding any kind of suitably surgical tweezers. This led to research about a better pair of tweezers that might be available, something more precise than the normal and blunt dime-store instruments that most people used in those days. He became intrigued with tools used in industrial applications. After a series of twists and turns—characteristic of innovation when ideas from one industry are translated to another—he hit upon a pair of tweezers that was being used on the assembly line of an electronics company. He was able to adapt these tweezers to the more medical use of removing splinters. Time passed and the idea took another turn, as LaMagna, at the suggestion of an ex-girlfriend, stumbled into an even bigger market: precision tweezers for women's personal beauty care. It turned out there was a real need for a more sophisticated and specialized tweezers among the trade who served beauty-conscious women. Before long, the initial tentative purchases of a few buyers turned into a steady stream of orders.

Like so many entrepreneurs, Dal LaMagna pursued his new idea with a vengeance, but insisted on doing it all himself. Working out of a small family bungalow in Long Island, he made deals with suppliers, figured out how to create packaging, and went door-to-door pitching his product in small-scale beauty salons and then also to electrologists. He also started up a mail-order business, all out of the 400-square-foot bungalow. He was tireless and worked hard to earn some early successes; one day, one of his better beauty shop customers joked to her colleagues as he came in the door, "Here comes the Tweezerman!" Ever iconoclastic, LaMagna decided the name was better than the current Dal LaMagna Grooming—and just irreverent enough to become a new and distinctive brand. With his customer's joke, the new name of the company was born.

In the early 1980s, Tweezerman began to grow steadily, and it seemed as if Dal LaMagna might at last be on his way to creating a business that would do more than merely support him. In the first year, he pulled in about $1,800; five years later, he was booking close to $1 million annually. But he was basically working himself to a frenzy to make that happen.

However, during those first few years, LaMagna began to be more reflective. He thought back to his earlier ventures, both the many failures and the occasional brief successes he had known, working with other people. Though he had operated largely as a solo entrepreneur, he had overseen employees in a few of his earlier jobs and ventures, and had developed some appreciation of the difference that good people—or bad people—could make to a company. As he recalls, looking back, "I sort of had this epiphany. I suddenly realized what my own time was worth, and I wasn't taking advantage of what I could do when I had to do everything alone. All along I had really just been sort of a promoter, selling this or that crazy idea. And it hit me then. I had to build a company. I needed to start to hire people, and I needed to get good at picking people I could trust and who could do the job. And then keeping them. And delegation became my new mantra." Lisa Bowen, who eventually became the president of Tweezerman, remembers her boss from the early days: "At first he was a micromanager. Tried to do everything. But as he brought on more people, he changed. He realized the power of trusting people. And he did. That kind of trust of employees is priceless."

From Compulsive to Responsible Capitalism

LaMagna's realization about the power of people and organization is not unlike the transition that many successful entrepreneurs go through—but his passage from solo promoter to company builder had its own special twist. A student in the early 1970s, he had, early in his professional career, developed some social consciousness, and remembered vividly earlier experiences in which he recognized the value of treating employees and colleagues fairly. As hungry as he was for financial success, he also wanted to now build a company "for everyone to be treated in a fair and just manner—in the way I would like to be treated." His reasoning was shaped not only by a personal sense of justice or utilitarianism but also in reaction to the accelerating love affair the country began to have with business and markets in the 1980s. Way ahead of his time with his use of the phrase *responsible capitalism*, he soon made Tweezerman a personal cause to challenge the then celebration of the stark pursuit of profit and shareholder value: "I didn't care if I missed the gravy train. I had a group of wonderful employees now and they were my concern. My sisters Seri and Teri had joined the business. Yvonne Leslie came from West Virginia with her three children. We were a big family. I was intent on proving Milton Friedman wrong—corporations should not exist for the sole benefit of the shareholders but for the benefit of all stakeholders."[3]

Many of Tweezerman's first employees were in fact recruited out of the small Long Island beach community (near Port Washington) where LaMagna's bungalow and office was based. Tweezerman's president, Lisa Bowen, for example, first joined LaMagna at age eighteen, a summer intern hired as a friend of the family from the same bungalow colony. In the first years of the company, he brought much of the same "community thinking" to the development of the company culture. Planning was done in what LaMagna described as "Quaker-style meetings," and the company members soon decided, together, that a portion of their first profits would be donated to local charities.

From the very start, LaMagna also shared profits with his employees, and took opportunities to empower people while also inspiring them. He also learned about, and quickly embraced, the concept of *open book management*—helped along by his enthusiastic reading of Jack Stack's *The Great Game of Business*.[4] LaMagna put into practice its fundamental democratic workplace principles: sharing financial data with employees, encouraging them to take leadership to move measures toward greater performance, and sharing the resulting prosperity with all. At

Tweezerman this translated eventually to more formal profit-sharing programs among employees, and an extra staking of his steering committee in ownership of the company. The steering committee itself, at first simply an informal gathering of key managers, became a more formal body over time, engaging with the CEO on a regular basis, and actively contributing to all major decisions—strategy, personnel issues, company facilities, and the like. "We made decisions," LaMagna proudly recalled, "not by consensus but majority. And I did not always get my way."

In this committee, and indeed across the company more broadly, the founder worked to create a climate of open discussion, problem solving, the right to make mistakes, and the right to dissent. Frank Suttell recalled that "with Dal, the basic theme was always 'don't blame the person, find the solution.' You could make a mistake, and there was no capital punishment. Nobody had to sugarcoat reports." Lisa Bowen remembers how "Dal never lost his temper. We all trusted him, and he had an open-door policy that was real. We were constantly training employees to understand our numbers and business progress. And all of us grew over time because of the responsibility we were given, and our exposure to others as we worked on problems together." The *Tweezerman Employee Handbook* codifies this way of working, simply listing principles such as "involve all employees in ownership of the company," "equal opportunity in all employment related matters," "open communication," "encourage individual growth," and "utilize employee talents to the fullest."[5] The difference at Tweezerman from many other companies that post similar concepts on conference room walls is that Dal LaMagna really believed these things. And both in action and in his personal leadership, he actually reinforced this culture every day.

The Bumpy Road to Walgreens

The culture and collaboration of the enterprise Dal LaMagna built equipped the company well for the challenges of growth—but the journey upward was no simple climb. In 1989, Tweezerman, whose reputation for quality and service was steadily growing, had a major breakthrough. The company started a relationship that led to its biggest deal to date: Sally Beauty Supply, a Texas-based chain that was "the quintessential seller of beauty products," serving primarily the professionals of the beauty profession. When Tweezerman closed a distribution contract with Sally, it in a stroke added eight hundred outlets to its sales network, and in the first year boosted revenue by over 10 percent, much of it now falling directly to the bottom line. The deal also reenergized LaMagna, who was wondering whether he could still keep pursuing growth for his then $6 million company. Conversations with his steering committee continued to brainstorm about the much bigger prize of full-fledged retail drugstore distribution—Eckerd, CVS, Walgreens, and the like—but the Tweezerman team kept being thrown back. LaMagna stated the problem simply: "The big problem for Tweezerman going into chains was that Sally did not sell professional beauty products if they were also available in chain drugstores. Period."

But ever resourceful—getting some ideas from both his team and Mike Renzulli, the president of Sally Beauty Supply, with whom he had built a close working relationship—Dal LaMagna found a palatable compromise for his then biggest account: "What if Tweezerman were to package its products for retail outlets in a different way, and sell them under a different name—'Finer Touch'?" Renzulli nodded OK, and before long the Tweezerman team had a deal with a small retail chain called Drug Emporium in Dallas—which became an immediate disaster when the new customer started dramatically discounting the Tweezerman products. To protect the Sally account, LaMagna sent Tweezerman's sales representative in the area into the Drug Emporium stores to buy out every piece of Tweezerman products. Then because Drug Emporium was late in paying its invoices to Tweezerman, LaMagna had an excuse to close the account. A deal to sell the Finer Touch line to the even larger chain Rite-Aid got off on a good foot, but then suddenly exploded when this customer insisted on an extra discount that the team refused to give. "After we said no to the buyer," recalls Dal LaMagna, "we got back ten pallets of unsold product."

Next in line was another chain retailer, Eckerd. "Another lesson learned the hard way," recounted La Magna. "Don't sell a big customer if you can't deliver the product." The small company had no sooner started celebrating the sale when it realized that Eckerd wanted the product in its stores within thirty days. Tweezerman did not have the inventory in stock, and it would have needed three months to fill the order. Eckerd canceled the sale.

But the setbacks only hardened the determination of the Tweezerman team, and living the culture of "don't blame, find the solution," they prepared for another big sales effort. Through their earlier disappointments, the steering committee members of the young company learned what it would take, and what risks they had to prepare for, as they developed plans for the next attempt. After some further industry research, and networking among salespeople, customers, and partners, LaMagna and his people turned toward Walgreens—with a reputation for more predictable expectations about discounting and more accommodating financing relationships with suppliers.

Values and Problem Solving for the Opportunity

The steering committee met periodically, following the easy give-and-take of its operating style set by its CEO. Sometimes the members of the committee met in LaMagna's office, other times in the Tweezerman conference room, and other times their conversations simply took place in hallways or on the shop floor, less a meeting than an informal exchange among two or three of them at a given time. But despite the informality, the committee guided its discussions with particular values and by a few shared principles—"commitment to excellent products, commitment to customer service, and find ways to expand the market." As long as those kinds of beliefs were honored, debate could rage. In this particular quest, the conversations also followed a clear purpose and goal—how would Tweezerman get ready for, and be able to deliver on, a contract negotiation with Walgreens? From their past experiences, and the growing knowledge of all of them about the ins and outs of the industry, selling to Walgreens was still a big risk: financial exposure in extra inventory, uncertainty about a significant demand for manufacturing, volatility in the customer space, and the ongoing arrival of new competitors and innovations that could undercut the Tweezerman franchise in a flash.

The steering committee did not take the risks lightly. The members worked hard to take full advantage of what they had learned and what each of them was bringing to the table. All understood that this would have to be a well-coordinated and multivariable operation to execute a deal that LaMagna would sell. Each member of the committee explored and worked on the implications of a huge new contract for his or her particular oper-ating area. "We talked everything through, again and again, until we had the answers," recalls Lisa Bowen. Each steering committee member played their part and made their arguments for how to move ahead. Suttell, the CFO, analyzed financing implications and loans for inventory manage-ment, assuming they would be considerably ramping up product units. Bowen, the president, laid plans for increased production. Teri Schiano, head of product development, worked through the packaging and graphics for the different brands that would be needed to address customer needs while still preserving the Sally relationship. Laura Costin, overseeing IT, investigated how Tweezerman systems would integrate with Walgreens' electronic data input processes and bar coding. Seri LaMagna negotiated and smoothed the way with vendors on which Tweezerman depended for manufacturing. Lori Skroski, the vice president of sales, was a constant worrier about—and manager of—the still critical relationship with Sally Beauty Supply.

The meetings, as described by members of the steering committee, were iterative small steps in pursuit of a decision—a series of explorations, discussions, and problem-solving sessions all organized around the core questions of "How would we do this?" and "Can we get ready to do so?" The managers each made ongoing contact with their vendor and customer stakeholders, and the Sally account was tended carefully at every step of the way. With each meeting, new information was shared, new barriers and risks identified, and new solutions suggested and debated. The meetings were by no means always harmonious or driven by some sense of "needing to agree with Dal." As two small examples, Dal LaMagna recalls some "pretty strong opposition along the way by Lori about the risk to the Sally account." He also recalls "a lot of backing and forthing about the packaging and branding decisions."

By this time in his development as a leader, LaMagna was enjoying the benefits of knowing not only his strengths but also his own weaknesses. And he similarly appreciated the strength of a complementarily skilled and empowered team: "I realized how important it was to have the backing and knowledge of the people who had to work together and make this kind of decision work."

Core to the success of the ongoing problem solving was not just the trust engendered by the values of open debate and "permission to be wrong," but also the sense of mutual accountability across the steering committee. Because the decision of selling a deal to Walgreens was centrally dependent on how it would actually be implemented, the several leaders had to trust in the expertise and commitment of each other. All came to realize that this would be no decision made in an execution-free vacuum, and all similarly understood that they would have to depend critically on one another to assess the viability of making the move and then being able to deliver on it. The judgment being brought to bear was not just about assessing strategic benefits and costs but also each leader's ability to pull off the initiative safely and efficiently. Large national vendors could easily bankrupt new small suppliers that failed to deliver as promised, or leave them hanging with a sudden change of mind. The Tweezerman team had to understand every element of risk and every dimension of necessary performance against contract in order to succeed. And they had to fundamentally believe in one another to make it all happen.

To Walgreens . . . and Beyond

After months of debate and planning; hours spent understanding how they would handle the branding, packaging, production, and inventory; and a fair share of trial and error with various ideas to overcome many small and not-so-small obstacles, the steering committee finally felt ready to make a final decision. LaMagna recalled, "We finally came up with the concept to drop the Finer Touch brand and create Tweezerman Limited for Walgreens and the chain drugstores; and to make it all work, we also renamed Sally's and the beauty industry products Tweezerman Professional. Mike Renzulli at Sally's approved the approach as long as the packaging for the two lines was distinctive."

CFO Frank Suttell remembers the final decision with the group, sitting, as so often was the case, in LaMagna's simply furnished office. The mood in the room was lighthearted but with an undercurrent of some tension for the big question still before them, as they sat casually on the secondhand chairs in a circle. They were patient with CEO Dal LaMagna's occasional penchant for multitasking on his computer during lulls in the conversation—but everyone knew he was listening carefully, as each member of the committee reported that his or her investigations and preparations indeed checked out. As they spoke in turn, each began to realize that everything was now in place; Tweezerman could deliver on a big Walgreens deal. The room momentarily fell quiet.

Suddenly Suttell broke the silence: "So if everything is so ready, where's the purchase order?" His colleagues burst into laughter, knowing their CFO had comically but importantly "called the question." At this moment, Dal LaMagna, as just one more guy in the circle, joined the laughter. He waved his hand to emphasize the green light was now flashing, and the company was ready to take a very big strategic step.

Suttell's ironic directness signaled the future to come. In 1998, Tweezerman, a rising but still relatively small entrepreneurial venture, would close the biggest deal of its young life—moving its product line beyond the specialty shops of the professional beauty industry to a major chain of retail drugstores. Within weeks Tweezerman was shipping to the shelves of Walgreens, a move that tripled the number of locations where its products were sold, added millions of dollars to its revenue base, and started a double-digit growth expansion into related retail distribution that more than doubled its annual sales in the next five years. "It was," founder and CEO Dal LaMagna recalled, "a really big and successful decision—but also with a lot of risks. But we won out and it changed forever who we were in the industry."

By the year 2000, thanks to the Walgreens deal, Tweezerman had reached a higher-than-ever level of growth. It never looked back, expanding to other retail chains too and adding millions of additional dollars to its company volume. In 2004, Tweezerman decided to sell itself to an acquiring German company (Zwilling J.A. Henckels), having risen to become a worldwide dominant brand, with thousands of customers and a reputation for unmatched quality and innovation. Every member of the steering committee and most members of the company reaped significant growth in their personal fortunes. LaMagna himself went on to other business ventures, as well as embarking on a range of charitable and political initiatives.

Reflections on Organizational Judgment at Tweezerman

Though there are many elements of this story that combined to make the Walgreens sale a successful decision, the collaborative culture, the values of people looking for solutions rather than blame, and a spirit of mutual accountability that Dal LaMagna built at Tweezerman were especially critical. If we consider organizational judgment to be a fundamental capability—one that increases the chances of capturing opportunity and minimizing risk—the case of Tweezerman demonstrates how important it is that leaders who share a common performance objective develop trust and dependence upon one another in order to achieve that capability.

The founder not only fostered that trust and accountability in the company, but also encouraged the shared experience and learning as he and his team worked shoulder to shoulder through the years, often coming to wisdom "the hard way."

The Tweezerman story has echoes of many different findings by management researchers in recent years. The functioning of the steering committee, and Dal LaMagna's working relationship with its members, affirms what so many researchers who have studied leadership teams and other groups that function effectively have taught us: there is unusual power in people with complementary skills working together toward a common performance objective, when coupled with true sense of mutual accountability, trust, and shared understanding.[6] Groups perform and find solutions best when leaders and the behavior they model indicate that it is "safe to fail" and also that there is respect for the fairness of process—when everyone has a chance to be listened to and heard, and when decisions are arrived at (and explained) in an evenhanded and egoless way.[7] In recent years, there has also been increasing research that highlights how "strategy" and "implementation" are not neatly separable and sequential domains, but must be made together, with the needs of executing something considered hand in hand with decisions about whether to do it.[8] Tweezerman's decision making centrally linked not just the questions of *what* and *whether*, but also *how*. The steering committee, faced with the potential strategy of seeking growth with Walgreens, had no choice but to wrap that question with the same-time questions about how to actually do it.

As we have seen before, so much of the judgment of this company goes back to broader questions of its organizational culture and the context for good decision making created by the founder. In interviewing members of the Tweezerman team, we found it notable how often they discussed their culture and showed real self-awareness about how important it had been for their ultimate success. Its special nature is perhaps best summarized by CFO Frank Suttell:

> We evolved a culture where everyone there could be himself. Nobody was posing; there was no destructive competition or undermining one another. We depended on each other. People acted and spoke freely; they could tell their leaders 'Go mine salt,' if they wanted to, and they wouldn't be fired. We all realized that it's how people can be their best. It helped us make some really good decisions.

Conclusion

Final Reflections and Some Implications for Tomorrow's Leaders

W E DEVELOPED THE stories in this book to highlight an underappreciated dimension of decision making—*organizational judgment*. As we first argued in the introduction, we were guided by the belief that the traditional paradigm of decision making—where an all-seeing and wise CEO "makes the call" alone—is being superseded by more participative and data-intensive approaches, and therefore that this concept and capability is something every leader today can benefit from. We think that more decision making will be made in this way in the future—and is already being made this way—because of the changing context in which all organizations now operate. Today's global economy and more rapid pace of business are raising the stakes for making good decisions and also punishing bad decisions; and the complexity of factors that must be considered by any decision maker also continues to rise.

Rising Complexity and Opportunity

Part of that complexity includes not just problem but opportunity. More potentially relevant information about any decision is available than ever before, and new technologies and analytical capabilities (including mechanisms to tap into the "wisdom of crowds" and collective problem solving) are being deployed to help organize, synthesize, and prioritize it. But armed with more and better information, decision makers in turn face even more choices and nuances about what they must decide and why.

Another aspect of the new complexity is the ongoing knowledge revolution. More than just information, knowledge—in the heads and hands of professionals—is increasingly appreciated as the source of value creation for businesses and enterprises. How can organizations mobilize that in order to make better decisions? Part of this same revolution is that organizations are (to use the now popular vernacular) "getting flatter"—meaning, in varying ways, leaders have broader spans of managerial control, and structures and values are less hierarchical, with more authority for decisions more widely distributed in enterprises. This shift, chronicled for the last several decades, has allowed businesses to "get closer to customers," improve productivity, solve problems more quickly, and innovate more rapidly. But here again, another dimension of complexity enters the fray: when the knowledge needed for a good decision is more decentralized, together with the authority to apply it, how can organizations mobilize this knowledge in a rationale and practical way?

Moving from the traditional model of single decision maker to a more collective and participative model has obvious challenges—its own kind of complexity, possible decline of speed and nimbleness, and, in the worst cases, a nagging sense among all that "that no one is really in charge." But the great advantage of a more collective information- and knowledge-intensive approach is that, done well, it offsets the litany of pitfalls one person making a decision can fall into. Each year, thanks to the research of behavioral and neuroscientists, that list gets longer. We know more and more about why we, as individual actors, can make bad decisions. Techniques to offset the biases and sometimes dangerous heuristics that single leaders use to make the call are also well studied—recommendations such as using outside advisers, constructing what-if alternative scenarios, encouraging constructive conflict among members of a leadership team, and so forth. But for us the question remains not just about techniques but about living practice, and living practice across an entire organization. What does it look like when an organization develops the ability to make better decisions through a broad-based approach, one that is embedded in the way it operates? How does it play out in actual day-to-day work? And what can be learned from cases and stories where organizations seem to have developed, or started to develop, this capability? The preceding chapters have tried to answer these types of questions.

Learning from Success

Unlike authors of many other books on decision making, we have avoided the finger-pointing lessons of bad decisions that led to this or that catastrophe. Instead of trying to teach through negative example, we have focused on cases where answers to a particular dilemma or challenge that an organization faced came out well, trying to understand what allowed its leaders and people to make the call successfully. In every case, we were looking for more systemic conditions, processes, values, and mind-sets that suggested that the organizations studied had built some enduring capability—to capture value more often than not when decisions are required, with a diminished risk of failure. Here, and throughout this book, we use the word *capability* because we believe that organizational judgment is not a onetime lucky or even informed decision. Rather, it reflects the ongoing strength and will of an enterprise to perform in a competitive world, where bad choices can lead to ruin and good choices to greater opportunity. It has been our goal to analyze and understand the nature of the capability in the cases we have studied, and bring those insights to our readers.

Beyond the Simple Maxim or Framework

But we have resisted trying to create some simple, one-size-fits-all decision-making maxim or framework to define and prescribe this capability. All too often, advice about decision making involves only one type of intervention—employing only intuition, or knowledge management, or analytics, or the wisdom of crowds. Use only one of these approaches, we are urged, and it will be sufficient in itself to yield better decisions for individuals and organizations. We have avoided this classic business book temptation for a couple of reasons. First, we believe there are many routes to better judgment, and in fact most organizations should intervene with each of these tools at different times and in different situations. Second, the patterns of this capability, if in fact they are new and emerging, are not yet fully formed in a way that can be simply defined; there is more to learn from stories than a (perhaps still incomplete) checklist of "things one must do." Third, in the cases we have studied, there is so much context-specific application and practice, we are wary of removing learnings and promising approaches from the specific organizational and market conditions in which they seem to thrive. Instead, we have selected and developed a series of cases that, taken together, start to form a mosaic of ideas and emerging practices. Understanding these in their appropriate contexts can inform the design and development of other organizations seeking to develop collective judgment—without stipulating any step-by-step prescriptions.

But as we also reflected in our introduction, the cases taken as a whole do reveal a few broad themes that we have highlighted as we structured the book. Good organizational judgment usually involves reframing that reminds us that, like the human body, organizations must both perform in the present and maintain or renew their potential for future performance.

We would argue that organizational judgment is, in fact, one other dimension of organizational health—as a capability, it offers the potential for better future decisions. And what capability could be more important than that? Like any capability, and like health itself (organizational and human), it must be exercised and maintained. Organizations that build judgment do so with a journey of continuous improvement, and are constantly learning through practice, both how to improve it and how to maintain it for the future. In every case of our study, we see judgment that has been built to be sustainable, and used repeatedly to improve decisions on the horizon beyond the challenge of the immediate moment.

Civilizations, both east and west, have long celebrated wisdom and its applications to problems. Whether it is King Solomon, Confucius, or the wizened Nestor in Homer's poetry, we admire the icon of he (or she) who judges fairly and with deep understanding of what has been and now should be. That hero worship continues in the world of organizations today—the all-powerful, all-knowing CEO who makes the big decisions alone lives on, both in imagination and in the pages of the business press. But we are also beginning to witness an evolution of a new kind of wise man (and woman): not one who does it all alone, with the power of unique insight or intelligence, but rather one who understands, embraces, and takes full advantage of the collective judgment of many others as well as the power of new tools and information, and values the ability of organizations and networks to provide potentially better answers than the big "solo call." We hope this book can be a small piece of Darwin in fostering more of this evolution.

decisions as a participative process of problem solving. It takes advantage—and often considerable advantage—of the widening array of data now available in the world, and the advancing technological and analytical tools to interpret it. It is shaped by, and often itself shapes, powerful organizational culture based on values such as participation, deliberation, diversity of thought, constructive challenge and debate, and the like. And, as our fourth crosscutting theme highlights, good organizational judgment is often created by leaders—not as great "deciders" themselves, but as more egoless developers of the right context and structures to allow their organizations to find solutions more collectively. As several of our stories show, creating that context is often its own form of both organizational change and personal transformation for the leaders themselves.

History and current life both have their share of grand decisions. However, with perhaps one or two exceptions, the stories we have collected are not necessarily about major turning points for the course of civilization. Nonetheless, they were all important decisions for the actors involved, and had their own fair share of risk and uncertainty that had to be managed. We believe that building great organizational judgment has everyday application and should not be reserved only for grand historical moments. So what action steps can leaders take to build great judgment in their organizations?

Leaders Building Judgment

Here again, we resist the quick checklist, but a few observations, reflecting upon our case studies, might offer some guidance.

Begin by Recognizing the Need and Opportunity

Every case, in one way or another, exhibited an organization whose leaders understood that they needed to go beyond their own limitations and take advantage of a broader set of ideas, concepts, and wisdom. They took on the challenge of letting go of at least some of their own power and prerogative, at some level, in exchange for the deeper set of resources that comes from engaging and authentically collaborating with, and learning from, others to get to better decisions. They did so also believing that such an approach promised better outcomes and more chances for future success in all that their organization strives for. Whether Christine DeVita in The Wallace Foundation, Pete Gorman in the Charlotte-Mecklenburg Schools, the CEO of Media General, or the engineers in NASA—every leader confronted and acted upon the challenge to improve their enterprise's decision making by going beyond their own abilities and interests.

Be Intentional and Invest in Capability

In no case did we see an enterprise that had or was developing this kind of judging capability by accident. The capability for an organization to per- form in this way is invested in, built, and earned, rather than resulting from luck or a little bit of tinkering here or there. Even the ancient Athenians and McKinsey & Company, which had well-established processes and val- ues within which decisions developed, reflect organizations in which the capability was deliberately built over time. Our other cases (Cognizant, Charlotte-Mecklenburg Schools, Partners HealthCare, Tweezerman) show leaders and organizations very consciously building that capability for the future.

Consider the "Architectural Elements" Within the Cultural and Market Context

Whether using analytical software, blogging across the enterprise, embracing more democratic approaches to employee or managerial participation, employing a new problem-solving process, changing how to engage a leadership team, or using a different organizational design, our cases show enterprises that built judgment by assembling and com- bining different pieces of infrastructure and process into a new kind of "system" to better find solutions to problems. Though not always done

consciously, in the end they all created a mechanism that embraced collective intelligence and understanding. If perhaps too fancy a wo *architecture* can still be seen among the different dimensions of p working together that, as constructed and operated, provided a b way of coming to a decision.

That architecture, however, varies from organization to organiza based on a variety of variables. These might include the cultural traditi of the enterprise, the particular market conditions in which it opera and the stage of development and sophistication about decision makin, aspires to. Context must guide which pieces are assembled and how. The is no one-size-fits-all blueprint, but some kind of blueprint (implicit explicit) is nonetheless visible in every case.

Be Ready for Change

As the previous themes would naturally suggest, taking steps in the indi cated directions will change the status quo. Power is redistributed, values are reinterpreted, people not used to giving their opinions or being lis- tened to are suddenly invited to center stage. New technology comes in with more and new information, old prejudices are made visible, former reporting relationships are muddied by a mandate to share more knowl- edge across boundaries. Building organizational judgment is transforma- tional, not just a new set of practices "bolted on" to the old way of working. And, as mentioned already, it will be transformational not just for your organization, but also very likely for you as a leader.

Understand That, Like Health, Organizational Judgment Needs Exercise and Continuous Maintenance

A recent book by Scott Keller and Colin Price, *Performance and Health*, distinguished the processes and practices that organizations use to per- form current strategy versus deeper and more subtle dimensions that they labeled its *health*—"the ability of an organization to align, execute, and renew itself faster than the competition."[1] It is a useful construct

Notes

Introduction

1. *BusinessWeek*, "Gerald Levin Looks Ahead," November 6, 2000.

2. Andrew Edgecliffe-Johnson, "Levin Apologizes for 'Worst Deal of Century,'" *Financial Times*, January 4, 2010.

3. An overview of the Microsoft–Yahoo! negotiations is available in summary form and in a number of *New York Times* articles; see http://topics.nytimes.com/top/news/business/companies/yahoo_inc/yahoo-microsoft-deal/index.html.

4. Interview on CNBC "Squawk Box" program, September 10, 2009, online at http://www.nbcbayarea.com/news/local/Bartz-to-CNBC-You-Think-Im-Stupid-58503652.html.

5. For a comprehensive discussion of Digital's problems, see Edgar Schein, *DEC Is Dead, Long Live DEC* (San Francisco: Berrett-Koehler, 2003).

6. "Digital Equipment Corporation: A Case Study," Venture Navigator, online at http://www.venturenavigator.co.uk/content/158.

7. Oral history interview with Ken Olsen, September 1988, online at http://americanhistory.si.edu/collections/comphist/olsen.html#tc20.

8. Greg Grandin, *Fordlandia: The Rise and Fall of Henry Ford's Forgotten Jungle City*, (New York: Metropolitan Books, 2009).

9. More on the Jobs–Sculley issue is available at http://www.mac-history.net/the-history-of-the-apple-macintosh/showdown-at-apple-john-sculley-vs-steve-jobs.

10. Steve Lohr, "Without Its Master of Design, Apple Will Face Many Challenges," *New York Times*, August 24, 2011, online at http://www.nytimes.com/2011/08/25/technology/without-its-master-of-design-apple-will-face-challenges.html.

11. There is an a-to-z *list of cognitive biases* under that term in Wikipedia. For more detail on the major biases that affect human decisions, see Wray Herbert, *On Second Thought: Outsmarting Your Mind's Hard-Wired Habits* (New York: Crown Publishers, 2010).

12. Daniel Kahneman, Dan Lovallo, and Olivier Sibony, "Before You Make That Big Decision," *Harvard Business Review*, June 2011.

13. Thomas Carlyle, *On Heroes, Hero-Worship, and the Heroic in History* (Fredrick A. Stokes & Brother, New York, 1888) 1–2.

14. Data from an AFL-CIO survey of 299 CEOs, and the U.S. Bureau of Labor Statistics, May 2009 Occupational Employment and Wage Estimates, national cross-industry estimate of median annual compensation for all occupations.

15. James Surowiecki, *The Wisdom of Crowds: Why the Many Are Smarter Than the Few and How Collective Wisdom Shapes Business, Economies, Societies and Nations* (New York: Little, Brown, 2004).

16. Mehrdad Baghai and James Quigley, *As One: Individual Action, Collective Power* (New York: Portfolio, 2011).

17. Thomas H. Davenport and Jeanne G. Harris, *Competing on Analytics: The New Science of Winning* (Boston: Harvard Business School Press, 2007).

18. The Gottman story is described in Malcolm Gladwell, *Blink* (New York: Little, Brown, 2005), 18–27.

19. Robert Half Technology, "Whistle—But Don't Tweet—While You Work," news release, October 6, 2009.

20. This survey is described in Thomas H. Davenport, Jeanne G. Harris, and Robert Morison, *Analytics at Work* (Boston: Harvard Business Press, 2010), 1.

Chapter 1

1. Development of this case was led by Larry Prusak, with the helpful assistance of Don Cohen, managing editor of the National Aeronautics and Space Administration's *ASK Magazine*. In addition to interviews with Ed Hoffman, director of NASA's Academy of Program/Project and Engineering Leadership, and Mike Ryschkewitsch, NASA's chief engineer (May 7, 2010), the authors have drawn on published NASA materials about STS-119, including the internally published case study "Collaborative Problem-Solving: The STS-119 Flow Control Valve Issue," available at http://www.nasa.gov/pdf/468375main_STS-119_flow_control_valve.pdf. All quotations not attributed to other sources are drawn from interviews and these noted sources.

2. The commission's findings are available at http://history.nasa.gov/rogersrep/genindex.htm.

3. Diane Vaughn, *The Challenger Launch Decision* (Chicago: University of Chicago Press, 1996), xiii.

4. The report is available at http://www.nasa.gov/columbia/home/CAIB_Vol1.html.

5. See recently, Dan Lovallo and Olivier Sibony, "The Case for Behavioral Strategy," *McKinsey Quarterly*, March 2010, 1–16.

6. For a good recent discussion on this theme, see Jeffrey Pfeiffer and Robert Sutton, *Hard Facts, Dangerous Half-Truths, and Total Nonsense: Profiting from Evidence-Based Management* (Boston: Harvard Business School Press), 2006.

7. Bryan O'Connor, "Some Safety Lessons Learned," *ASK Magazine*, no. 35 (Summer 2009): 5–9.

8. See also, for example, Amitai Etzioni, "Humble Decision-Making," in *Harvard Business Review on Decision Making* (Boston: Harvard Business School Press, 2001), 45–57.

9. Karl E. Weick and Kathleen M. Sutcliffe, *Managing the Unexpected: Resilient Performance in an Age of Uncertainty* (San Francisco: John Wiley & Sons, 2007).

Chapter 2

1. Erica Burrill, one of Greg Burrill's daughters, was in an MBA class of mine (Tom) at Babson College. She introduced me to her father, whom I interviewed on two occasions. I also interviewed Erica and her sister Vanessa for this chapter.

2. Brian Lee, "A Family Home—Burrill's Build Neighborhoods with Extras," *Worcester Telegram and Gazette*, November 11, 2009.

Chapter 3

1. This case was developed with the input and interviews of the following former and current McKinsey & Company partners and staff over the course of 2010–2011: Dominic Barton, Michael Conway, Luis Cunha, Dolf DiBiasio, Jennifer Futernick, Fred Gluck, Jim Goodrich, Robert Harvey, Michelle Jarrard, Jon Katzenbach, Brian Rolfes, Margaret Snow, Jerome Vascellaro, Dave Wenner, Terry Williams, Kristina Wollschlaeger, and Rodney Zemmel. Full disclosure: Brook Manville, who drafted this chapter, and Tom Davenport were both members of McKinsey staff during this period and were nontraditional hires; some observations stem from Brook's own memories of the events described.

2. The McKinsey London office can fairly be said to have played an additional complementary role in the broadening talent strategy in the firm. It was that office that started, in 1982, a business analyst program, an early step to find more non-MBA talent—in this case,

academically excellent undergraduates; the program was adopted firmwide in 1985. It was also in 1985 that the firmwide McKinsey Fellows program was launched, which institutionalized some of McKinsey's earliest efforts to attract talent from other non-MBA degree programs—though primarily Rhodes and Marshall scholars at first.

3. This section is based not only on interviews with Fred Gluck and related other discussions cited above, but also on a recent, helpful history of strategy development during these years, with a particular focus on McKinsey and its various competitors; see Walter Kiechel III, *The Lords of Strategy: The Secret Intellectual Strategy of the New Corporate World* (Boston: Harvard Business Press, 2010), 95–115.

4. There's a rich decision-making literature about the importance of *safe space*: creating a psychological welcoming environment for learning as an input to decision making. One prominent contributor here is Amy Edmondson—e.g., her now classic article "Psychological Safety and Learning in Work Teams," *Administrative Science Quarterly* 44, no. 2 (June 1999): 350–383. See also, more recently, Amy Edmondson, "Strategies for Learning from Failure," *Harvard Business Review*, April 2011, 48–55.

5. Jarrard also notes that while the percentage of APDs has increased, so has the absolute number hired today in McKinsey, versus those hired in the early '90s (since the total number of associates hired is notably larger).

6. For example, estimates of Kennedy Consulting Research & Advisory, cited by Kiechel, *The Lords of Strategy*, 260.

7. See, for example, Edgar Schein, *Organizational Culture and Leadership* (San Francisco: Jossey-Bass, 1985); and John Kotter and James L. Heskett, *Corporate Culture and Performance* (New York: Free Press, 1992). Good insight into McKinsey's own culture can be found in Elizabeth Hass Edersheim, *McKinsey's Marvin Bower* (New York: Wiley, 2004).

Chapter 4

1. This chapter is based on interviews by Tom Davenport of John Glaser, Blackford Middleton, Tonya Hongsermeier, Jeffrey Schnipper, and a Partners cardiologist who wished to remain unnamed.

2. The CIRD Web site is at http://www.partners.org/cird/.

3. U.S. Agency for Healthcare Research and Quality, "Perspectives on Safety: Conversations with . . . Lucien Leape, MD," online at http://www.webmm.ahrq.gov/perspective. aspx?perspectiveID=28.

4. John Glaser is now CEO of Siemens Healthcare, a position he assumed in mid-2010.

5. This and other details of the Partners LMR/CPOE systems are derived from Richard Kesner, "Partners Healthcare System: Transforming Health Care Services Delivery Through Information Management," case study 9B09E023 (London, Ontario, Canada: Richard Ivey School of Business, 2009).

6. William W. Stead and Herbert S. Lin, eds., *Computational Technology for Effective Health: Immediate Steps and Strategic Directions* (Washington, DC: National Academy of Sciences, National Academies Press, 2009), 3.

7. Jack Beaudoin, "Eligible Provider 'Meaningful Use' Criteria," *Healthcare IT News*, December 30, 2009, online at http://www.healthcareitnews.com/news/eligible-provider-meaningful-use-criteria.

8. "HPM and IT: A Successful Working Partnership: Q&A with James Mongan and John Glaser," *Partners IS Newsletter*, Winter 2010, 1.

9. The source of the Cole and Mort comments on the Smart Form is Blackford Middleton, Jeffrey Schnipper, and Lana Tsurikova, "Improving Care for Acute and Chronic Problems with Smart Forms and Quality Dashboards" (presentation at the National Web Conference on Smart Forms and Quality Dashboards, U.S. Agency for Healthcare Research and Quality, July 19, 2007).

10. Clement J. McDonald, MD, "Protocol-Based Computer Reminders, the Quality of Care and the Non-Perfectibility of Man," *New England Journal of Medicine* 295 (1976): 1351–1355.

Chapter 5

1. This chapter draws heavily on Robert G. Eccles and Thomas H. Davenport, "Cognizant 2.0: Embedding Knowledge and Community into Work Processes," case 9-410-484 (Boston: Harvard Business School, 2010). It involved interviews by Tom Davenport with Sukumar Rajagopal and Alan Alper (who both patiently answered many e-mails), Malcolm Frank, Francisco D'Souza, and several Cognizant project managers, and a visit to a Cognizant client conference.

2. For more information on Cognizant's founding and business strategy, see Robert G. Eccles, David Lane, and Prabakar Kothandaraman, "Cognizant Technology Solutions," case 9-408-099 (Boston: Harvard Business School, 2008).

3. Bala Iyer, "Successful IT Services Delivery Using Knowledge Management: The Case of Cognizant Technology Solutions," case study (Wellesley, MA: Babson College, 2007).

4. Sujata Dutta Sachdeva, "Netting Biz: Blogging Bug Bites Big Bosses," *Times of India*, October 7, 2007.

Chapter 6

1. All students' names have been disguised to protect their privacy.

2. This chapter is based on interviews by Tom Davenport with Dr. Peter Gorman, Dr. Robert Avossa, and Farrah Santonato in the CMS district headquarters; and Chuck Nusinov, Christa Olech, Donna Helms, and several other teachers and classroom facilitators at David Cox Road Elementary.

3. Kathryn Parker Boudett, Elizabeth A. City, and Richard J. Murnane, eds., *Data Wise: A Step-by-Step Guide to Using Assessment Results to Improve Teaching and Learning* (Boston: Harvard Education Press, 2005).

4. Nick Anderson, "Education Chief Calls On Schools to Share More Data," *Washington Post*, August 26, 2010.

5. Richard DuFour, "Schools as Learning Communities," *Educational Leadership* 61, no. 8 (May 2004): 6–11.

6. Gorman became senior vice president of News Corporation's Education Division. Avossa was named superintendent of the Fulton County School District in Georgia. Nusinov became head of school at the Countryside Montessori School in Charlotte.

Chapter 7

1. Readers not schooled in the scholarship of ancient Greek history should know that the actual chronology and certain specific facts about the decision here described—and more generally many of the events surrounding the prelude, course, and aftermath of the ensuing battle of Salamis—have been long debated by professional historians. In addition to voicing at least some skepticism about the reports of the main sources, scholars also disagree about the veracity and implied chronology of another critical primary source: a stone inscription first published in 1960—the so-called Themistocles Decree—which appears to provide the details of the original democratic resolution framing the decision herein described; see M. Jameson, "A Decree of Themistocles from Troizen," *Hesperia* 29 (1960): 198–223.

In retelling the story of this historical decision, its timing, and its ensuing results, I (Brook) have largely followed the reconstructed sequence of events of Barry Strauss in his authoritative study, *The Battle of Salamis: The Naval Encounter That Saved Greece—and Western Civilization* (New York: Simon & Schuster, 2004). I (Brook) have also benefited from the reconstruction (generally consistent with Strauss) of Frank J. Frost, *Plutarch's Themistocles: A Historical Commentary* (Princeton, NJ: Princeton University Press, 1980), especially pp. 101–104. Though the interpretation offered here would certainly have its scholarly challengers, the view advanced aligns with historians' majority consensus of what likely happened.

2. This case was developed on the basis of classical primary sources including Herodotus, *The Histories* (translated by Aubrey de Selincourt, revised edition by A. R. Burn [NewYork: Penguin Books, 1972]) and Plutarch, *Life of Themistocles* (available in Plutarch, *The Rise and Fall of Athens*, translated by Ian Scott-Kilvert [New York: Penguin Books, 1960], 77–108), and other secondary works referenced below. Thanks to professors Josiah Ober of Stanford University and Barry Strauss of Cornell University, who, as leading historical researchers in many of the relevant questions addressed in this study, provided advice and counsel on earlier drafts. I (Brook) have, as indicated, also benefited greatly from their published work, as cited.

3. For example, James Surowiecki, *The Wisdom of Crowds: Why the Many Are Smarter Than the Few and How Collective Wisdom Shapes Business, Economies, Societies and Nations* (New York: Doubleday, 2004); Don Tapscott and Anthony D. Williams, *Wikinomics: How Mass Collaboration Changes Everything* (New York: Portfolio, 2006); and Clay Shirky, *Here Comes Everybody: The Power of Organizing Without Organizations* (New York: Penguin, 2008).

4. On some radically democratic organizations, see examples cited in Brook Manville and Josiah Ober, *A Company of Citizens: What the World's First Democracy Teaches Leaders About Creating Great Organizations* (Boston: Harvard Business School Press, 2003), 187, note 3. On the general trend toward organizational flattening, and team-based and more collaborative work, see Jon Katzenbach and Douglas K. Smith, *The Wisdom of Teams* (Boston: Harvard Business School Press, 1992); Frances Hesselbein, Marshall Goldsmith, and Richard Beckhard, eds., *The Organization of the Future* (San Francisco: Jossey-Bass, 1997); Peter Drucker, "The Coming of the New Organization," in *Harvard Business Review on Knowledge Management* (Boston: Harvard Business School Press, 1998), 1–19; Ron Ashkenas et al., *The Boundaryless Organization*, 2nd ed. (San Francisco: Jossey-Bass, 2002); and Morten T. Hansen, *Collaboration: How Leaders Avoid the Traps, Create Unity, and Reap Big Results* (Boston: Harvard Business Press, 2009).

5. One recent exception was work Brook did with professor Josiah Ober, examining exactly this question: Manville and Ober, *A Company of Citizens*, cited above in note 4; the book and other related investigations have helped shape this case study. See also Ober's more recent work that pushes deeper into the mechanisms of decision making and has further contributed to this case: Josiah Ober, *Democracy and Knowledge: Innovation and Learning in Ancient Athens* (Princeton, NJ: Princeton University Press, 2008).

6. Interview with professor Barry Strauss, Cornell University, June 13, 2010. For the famous and similar opinion of Herodotus himself, see *The Histories* Book 7, section 139: "One is surely right in saying that Greece was saved by the Athenians. It was the Athenians who held the balance: whichever side they joined was sure to prevail . . . It was the Athenians who—after God—drove back the Persian King."

7. The only known example of a Greek people having ever done this before (cited by Herodotus) was the city of Phocaea in Asia Minor. In 540 BC its people took solemn vows to abandon their homeland, to avoid becoming Persian subjects. But eventually half the citizens relented, returned home, and became slaves to the oriental empire; the other half suffered greatly in exile, eventually resettling in Italy. So abandoning Athens was not an idea to be taken lightly.

8. Herodotus, *The Histories* Book 7, sections 140–143 recounts the story that follows.

9. This and the discussion that follows owe much to Ober, *Democracy and Knowledge*, 27.

10. On mixing and its importance to creating democratic culture, see Aristotle, *Athenaion Politeia*, sections 21.2-4 (accessible in Kurt Von Fritz and Ernst Capp [ed. and trs.]),

Aristotle's Constitution of Athens and Related Texts (New York: Hafner Publishing Co), 90. For details of Cleisthenic reforms, see Philip Brook Manville, *The Origins of Citizenship in Ancient Athens* (Princeton, NJ: Princeton University Press, 1990), 184–209; and Ober, *Democracy and Knowledge*, 139–167.

11. It's interesting to see how many of the practices and processes invented by and used by ancient Athenians in their democracy map to contemporary synthesis of good decision making; for example, W. Chan Kim and Renée Mauborgne, "Fair Process: Managing in the Knowledge Economy," *Harvard Business Review*, July–August 1997, 65–75; Peter Drucker, "The Effective Decision," in *Harvard Business Review on Decision Making* (Boston: Harvard Business School Press, 2001), 1–20; J. Edward Russo and Paul J. H. Schoemaker, *Winning Decisions: Getting It Right the First Time* (New York: Fireside Press, 2002); and Max H. Bazerman and Don A. Moore, *Judgment in Managerial Decision Making*, 7th ed. (New York: Wiley & Sons, 2009).

Chapter 8

1. I (Tom) first learned about Mabel Yu from Jeremy Mercer's story, "In Praise of Dissent," *Ode*, July–August 2010, online at http://www.odemagazine.com/doc/71/in-praise-of-dissent/. After that, I interviewed her several times, and also interviewed her direct supervisor at Vanguard, Bill Roberts, and the head of fixed income investments, Bob Auwaerter.

2. John C. Bogle, "A Tale of Two Markets" (remarks at the Trinity University Policymaker Breakfast Series, San Antonio, TX, April 16, 2001); transcript at http://www.vanguard.com/bogle_site/sp20010416.html.

3. Sigma Investing, "Review of Common Sense on Mutual Funds," http://www.sigma-investing.com/reading-materials/common-sense.

4. A longer overview of the power of dissent (beginning with Mabel Yu's dissent) is provided by Mercer, "In Praise of Dissent."

5. Irving Janis, *Victims of Groupthink*, 2nd ed. (Boston: Houghton-Mifflin, 1972).

6. Charlan Nemeth, "Jury Trials: Psychology and the Law," in *Advances in Experimental Social Psychology*, ed. Leonard Berkowitz (New York: Academic Press, 1981), 14:309–367.

7. Charlan Nemeth, John Rogers, and Keith Brown, "Devil's Advocate vs. Authentic Dissent: Stimulating Quantity and Quality," *European Journal of Social Psychology* 31 (2001): 707–720.

8. Elizabeth MacDonald, "The Credit Rating Agencies' Moment of Shame," Fox Business, October 23, 2008, http://www.foxbusiness.com/markets/2008/10/23/credit-rating-agencies-moment-shame#ixzz1ACAVxikH.

9. "The Watchmen," *This American Life*, National Public Radio, June 5, 2009, transcript at http://www.thisamericanlife.org/radio-archives/episode/382/transcript.

Chapter 9

1. This chapter draws from interviews by Tom Davenport with Chuck Hollis, David Goulden, Michelle Lavoie, and Polly Pearson. Thanks also to Lesley Ogrodnick of EMC corporate public relations for shepherding the chapter through the approval process and arranging interviews.

2. Chuck Hollis, "EMC|ONE: A Journey in Social Media" (white paper, EMC, December 2008), online at http://chucksblog.emc.com/content/social_media_at_EMC_draft.pdf. Hollis's "general" blog is at http://chucksblog.emc.com; his blog about EMC's social media journey is at http://chucksblog.emc.com/a_journey_in_social_media/.

3. From an interview with David Goulden: Jack Sweeney, "EMC's Cost Transformation Journey," *Business Finance*, March 24, 2010, http://businessfinancemag.com/article/emcs-cost-transformation-journey-0324.

Chapter 10

1. This case was developed from Media General materials and interviews with CEO Marshall Morton and other members of his executive team (August 2010), and with helpful discussions with Media General board member Scott Anthony, managing director of Innosight (August–September 2010). Special thanks to Kevin McDermott of Collective Intelligence, who introduced this case and contributed substantially to its development; and Lou Anne Nabhan, Vice President, Corporate Communications, who greatly facilitated our research.

2. Internal Media General memorandum of Marshall Morton, May 13, 2008.

3. The different dimensions of diversity and its contribution to superior problem solving were helpfully explored recently by Scott Page, *The Difference: How the Power of Diversity Creates Better Groups, Firms, Schools, and Societies* (Princeton, NJ: Princeton University Press, 2007).

4. The dissident directors also, it should be noted, closed out the majority of their stock holdings and left the board in April 2009.

5. For example, Karl E. Weick, *Sensemaking in Organizations* (Thousand Oaks, CA: Sage Publications, 1995); David Nadler et al., *Leading Executive Teams* (San Francisco: Jossey-Bass, 1995); Andy Boynton and Bill Fischer, *Virtuoso Teams: Lessons from Teams That Changed Their Worlds* (Upper Saddle River, NJ: Financial Times Press, 2005); and Michael Roberto, *Why Great Leaders Don't Take Yes for an Answer: Managing Conflict and Consensus* (Upper Saddle River, NJ: Wharton School Publishing, 2005).

6. On cognitive and heuristic traps, see Max H. Bazerman and Don A. Moore, *Judgment in Managerial Decision Making*, 7th ed. (New York: John Wiley & Sons, 2009), 13.

7. For example, Ronald A. Heifetz, *Leadership Without Easy Answers* (Cambridge, MA: Belknap Press, 1994); Warren Bennis and Patricia Ward Biederman, *Organizing Genius: The Secrets of Creative Collaboration* (Reading, MA: Perseus Books, 1997); Robert K. Greenleaf, *Servant Leadership: A Journey into the Nature of Legitimate Power and Greatness*, 25th anniversary ed. (New York: Paulist Press, 2002); and Linda Hill, "Where Will We Find Tomorrow's Leaders?" *Harvard Business Review*, January 2008, 1–7.

Chapter 11

1. This case was based on Wallace Foundation publications and a series of discussions with (then but now retired) president Christine DeVita and members of her executive team, conducted during June–September 2010. Thanks are owed to all interviewed and especially for the guiding support of DeVita. Also special thanks to Lucas Held, vice president of communications, who helped with earlier drafts and factual corrections in the case.

2. The new board directive was further helped along a few years later with the passing of the No Child Left Behind Act in 2001—which considerably increased the need for leader accountability in public schools.

3. Russ Mitchell, "Schools Face Uphill Challenge to Improve," CBS News, January 31, 2010, http://www.cbsnews.com/stories/2010/01/30/eveningnews/main6158370.shtml.

4. Kenneth Leithwood et al., *Review of Research: How Leadership Influences Student Learning* (Center for Applied Research and Educational Improvement, Ontario Institute for Studies in Education, The Wallace Foundation, 2004).

5. Karen Seashore Louis et al., *Learning from Leadership: Investigating the Links to Improved Student Learning; Final Report to the Wallace Foundation* (University of Minnesota and The Wallace Foundation, 2010). See also Bradley S. Portin et al., *Leadership for Learning Improvement in Urban Schools* (Seattle, WA: Center for the Study of Teaching and Policy, University of Washington, 2009).

6. "Education Leadership: An Agenda for School Improvement" (publication from The Wallace Foundation's Annual Conference, Washington, DC, October 14–16, 2009), 21.

7. As commonly happens when one interviews multiple participants in a bygone event, without any written record or notes available from the original time, opinions differ about

the timing and sequence of activities. What's presented here was agreed in summary to have occurred by the team at The Wallace Foundation, with the caveat that some of the account may stand as a composite or an approximation of what was actually said and transpired.

8. Though DeVita noted that at Wallace, research and evaluation had always reported directly to her—but had not originally been integrated as part of an interdisciplinary team approach, as later developed.

9. Knowledge Center, The Wallace Foundation, http://www.wallacefoundation.org/ KnowledgeCenter/Pages/default.aspx.

10. For example, discussions such as Jay R. Galbraith, *Designing Organizations: An Executive Briefing on Strategy, Structure, and Process* (San Francisco: Jossey-Bass, 1995); and David A. Nadler and Michael L. Tushman, *Competing by Design: The Power of Organizational Architecture* (New York: Oxford University Press, 1997).

11. See recently, for example, articles in *Harvard Business Review on Collaborating Across Silos* (Boston: Harvard Business Press, 2009); and Morten T. Hansen, *Collaboration: How Leaders Avoid the Traps, Create Unity, and Reap Big Results* (Boston: Harvard Business Press, 2009).

Chapter 12

1. This case was developed with the help of Tweezerman founder and CEO Dal LaMagna, interviewed by Brook Manville on January 11, 2011, whose quotations in what follows are drawn from that and related discussions. Also interviewed and helpful to the reporting of the case were Frank Suttell, former CFO (January 12, 2011), and Lisa Bowen, former president (January 17, 2011), whose quotations are drawn from those conversations.

2. Dal LaMagna, *Raising Eyebrows: A Failed Entrepreneur Finally Gets It Right* (New York: John Wiley & Sons, 2010).

3. Ibid., 215–216. It's interesting to note how many years it took before concepts comparable to responsible capitalism started to become mainstream; e.g., recently, Michael E. Porter and Mark R. Kramer, "Creating Shared Value," *Harvard Business Review*, January–February 2011, 62–77.

4. Jack Stack (with Bo Burlingham), *The Great Game of Business* (New York: Currency Doubleday, 1992).

5. *Tweezerman Employee Handbook*, as provided by Dal LaMagna, January 2011.

6. For example, Jon R. Katzenbach and Douglas K. Smith, *The Wisdom of Teams: Creating the High-Performance Organization* (Boston: Harvard Business School Press, 1992); and J. Richard Hackman, ed., *Groups That Work (and Those That Don't): Creating Conditions for Effective Teamwork* (San Francisco: Jossey-Bass, 1990).

7. We've made this point in earlier chapters (e.g., the NASA case study, chapter 1) and revisit it here. In addition to previous references noted, see E. Allan Lind and Tom R. Tyler, *The Social Psychology of Procedural Justice* (New York: Plenum Press, 1988); and W. Chan Kim and Reneé Mauborgne, "Fair Process: Managing in the Knowledge Economy," *Harvard Business Review*, July–August 1997, 65–75.

8. For example, Larry Bossidy and Ram Charan, *Execution: The Discipline of Getting Things Done* (New York: Crown Business, 2002); and G. L. Neilson, K. L. Martin, and E. Powers, "The Secrets to Successful Strategy Execution," *Harvard Business Review*, June 2008.

Conclusion

1. Scott Keller and Colin Price, *Performance and Health. An Evidence-based Approach to Transforming Your Organization* (New York: McKinsey & Company, 2010).

Index

Acknowledgments

A book like *Judgment Calls*, based on a complement of different case studies, could not have come into being without the help and support of many people. We've attempted to thank many of the people who shared their knowledge and experiences with us in the footnotes of the chapters in which their cases appear. With apologies to those not mentioned in those notes, these acknowledgments will likely recognize and thank only a small portion of folks to whom we owe our gratitude. We begin with our colleague Larry Prusak, whose first discussions with us helped spark and develop the idea for this book. The foreword Larry wrote for this book further reflects his interest and passion for the topic, and we benefited from his good insights and ideas throughout our research and writing. Julia Kirby was a wise and encouraging editor and friend, and her suggestions and good judgment about this book about judgment made the volume much more interesting and coherent. Leila Lamoureux was our invaluable editorial assistant, who aided us greatly in assembling and quality-controlling our manuscript. Thanks also to the anonymous readers, editors, and production staff of the Harvard Business Review Press (including Jacque Murphy, Justin Fox, Jennifer Waring, Stephani Finks, and Kevin Evers), whose ideas, suggestions, and cover designs also added significantly to the final volume.

We would also like to thank, in addition to the executives we interviewed and noted in individual chapters, the many contacts and communications professionals at different organizations who worked with us on specific case studies. For work led by Tom Davenport, these include Erica Burrill (WGB Homes), Lesley Ogrodnick (EMC), Sukumar Rajagopal (Cognizant), and Bill Roberts (Vanguard). For Brook Manville, these include Lucas Held

(The Wallace Foundation), Ed Hoffman and Don Cohen (NASA), Connie Jordan (McKinsey & Company), Lou Anne Nabhan (Media General), and finally Herodotus of Halicarnassus, though he was quite delinquent in returning emails.

Each of us owes a debt of thanks to our families. Brook's family—Margarita, Sabrina, Laura, and Martin—like spouses and children of authors everywhere, patiently put up with him spending too much time away, working on yet another blankety-blank new book. Tom's family is more or less inured to a constant book project, but he wishes to thank his wife Jodi for her enthusiastic support of his trying to write like Malcolm Gladwell (though Tom fears it didn't quite work out that way) and his sons Hayes and Chase for their interest in the content. He dedicates his struggles on this book to family member Kim Bunch, who has struggled successfully with far more difficult challenges.

Thomas H. Davenport
Brook Manville

About the Authors

Tom Davenport is the President's Distinguished Professor in Information Technology and Management at Babson College, the Research Director of the International Institute for Analytics (www.iianalytics.com), and a Senior Advisor to Deloitte Analytics. In 2012–2013 he will be a visiting professor at Harvard Business School.

Tom has written, coauthored, or edited fourteen other books, including the bestselling *Competing on Analytics: The New Science of Winning* (with Jeanne Harris). He also authored the first books on business process reengineering and achieving value from enterprise systems, and the bestseller *Working Knowledge* (with Larry Prusak), on knowledge management. He has written more than one hundred articles for such publications as *Harvard Business Review, MIT Sloan Management Review, California Management Review*, the *Financial Times*, and many other publications. Tom has also been a columnist for *CIO, InformationWeek*, and *Darwin* magazines. In 2003 he was named one of the world's "Top 25 Consultants" by *Consulting* magazine, and in 2005 was named one of the world's top three analysts of business and technology by readers of *Optimize* magazine. In 2007 and 2008 he was named one of the one hundred most influential people in the IT industry by Ziff-Davis magazines. In 2011 he was named one of the top thirty management educators in the world—the "A-List"— by BusinessEducators.com. His blog at Harvard Business Online is http://hbr.org/search/Tom%20Davenport.

Brook Manville is Principal of Brook Manville, LLC, an independent consultancy focused on strategy, organization development, and executive leadership for mission-led organizations in all sectors. To learn more, go to www.brookmanville.com. Earlier in his career he was Executive Vice

President of the United Way of America, Director of Strategy and Learning for Saba Software, and a partner of McKinsey & Company, where he served as the firm's first Director of Knowledge Management and also worked with clients as a specialist in Organization.

Brook began his career as an academic historian (PhD, Yale) and has also worked in media, online information services, and journalism. He is widely published in the fields of organization, knowledge management, and learning. He is the author (with Josiah Ober) of *A Company of Citizens: What the World's First Democracy Teaches Leaders About Creating Great Organizations* (Boston: Harvard Business School Press, 2003).

Brook lives with his wife and three children in metropolitan Washington, D.C.